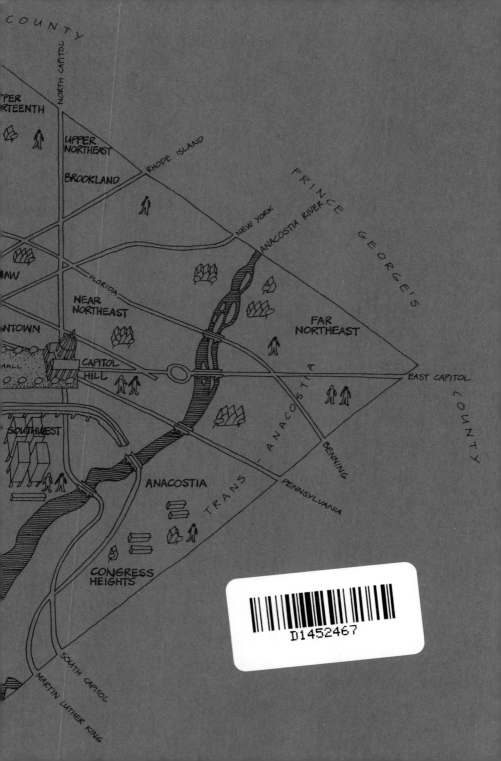

Captive Capital

Colonial Life in Modern Washington

Captive Capital

COLONIAL

LIFE IN MODERN

WASHINGTON

SAM SMITH

Photos by Roland L. Freeman

Indiana University Press

Bloomington / London

Published in Canada by Fitzhenry & Whiteside Limited, Don Mills, Ontario

Manufactured in the United States of America

DRAWINGS AND ENDPAPER MAPS BY JOHN WIEBENSON

LIBRARY OF CONGRESS CATALOGING IN PUBLICATION DATA

Smith, Sam, 1937–
    Captive Capital; colonial life in modern
      Washington.
    Bibliography: p. 293
    1. Washington, D.C.—Social conditions.
  2. District of Columbia—Politics and government.
  3. Urban renewal—Washington, D.C. I. Title.
HN80.W3S45   309.1'753   73–15406
ISBN 0–253–11070–X

To Julius Hobson

WHO REFUSED TO GO GENTLE

INTO THAT GOOD NIGHT

CONTENTS

*Life Inside the Monument, photographs
by Roland L. Freeman, page 95*

vii

PREFACE

ACRES OF TREES HAVE FALLEN TO CONSTRUCT PAPER monuments to Washington's marble ones. Still more have been turned to description of Washington's national political life. But the nature of the capital as a place—as a community—remains hidden from view; and what is seen is often misunderstood, leading visitors to appreciate the city less than they might and residents to endure more suffering than they should.

Washingtonians suffer because, while they live in the capital, they also live in a colony. Recent legislation has granted the District the right to elect a mayor and city council, but control over the budget, courts, prosecutor's office, police and planning will remain wholly or partially hostage to the federal government. Further, the city continues to be without voting representation in either the Senate or the House; and since the limited suffrage granted may be revoked by simple act of Congress, it is conditional on local policy being acceptable to Capitol Hill and the White House. (A special White House assistant for DC affairs warned local politicians against indulging in partisan politics and promised that the administration would exercise "oversight" to "see that self-government works.")

Thus the city has been permitted the externals of self-determination, elections, without its heart, power. We are left still far short of the local autonomy that other Americans enjoy. In fact, even with the most recent reforms, the District, more populous than 20 percent of the states of the union, remains with considerably less control over its destiny than either the Virgin Islands or Puerto Rico. In essence we have been granted participatory colonialism. The style is democratic but the substance is still deeply autocratic.

As Congressman Edith Green, no flaming liberal, said during the House debate on the home rule bill, "In the long haul, we must do one of two things. We must face up to full citizenship rights and seriously consider retrocession of all the District of Columbia except the federal enclave to Maryland. . . . The other alternative as I see it is statehood. So I would contend that whatever we do today and tomorrow is going to result at best in an interim measure and that we are really not settling anything."

Despite their colonial situation, however, Washingtonians have managed to create a city that is one of the most attractive, civil, interesting, and pleasant in the country. Too many, in fact, have been led to conclude that because of these qualities living in a colony can't be all that bad. But it is the nature of man to fill the hollows of the soul. Misery can be mitigated by decency and poverty can exist on a tree-lined street. The best of Washington thrives despite its political status rather than because of it, and the city becomes like Emerson's description of life, "evermore beauty and disgust; magnificence and rats."

I have lived with the magnificence and the rats for more than twenty years. It is hard to be coldly analytical in their company; and while I have attempted in this book to rationalize my emotions, I have not attempted to obscure them. Anyone seeking a dispassionate view of the capital will have to look elsewhere. I am, without apology, a Washingtonian. I was born here and, though my family moved away when I was nine, I don't think I ever doubted that I would return. I recall visiting Washington as a teenager, stepping out of Union Station, and saying to myself, "I'm home." That mysterious affliction known as "Potomac fever" affects even the young, even those too young to be addicted to the proximity of power, the alleged cause of the disease. It was just that Washington seemed what a city ought to be—exciting yet verdant, crowded yet spacious, hospitable to the stranger, and tolerant of diversity.

After college I returned, but for a number of years accepted the common local view that there was not much to be done about the city's status and so merely enjoyed Washington's virtues and ignored its problems. Then in the mid-sixties I found myself drawn to the Free DC Movement, organized by the local chapter of the Student Nonviolent Coordinating Committee. Since that time the city has been my vocation and avocation.

The biases created by various influences and experiences will be clear enough to the reader, but a few should be made explicit. In 1966 I started the *Capitol East Gazette*, a neighborhood newspaper which later became the *DC Gazette*, an alternative biweekly. I have participated in fights against freeways and mass development and in the battle for self-government. I have been an active member of the Statehood Party, and for four years was an increasingly disgruntled member of the DC Democratic Central Committee.

I have willingly and with malice aforethought violated the canons of journalistic detachment and objectivity, preferring involvement and reasoned subjectivity; believing that, while there may be two sides to every question, the truth does not usually lie in the middle, nor can the search for it be a purely vicarious experience.

I am also white and comfortable. In a city that is 71 percent black, with many of its residents struggling to get past the next utility bill, my perspective is suspect. On the other hand, one needn't touch a stove to know it's hot.

Besides, the sort of injustice perpetrated against the city of Washington, closely tied as it is to racial misconceptions and prejudices, is largely the responsibility of white America. We made this mess and we should, if we can summon up the decency, attempt to resolve it. The so-called black community understands the problem; it is the white community that doesn't to whom this book is largely addressed.

I have been helped in writing this book by a large number of people through conversations, example, and mutual experience over the years; but three persons provided direct and crucial aid, intervening in behalf of accuracy, balance, and clarity. Carl Bergman, formerly an aide at the DC Council, provided valuable information and criticism. My wife, Kathy Smith, did most of the research for the chapter on Washington history; she and Jean Lewton, associate editor of the *DC Gazette*, helped with the editing and preparation. A portion of the last chapter was originally published by the *Washington Post* as "The Case for Statehood." Much of the historical material is based on information contained in Constance McLaughlin Green's three excellent books, *Washington: Village and Capital, Washington: Capital City*, and *The Secret City*.

The end papers and drawings were done by John Wiebenson, an architect who came to Washington in 1967 via Denver, the Harvard School of Design, and San Francisco. Wiebenson helped in designing Resurrection City for the Poor People's Campaign in 1968 and has taught at Yale and the University of Maryland. He was a leader in the fight to save Washington's Old Post Office Building and created a popular map of the Adams-Morgan neighborhood. He draws cartoons for the *DC Gazette* as well as an urban planning comic strip, "Archihorse."

The photographs were taken by Roland L. Freeman, who has been photo editor of the *DC Gazette* since 1967 and a freelance photographer who has handled assignments for *Time, U.S. News & World Report, Paris Match* and the United States Information Service. A member of the White House News Photographers Association, the Society of Photographers in Communications, and a Friend of Magnum, Freeman was the first photographer to receive a grant from the National Endowment for the Humanities. He also has had an exhibition at the National Collection of Fine Arts.

To all of the above goes much of the credit and none of the blame for what follows.

Captive Capital

Colonial Life in Modern Washington

1 / *Life Inside a Monument*

Fᴏʀ ɴᴇᴀʀʟʏ ᴏɴᴇ ᴀɴᴅ ᴛʜʀᴇᴇ-ǫᴜᴀʀᴛᴇʀ ᴄᴇɴᴛᴜʀɪᴇꜱ, the city of Washington has served as house-servant to the national government, garbed in gaudy livery that veils its menial status. Washington does not participate in the Union, it waits on it. It stages a pageant of democracy without sharing in the democracy that is portrayed.

To most of the eighteen million tourists who visit Washington every year, the arrangement has been more than satisfactory. To stand, even for a moment, where the most powerful have stood is worth the wait. To visit the other side of the television screen and see the stage sets of the evening news is enthralling.

And if the aura of the awesome and the trip into the media's eye is not enough, the physical city looms over every block the tourist is likely to see, proclaiming in cold, intimidating marble that this is the Capital of the Free World. The tourist, who is not likely to meet a president during a lifetime, can arise early to stand long in line and be hustled through White House rooms where presidents have stood, perhaps as recently as last evening. Squads of high school students on spring tours can step out of buses at the foot of Capitol Hill and march respectfully up for a glance—no talking, reading, or leaning on the rail in the gallery, please—of the "world's greatest deliberative body," impressive even if you can't hear what those two senators are saying to each other and there are only three others on the floor and you don't recognize any of them anyway.

Then there is the majesty of the Supreme Court, the mystery of the FBI, the strength and grace of Abraham Lincoln, and the Smithsonian's mementos of our history and technology. And for those too jaded, a pair of giant pandas have been installed at the National Zoo.

What lies beyond, the community that supports this pageant, is considered a strange and fearful place inhabited by muggers and rapists. The tourists heed the advice of room clerks, cab drivers, and tour guides not to stray far from the Mall or their hotels.

For the temporary residents who float in and out of Washington with the tides of national administrations, the arrangement is at least adequate and sometimes exhilarating. From the first diplomatic reception attended by the new Assistant Undersecretary, from the first Georgetown cocktail sipped by the neophyte Hill receptionist, from the first confidential file touched by the newly arrived FBI clerk, Washington raises the curtain on heady experience. To those passing through, Washington is not so much a city as an event. It is democracy's Disneyland, where senators, rather than Pluto and Donald Duck, pop out at you in unlikely corners. Charles McDowell, Jr., a Washington correspondent who likes to gaze out of his National Press Building office window, recalls: "Once I perceived John Connally of Texas, Jacob

Javits of New York, Sonny Jurgenson of Washington, David Brinkley of NBC, and a red-bearded man from somewhere wearing a sandwich board that said, 'The man with the Plan: Jesus in '72,' all within the space of a couple of hours, each alone, each on some mission of his own among ordinary mortals in the street."

Washington is also a period—the New Frontier, the Nixon Era—rather than a place. It is who you know rather than where you are. It is not a community to discover but a stage upon which to act. And if you are important, it is not where you are from. As Russell Baker of the *New York Times* once noted, John F. Kennedy spent most of his adult life in Washington but remained "from Boston." Lyndon Johnson lived thirty-five years in DC but was "from Texas."

Yet to those who call Washington home, those who stay when others leave, the bulk of the 750,000 residents of the capital, the functions assigned the city have been at best barren and at worse the source of bitterness that only habit conceals. To the Washingtonian, the oft-made declaration that "Washington belongs to all the people of the nation" has the sound of a sponging cousin asserting that your house belongs to all the family. For the residents of Washington, the city is not the capital of the free world, but a colony.

The democratic values cited so frequently in official halls do not apply inside the District line. Article 1, Section 8, of the Constitution states:

The Congress shall have power . . . to exercise exclusive legislation in all cases whatsoever, over such District (not exceeding ten miles square) as may, by cession of particular States, and the acceptance of Congress, become the seat of the government of the United States.

Although the clause was designed to prevent the ceding states from exerting residual control over the Dis-

5

trict, it has been interpreted over the years as a rationale for denying the District political influence over its own affairs.

The District today has nearly sixty times its 1800 population. It is larger than were any of the thirteen original states at the time of their union. It is larger than ten present-day states and has more people than twenty independent nations of the world that vote equally with the United States in the UN General Assembly. Yet the District's every act, from dog licensing to levying taxes, requires the implicit or explicit consent of non-Washingtonians in Congress and the White House. DC acts only by the grace of the crown. Even during periods in which the city enjoys what has come to be known as "home rule," its right of self-determination is conditional on good behavior. When, as in 1874, the city fails to please Congress, the national legislature needs only to pass a simple act to cancel the local power that it has granted.

Thus it is not rhetorical whimsy to describe Washington DC as a colony. It is a colony—a lonely and forgotten colony. Even during the tumultuous years of the sixties, when the streets of the nation repeatedly overflowed with protests against the numerous offenses of the national government, the lack of self-government in the District of Columbia failed to make the demonstrators' list of concerns. The media ignored the city's status problem as well.

Washington began with a plan. To Pierre L'Enfant, whose plan it was, the scheme had to be drafted "on such a scale as to leave room for that aggrandizement and embellishment which the increase of the wealth of the nation will permit to pursue at any period however remote." Thus Pennsylvania Avenue was laid out through empty lots; the monuments, parks, and major buildings plotted in tidal flats and atop vacant hills; and over half of the land reserved for roads. Flying into Washington on a clear early evening, the visitor is welcomed by illuminated landmarks spotted about the neat grid of still visible streets to a capital of grandeur and order; even the native Washingtonian coming home leans close to the window to catch the prospect. The aggrandizement and embellishment has not yet obscured the foci of the original design. No high-rise towers dwarf the Washington Monument or crowd the Capitol. The plan has, to a large degree, survived.

But the plan was, at the start, an illusion. L'Enfant, like many planners after him, apparently believed that physical form can triumph over politics, tradition, economics, and culture. For years, however, Washington failed to respond to the design. The city was a place of power, not grandeur. The neatness of the street plan failed to be repeated in the life of the city. As late as Reconstruction, animals ran loose in the muddy roads of the capital. Only in the past few decades has there been an appropriate convergence of symbol and reality. As the power of the President expanded in this century, so did monumental Washington. Many of the major attractions of the city are hardly older than the visitor. The Lincoln Memorial was built in 1922. The classical columns of the Supreme Court were raised in the midst of the Depression as was the Archives building. The National Gallery was finished in 1941 and the Jefferson Memorial followed in 1942. In fact, it is difficult for the tourist to find—aside from the White House, Capitol, Washington Monument, or Library of Congress—a hallowed shrine that predates the administration of Warren Gamaliel Harding. The tone of monumental Washington is set by architecture of that most recent era during which Washington's hold over the nation and the world burgeoned.

The construction of large federal office buildings, the Pentagon, and the Supreme Court by the Roosevelt Administration heralded the new age of massive federal government. The dream of John Kennedy to turn Pennsylvania Avenue into a Champs Elysee warned that the days of presidents walking the streets of Washington before breakfast were over. And under Johnson and Nixon, the press of federal construction matched the appetites of those in power. In 1970, the National Capital Planning Commission projected a $1 billion building program to put the city in shape for the bicentennial of 1976. Included on the list of pending and proposed buildings were an ethnic museum; completion of offices in the area known as the Federal Triangle at a cost of $70 million; a new building for the Department of Health, Education, and Welfare; a $90 million annex to the Library of Congress; a National Square; a $65 million air and space museum; a national aquarium; three art museums; the John F. Kennedy Center for the Performing Arts; an arena and convention center; new court buildings; a museum of "American Architecture and Building Technology"; a $75 million FBI building; and the FDR Rose Garden.

Following on the trail of the freeway and federal office building boom of the fifties and sixties (including the construction of the grotesque and gargantuan Rayburn House Office Building in which, it is said, 1,800 people can go to the bathroom at the same time), the plans of the seventies indicated that L'Enfant had been prescient about the course of American democracy.

Monumental Washington, though, had gotten off to a bad start. The first of five architects of the Capitol had described his successor in these terms: "This Dutchman in taste, this monument builder, this planner of grand steps and walls; this falling-arch maker, this blunder-roof guilder, himself still an architect calls." A railroad station was plunked in the middle of L'Enfant's Mall. The Washington Monument stood as a decapitated obelisk for some thirty years before finally being topped. During the first three quarters of a century, Washington's federal buildings had consumed less than $60 million (those being the days when a dollar would still go across the Potomac).

Today, the monumentality is spreading rapidly. Fittingly, architect Nathaniel Owings evoked the memory of Pope Sixtus V to describe glowingly President Nixon's efforts to carry out the rebuilding of Pennsylvania Avenue. The former counsellor to the Inquisition, who as Pope had rebuilt Rome (and whose fiscal policies concurrently helped cause a recession in the papal states), seemed a worthy mentor for a plan that included a national square beside the Treasury Building and an imposing headquarters for the national police situated almost halfway between the seats of the executive and legislative branches.

The people of Washington have been inexorably swept up in the proliferation of federal temples. The construction of the Federal Triangle and beautification of Pennsylvania Avenue brought the removal of the city's Chinatown in the early thirties only to have the new location threatened four decades later, first by a proposed arena and convention center, and then by an international trade center. The bloating of office space around the Capitol Building destroyed houses, commercial establishments, and restaurants central to the life of the surrounding neighborhood. That sprawling monument to city planning, the Southwest Urban Renewal Project, laid waste to homes for 24,000 people and forced out hundreds of small businesses, some 60 percent of which never opened again. Further, since 1935 the aggrandizement and embellishment has removed some 2,200 acres, 8.5 percent of the land area of the city, from the local tax rolls.

But L'Enfant's dream has not only served national glory and contractor-contributors to presidential campaigns. It has also made a contribution to the ordinary resident. It led, in 1901, to a limitation on the height of buildings that has given Washingtonians the unusual urban pleasure of viewing the sky, although the privilege has been increasingly circumscribed by a curtain of smog. The height restriction has also restrained density, much to the annoyance of developers circling over the carrion of the city's urban renewal areas.

The numerous circles, the squares, and the green triangles where broad diagonal avenues cross the rectangular street grid have provided Washington with natural centers for congregation and recreation which add pleasure and civility to the city. Dupont Circle, for example, became during the sixties a meeting place of the free community, especially on balmy evenings as bongo drums and guitars filled its circumference and spilled over. The broad area adjoining the Mall is spotted on warm weekends with athletic contests ranging from ad hoc softball and football games to cricket and polo. In many other parks and squares, the heat of the summer brings mobile stages, rock groups, and choirs under the aegis of the National Park Service's "Summer in the Parks" program. Across from my onetime home on Seward Square, where the diagonals of North Carolina and Pennsylvania Avenues slice across a rectangle created by cross-streets, there are four small parks hewn out of the pattern, each finding a purpose—as a football field, dog run, or warm weather retreat for winos.

Curiously, the highest building in Washington is not even in the area delineated by the original plan. Taking advantage of the 350-foot elevation of Wisconsin Avenue in the northwest section of town, the National Cathedral looks out over the Washington Monument and the Capitol, a reminder of a time when it was the spiritual branch of WASP America's political headquarters down on Pennsylvania Avenue. But though the political power of Episcopalianism has waned, this extraordinary building intrudes on a remarkable number of vistas. You can see it from the Virginia side of the Potomac River.

Life Inside a Monument

For a block or two, driving along a ghetto street, you suddenly catch it in the rearview mirror. Across town, in the shadow of the Roman Catholic National Shrine, its heretical shape glares in the distance. And far to the east, on a hill in Anacostia, it reappears. The more than eighty years it has taken for its still incomplete form to rise above the city contrasts strikingly with the frenetic monumentality spreading over the central city.

There are other buildings that break with the classic image of Washington, but like the people of the city, they are obscured by the federal presence. Not a few of these buildings are threatened by some new agency headquarters or high-rise office building, like the romanesque revival Old Post Office Building and the turn-of-the-century Willard Hotel. There are smaller buildings, like the stately old homes ringing traffic circles, on what has now become prime commercial land, or the curious Octagon House and the twin towers of the Apex Liquor Store (a few steps away from a small statue to "Temperance"), which looks like a short-horn steer chewing its cud peaceably along Pennsylvania Avenue. Casting an eye away from the federal and the monumental, you can discover a Washington that has carried on its own business with more than a little grace and charm.

Beyond the center of the city are the ordinary houses of Washington. There are the typical three-story row houses, sixteen to twenty feet wide, and the later and wider two-story dwellings that even in the worst slums have a structural soundness that makes much contemporary construction seem flimsy. So solid does a large portion of Washington's housing look, it is sometimes difficult to convince visitors of the squalor behind many of the facades. Lacking tenements, Washington hides many of its problems until the sweaty nights of July and August drive young and old from the jammed interiors into the relative cool of the streets.

Although planners have tended to ignore the assets

of Washington's housing supply in their bias for slash and destroy urban renewal, those who can afford it have proved in places like Georgetown and Capitol Hill that the rehabilitation of the city's run-down row housing is quite practical. In such communities, white professionals have undertaken private renewal that has remade deteriorating streets into exciting urban neighborhoods. As in public renewal, however, the price has been heavy: the forced and largely unassisted removal of the poor, mostly black. Yet the physical success of these renovated communities suggests that ordinary people can renew a city as well or better than planners and that rehabilitation is more desirable than clearance.

In some neighborhoods, both black and white, detached homes predominate. The difference between the two is largely price, although one black businessman owns a $350,000 house in the heavily white Northwest and poverty-level whites hang on to their homes in scattered parts of black Washington. A rising black middle class has taken over large areas of formerly all-white housing ranging from the modest to the pretentious. Blacks got much of this housing as panicked whites fled —under what may ultimately be considered fire-sale conditions. The housing, having deteriorated in neither value nor condition under its new owners, has proved to be an unintended gift to the cause of black economic advancement. If one travels through Washington's middle-class neighborhoods after everyone has gone to bed, it is virtually impossible to tell whether the community is mostly white or black. It's said a high black official in the Kennedy Administration was mowing his lawn when a white woman drove up and asked him how much he got for doing the lawn. The reply: "I get to sleep with the lady of the house."

Most Washingtonians, however, don't own their own house. An extraordinarily high 70 percent of the units in the city are rented. These range from $200,000 large homes leased to top administration officials to public housing boxes badly maintained by the National Capital Housing Authority. Many row houses in both affluent and poor neighborhoods are rented, some to families living eight on a three-room floor and some expensive homes to groups of law students or secretaries sharing the costs. The rest of the renters live in high-rise apartments, including crowded flats with heat that doesn't function in the winter and water that may not run at anytime, as well as decayed luxury housing for white widows along Connecticut Avenue.

The houses of Washington are situated in what is left of the ten-mile square that originally comprised the District of Columbia. On a map, the square looks like a washed-out baseball diamond with north at second base. The area bounded by home plate, the pitcher's mound, short stop, and third base was ceded back to Virginia in 1846, leaving the District with sixty-nine square miles. The remaining city is sliced by two geographical lines. The first, running roughly north–south down the western part of the city is formed by Rock Creek and the surrounding 1,800 acres of Rock Creek Park. The other, running parallel to the first base line—cutting off a quarter of Washington's population from the rest, is the Anacostia River. The creek and the river are economic, political, and psychological barriers of critical importance to the city. "West of the Park" is a geographical term used by both whites and blacks. The 90,000 people who live there are mostly white, mostly well-off and nearly half Republican. If the area were a county, it would be the wealthiest one in the country. The 180,000 people living east of the Anacostia are mostly black, mostly engaged in a daily financial struggle and over 90 percent Democratic. While the population west of the park has remained steady over the past decade, the population east of the Anacostia has jumped as much as 22 percent in some sections, partially because of zoning policies as well as urban renewal and freeway construction in other parts of the city. This increase added enormously to the already overburdened public services of the area. West of the park schools are about the best in the city and children are bused in from other neighborhoods to fill classrooms. Across the Anacostia, schools are over-crowded and educational problems proliferate. West of the park crime is low; trans-Anacostia crime is high. About the only characteristic the two ends of Washington share is being bordered by streams so filled with sewage that a tetanus shot is advised if one falls into them.

About 60 percent of the people live between Rock Creek and the Anacostia. They live in comfortable middle-class (mostly black) neighborhoods in the north; in Washington's only truly polyglot communities, Adams-Morgan and Mt. Pleasant; in biracial but unintegrated Capitol Hill; in the high-rises of the new Southwest; and in the Shaw and Near Northeast areas—centers of the 1968 riots. Although the overall population density of the city is a modest 12,000 people per square mile, two-thirds of its residents live on one-third of the habitable land with densities in certain neighborhoods reaching 50,000 per square mile and higher.

Together, the people of Washington belie two great myths about their city, contradictory myths that somehow coexist. The first myth is that Washington is the home of the powerful. Most Washingtonians are powerless, and most of the powerful don't live in Washington but in the suburbs. Those who do reside in Washington are concentrated in the gilded ghetto of Upper Northwest and in the new apartment complexes of Southwest and Foggy Bottom. When the sententious writer for the *New York Times* notes, "The mood in the Capital these days is—" he is generally referring to his lunch partner that noon, but, granting a larger vision, he is undoubtedly talking about people, who, like himself, are white, male, and between the ages of twenty-five and fifty-five.

Life Inside a Monument

In Washington, DC, there are only 38,000 such persons, or about 5 percent of the population, not enough to fill RFK Stadium. No one asks the other 95 percent what their mood is.

On the other hand, there is the myth that Washington is a poor city. This stems in large part from the assumption that since the city is mostly black it must be mostly poor. But as George Grier of the Washington Center for Metropolitan Studies pointed out:

> Racial transition has not turned Washington from a white middle- and upper-income city to a black poor city. It is more prosperous today than ever before. The total number of black families in the District with annual incomes over $15,000 approximately tripled in the decade [1960–1970], even after the correction for inflation. The same was true for those earning over $12,000. The number with incomes of $8,000 or over more than doubled. There now are actually more black families at these higher income levels than there were white families with the same incomes in 1960.

The 1970 census found that 17 percent of all black families in the city earned more than $15,000 a year. But if an unusual number of Washington's blacks were doing well, a sizable minority could still feel, in Bill Mauldin's phrase, "fugitives from the law of averages." About a quarter of the black families and 60 percent of the unrelated individual blacks in the city earned less than $5,000 a year. Thus Washington is neither a poor nor a rich city but both. And in a city that is 70 percent black, the class divergence separates not only white from black but black from black.

Economist Leon Keyserling once pointed out that when the Titanic went down, the women and children were saved and the men drowned—not, as a modern sociologist or planner might conclude, because they had the special characteristics of being men, but because there were not enough lifeboats. Someone had to drown, a decision was made that it was to be the men. Short of a full-employment economy, we do the same thing ashore. With not enough jobs to go around, someone drowns—and blacks are right up at the top of the expendable list. In Washington, with a black majority and a better than average number of stable jobs for it, a better than average percentage of blacks get into the lifeboats, but there are still plenty of brothers and sisters who get left behind.

The nonparallel racial and economic divisions of the city muddy perceptions of Washington. The poor of the city must deal not only with white discrimination but also with black middle-class indifference. The poor are a pain to whites, but a personal embarrassment to many more affluent blacks, particularly those in power who must frequently choose between personal advancement and racial loyalty. One of the earliest and most profound discriminations that a poor black Washingtonian suffers may well come from experiences with a black middle-class teacher or principal convinced that the child is incapable of either learning or succeeding.

On the other hand, the problems of middle-class blacks are also obscured. Seen to be making it financially and free of much of the excruciating and explicit discrimination with which they grew up, they meet far subtler barriers at every turn. The black making it is not free at last, but only free until. Until he or she makes a mistake that a white could muddle through but may cost a black's job or chance for promotion or social status. Even the top ranking blacks in the city government feel under the gun. Appealing for more funds for the city's school system, black superintendent Hugh Scott once said, "I resent the notion that you give blacks power and then take away their resources." He quoted Dick Gregory's remark that if you want a man to pull himself up by his bootstraps, first give him some boots. There are

plenty of whites, Scott implied, who would not be unhappy to see him fail as the first black superintendent of
schools.

What is remarkable about Washington—given its colonial status; its massive shift in two decades from a city
65 percent white to a city 70 percent black; its great economic contrasts; the enormous pressures, forced migration and neighborhood destruction caused by urban renewal, development, and freeway construction; and the
anger and frustration at being so close to power yet without it—is that the District is one of the sanest and most
decent places in urban America. That it has not been
able to express these virtues through self-determination
is not only a crime against equity, it is a positive opportunity missed. Washington is not only ready to govern
itself; it is ready to help show a good many other cities
how.

Washington has a number of other advantages. Although it is no longer a sleepy southern town, the southern influence is engrained enough to discourage the
northern urban freneticism and pseudo-efficiency that
tends to drive the human out of our cities. That so many
Washingtonians are bureaucrats also helps to slow the
pace down, although it contributes dullness and bland-
ness at the same time. The bureaucrat advances at a
prescribed pace and through promotions that have more
to do with time than with combativeness or aggressive-
ness. Washingtonians don't have to hurry quite so much
because not many will get there any quicker if they do.

While retaining some of the civility and pace of the
south, Washington, in its transformation from a pro-
vincial town to contemporary city, managed to shuck the
terrible heritage of southern-style segregation early in
the civil rights struggle. By the time Martin Luther King
began his bus boycott in 1955, Washington had already
desegregated its public eating and theatre facilities.
When the Supreme Court school decision was handed

down in 1954, Washington moved quickly to follow the law. The Roman Catholic schools, in fact, had been quietly desegregated even earlier. This was not a matter of dealing with the implicit segregation that festered in the north, but striking at genuine, old-style southern apartheid that marred its every public institution.

By the time of the 1963 civil rights march, Washington was already far into its own civil rights revolution. The change was eased because Washington was simply a biracial city. Until the recent climb in the city's still small latino population, its ethnic politics were simple: you were either black or white. The problems found in cities with multiple ethnic minorities, each feeling threatened by one or more of the others, didn't exist. The whites' sharing of power with blacks was uncomplicated by such questions as whether the Jews would side with the WASPs, the blacks, or themselves; or whether the Poles would find themselves fighting off a coalition of blacks and white liberals.

Another advantage has been Washington's proximity to the national government. As the federal government insinuated itself more into the life of America's cities, so problems with the federal government increased. The DC activist has been able not only to learn how to deal with an intransigent local government but how to operate in federal offices as well. When the city refused to provide food stamp service to Near Northeast Washington, the community went over its head to the Department of Agriculture. When Congress threatened to cut day care funds, DC welfare mothers were on the picket line outside the Rayburn House Office Building. To people in Washington, "the federal government" does not reside in some mystical unreachable castle from which immutable laws are promulgated; the federal government is that building twenty blocks down the number 96 bus line. The resulting sophistication has stood Washingtonians in good stead even in the worst of colonial times.

The peek that Washingtonians have been permitted at local democracy confirms the suspicion that despite a bedrock Baptist black constituency and strong conservative leanings by a sizable minority of whites, DC has the potential, granted self-determination, to become one of the more progressive cities in the nation.

Since 1968, the city has elected its school board, although the privilege contains a large element of sham since the board has little control over its budget. Still, the city has shown its willingness to support major change. After throwing out an old-line, authoritarian school board president, the electorate chose in 1971 a board that included some of the most intelligent and progressive candidates one was likely to find anywhere in the country—among them Marion Barry, a much jailed ex-head of the local Student Nonviolent Coordinating Committee, who became president of the board. The board also included two black members of the radical DC Statehood Party and a white Roman Catholic priest. Even the white Jewish liquor store owner representing Ward Three, West of the Park, entered at least Consciousness II under the influence of the new majority.

Although the new board was hamstrung in its first term by constant budgetary crises, it was philosophically committed to concepts that embroiled other cities in deep conflicts: decentralization, community control, and major changes in the selection of teachers and principals.

Washington has also been allowed a nonvoting delegate in the Congress. One critic said it was like sending a eunuch to an orgy; someone else described the post as that of "congressional voyeur." Nonetheless, Washingtonians threw themselves into the selection of candidates with vigor. In the first delegate campaign, the candidates began on the right with a liberal Republican. The winner was a conventional black liberal Democrat named

Walter Fauntroy; his left-wing opposition had included three black Marxists and a white homosexual. The DC Statehood Party, whose platform is a mixture of populism, socialism, and anarchism, got 15,000 votes, a surprising total for a new party on the left. In fact, eliminating the mostly white Ward Three, the Statehood Party came within 240 votes of the Republicans in the rest of the city. And while the election of the ineffective Reverend Mr. Fauntroy could hardly be called inspired, in most other American cities Fauntroy, coming out of the Southern Christian Leadership Conference, would have been the radical of the campaign.

Washingtonians have been allowed to vote for president since 1964, but in typical fashion, even this right is circumscribed. The DC resident actually gets only a three-quarters vote for president, since the District is allowed three electoral votes, while under the formula used for states it would be entitled to four.

In the 1972 election, Washington joined Massachusetts in casting its electoral votes for George McGovern. In trans-Anacostia's Ward Seven and Eight, Nixon received only about 2,000 votes out of 25,000 cast. Even white Washingtonians cast a majority of their votes for McGovern. This last colony and one of the original ones stood together against the GOP onslaught.

The minimal contact with democracy permitted to Washingtonians, while failing to give the city control over its destiny, at least has granted it the first opportunity in nearly a century to discover itself politically. To those who live in communities that take elections for granted, it is difficult to appreciate the value of this. But for Washingtonians, accustomed to never being asked how they felt about anything, the chance to speak was exhilarating even if largely without effect.

As voting patterns accumulated, it became apparent that Washington was a liberal city with a larger than normal radical minority and a weaker than normal conservative minority. The 1971 nonvoting delegate vote revealed that the Baptist church initially was the most effective political organization in the still unpolitical city and that black liberals, like their white counterparts, were attracted to a candidate who would speak of change yet not be too energetic or disruptive in seeking it.

When the city's bible belt sent Baptist preacher Walter Fauntroy to Congress, it chose a man identified with the civil rights movement of the sixties but who, like his constituents, had tempered his politics as he advanced from positions of protest to positions of power. Fauntroy and his backers knew well that there was plenty of unfinished business, but they also had moved far enough not to want to risk the hard-earned gains by pushing too hard. And they warned those who were uneasy with their caution not to be "crabs in the barrel," pulling down the crab who was making his way up from the bottom.

Although Fauntroy drew white liberal support, his politics centered on blacks. His campaign staff knew that Fauntroy could afford to ignore white Washington and, except for visits to white fundraisers, he pitched his efforts and his extensive media campaign (financed heavily by white liberal and business interests) to blacks. This strategy did not hurt the flow of white liberal support or white money. Further, in his pre-election activities as a member of the appointed city council and as major-domo of the Shaw urban renewal area, Fauntroy was identified by the white business community as someone who was reliable, cooperative, and inoffensive; he might talk of 'nation-time,' but there was reason to be confident that the Board of Trade and developers would be cut in on the nation.

But if Washington's black voting majority felt comfortable with the respectable Fauntroy, it could also be appealed to by a more restless politician like School Board president Marion Barry. Since 1965 Barry had been involved in a string of confrontations, many of them involving police practices, that marked him as an agitator. When the young and then-single Barry took on incumbent black board president Anita Allen, the promise of real change in the city's troubled school system attracted enough support to put him in.

In a sense, the two candidates reflected the countervailing forces pulling at Washington's blacks: the urge for respectability and the need for change.

To the quarter of the city's voting population for whom either Barry or Fauntroy seemed too liberal, the local Republican party offered an alternative. But with the party organization remaining in the hands of old-line reactionaries, the GOP was unable to organize new support in the city.

Finally, the DC Statehood Party, formed in 1970 to run Julius Hobson, the city's leading and most effective militant, for the delegate post, found itself developing a black-white coalition that attracted the radical and the impatient, drawing best among young professionals to whom the pace of change in the city was altogether too slow. It capitalized upon the political generation gap among both whites and blacks to hold about 12 percent of the vote, placing it among the most significant local radical parties in the country.

The advent of real local politics, however, did not cover up the reality of DC's subjugated status. Those who did not run—congressmen, the White House, commercial and development interests, and the city's appointed commissioner and council—continued to hold the balance of power.

Not the least important of these was the business community. For years the Board of Trade functioned as a de facto coequal branch of local government. Congressmen wanting a local reaction to pending legislation or appropriations would first consult the board's executive vice president. Until 1972, the board opposed home rule for the city. It pressed for freeways, for zoning changes, and for renewal favorable to commercial inter- ests. Out of the board have been spawned other groups like a business organization that goes under the pre- sumptuous name of the Federal City Council, and an- other called Downtown Progress, a group dedicated to the renewal of the central city along lines familiar to most American urban areas, and whose board of direc- tors' membership tells as well as anything where much local power lies. In one recent year it included the presi- dent and/or chairman of twelve local financial institu- tions.

The media were represented by the president and/or chairman of the *Evening Star,* the *Washington Post,* Post-Newsweek Stations, the Evening Star Broadcasting Company, the now defunct *Daily News* and a vice presi- dent of the National Broadcasting Company.

Utilities representatives included the board chairman of the Washington Gas Light, the president and the chairman of the board of Potomac Electric Power Com- pany, and two vice presidents of the Chesapeake & Po- tomac phone company.

From the city's universities were the presidents of Howard, George Washington, Georgetown, and Federal City College. In addition there were various large real estate operators, the division managers of the largest su- permarket chains, department store heads, President J. Willard Marriott of the Marriott Corporation, and the area manager of Sears Roebuck.

Here was Washington's secret government. A ma- jority vote of this board was a mandate to the city gov- ernment, a mandate not often ignored except on those rare occasions when it ran counter to White House or congressional policy.

In development and transportation policies in partic- ular, the mandate reflected a myopic misreading of the needs and concerns of the city. Convinced that down- town was "dying," that the center city was a stagnant core, that Washington had become the hole in the suburban doughnut of a metropolitan area whose population had expanded 38 percent in ten years while the DC population had declined, the businessmen came up with the conventional solutions: more freeways, more parking, more high-rise office buildings, the elimination of small businesses occupying valuable land. They ignored the social, environmental, and economic costs of highway construction. They failed to see that developing a center city serving primarily nontaxpaying suburbanites added to the city's service burdens more than it added to the tax base. They failed to recognize that downtown, if it were to be viable, would need the eccentricity and variety that small firms offered and that downtown could not compete by imitating the services provided in a suburban shopping mall.

They made two other misjudgements. The first was that Washington was economically stagnant. While business and population were indeed booming in the suburbs, the city looked bad only in comparison. Atlee Shidler, of the Washington Center for Metropolitan Studies, has pointed out that far from being a hole in the doughnut, Washington is a bisected unit. If one plots economic indicators throughout the Washington metropolitan area, one discovers that both city and suburb are divided by a line that runs more north–south, than along any political boundary. This line separates high and generally more valuable land from the lower and poorer land. This division has existed since the earliest days. High and wealthy Montgomery County was where independent farmers once tilled fertile land. To the east lies the low, formerly tobacco cropland of far poorer Prince Georges County.

Today these areas continue to fulfill their historic roles and the adjoining portions of Washington follow suit. Northwest DC has more in common with Montgomery County, and trans-Anacostian DC is more like parts of Prince Georges County than either section of the city is like the other. Northwest's affluent Cleveland Park, established during the Cleveland Administration as a summer retreat, was rediscovered in the sixties as a chic neighborhood even as trans-Anacostia and Prince Georges were being reused as a catch-basin for the less fortunate.

The second misjudgement was the equation of Washington's racial change with economic deterioration. Those stores in downtown that were dying were in trouble because they continued to cater to a dwindling white market. On the other hand, some stores capitalized on the rising black market. Morton's department chain, which marketed to blacks, had four outlets before the 1968 riots. Two of them were destroyed in what a local black newspaper editor called "the great consumer rebellion of April 1968." But three years later, Morton's was doing more business with two stores than it had been doing with four. On Easter weekend in 1971, Morton's downtown outlet had to close its doors several times because of fire department limits on crowding.

Misjudgements stemmed in part from the suburban focus of those who made them. The economic power of the city rested with interests—commercial, financial, and media—whose major clientele was outside the city. The misjudgments proved expensive to Washington. They encouraged policies that attempted to regain a fleeing market instead of developing the new one. To anyone living in Washington during the sixties, it was clear that the business community had deserted DC residents for the lure of the suburbs. City supermarkets ran downhill; chain department stores let their downtown outlets deteriorate and, from the Board of Trade to the Urban Coalition, there came repeated warning that the city was on its last legs.

But the city refused to die. Local income mounted. Retail trade rose also, although at a much slower rate than in the suburbs. In selected areas, such as George-town and Capitol Hill, new strips developed and flour-ished in defiance of the fearful projections. Black busi-nessmen moved into corner laundries, mom and pop stores, and other establishments jettisoned by whites. On the average, Washington was doing better than ever. The tax base, contrary to the reports, was growing. But the progress could not keep pace with the city's proliferat-ing bureaucracy and expensive but ineffective programs. As the city did better, the city government did worse.

The prime victims of this divergence were the poorer residents of Washington. Almost without exception, the major new programs of the District were aimed at en-hancing the life of the middle and upper classes, partic-ularly those from the suburbs. The city encouraged high-rise office buildings for commuters, but its low income housing programs were minimal at best. It encouraged the construction of interstate freeways but let public transit fall apart. It enlarged the size of the metropolitan police force, adding considerably to the tax burden of local residents, but failed to take steps to deal with causes of crime like bad housing, poor schools, and un-employment. It sought white collar jobs for the city but not blue collar ones. The assumption was that if the upper end of the economy could be renewed, the poor would take care of themselves. In fact it was the middle and upper classes that, as could be expected, took care of themselves, while many of the poor continued to wallow in despair.

As the membership of Downtown Progress indicates, the media, rather than being a critic of the city's planning policies, was deeply involved in promoting them. It was, after all, the owner of the *Washington Post* who in 1890 had founded the Board of Trade in the first place. The *Washington Post*, widely considered outside the residen-tial city to be an ultraliberal journal of the first water (Joe McCarthy called it "Pravda on the Potomac"), was on local matters ultracautious and often downright conservative. It boosted the construction of civic circuses like the convention center and arena; it backed the building of more freeways; it encouraged slash and burn urban renewal; and it chastized those community groups and individuals who fought too vehemently against its pet projects. Although the *Evening Star* (later the *Star-News*) was editorially a much more conservative newspaper, many local activists in the sixties found that in the news pages, at least, they received a fairer and more accurate shake than in the *Post*. And while both papers engaged in behind-the-scene manipulation of local affairs (the *Post*'s editors helped LBJ choose Walter Washington as District Commissioner and one of them, Ben Gilbert, subsequently went on to be one of his key aides), it was the *Post*'s liberal posture combined with its often patronizing, ignorant, and business-oriented local coverage that galled those active in the community.

Increasingly, both papers turned away from the city as a source of news. With the overwhelming majority of their readership in the suburbs, the city pages became the "Metro" pages and DC residents found it harder and harder to discover what was happening in their own city.

Despite the city's growing black population, the aging *Afro-American* remained the major black print medium in Washington. An effete left-over from the days of "colored journalism," the *Afro* seemed resolutely indifferent to many of the issues and controversies that welled up in the black community; its surprisingly low circulation of less than 10,000 reflected a similar indifference towards it by the city's blacks.

For blacks, soul radio became one major source of communications, particularly WOL, which was relied upon by community organizations to stir up interest and by city officials to calm unrest, in between the shouts of DJ's like the popular Nighthawk. In 1972, WOL was the second most popular station in the metropolitan region.

Although Washington has more journalists per square mile than any American city, most of them are concerned with national affairs and the local problems of the city get short shrift. Aside from the superior national coverage of the *Star* and the *Post*, and the presence of four black radio stations, the local media is unexceptional: almost, it would appear from listening to top-rated WMAL radio, middle American circa 1955. Screaming announcers and cacophonous sounds have made less headway in Washington than in other places; the driving bureaucrat apparently prefers the gentle humor of WMAL's morning team, Hardin and Weaver, or Tom Gager, who plays the national anthem each day and programs middle-of-the-road music interspersed with lengthy interviews with directors of amateur classical music groups or retarded children benefit chairwomen. This is the town that spawned Arthur Godfrey with his gentle mocking of advertisers—like his complaints about the "dirty old bear," a stuffed symbol outside the store of a furrier who bought time on the show; and nobody on the air today has a more loyal audience than Hardin and Weaver or that other pair of satiric jockeys, the Joy Boys. Their success seems to stem in part from a covert cynicism about power and its institutions that may lurk in even the most loyal bureaucrat's breast.

While there are a large number of people in the communications business in DC and while it sometimes seems that everyone you meet either works for the government or writes about it, the impression is misleading. Less than a third of the city's labor force is employed by the federal government, fewer than the number in service-type jobs. Less than 5 percent of the DC jobs are in manufacturing.

There is another occupation, however, that strikes one as typical of the city: driving a cab. There's a cab for every eighty people in the city. With no limit on the number of licenses issued, it is easy to gain permission to operate a taxi. Many of the hackers drive only part-time and it is not unusual to find one's cab driven by a student, a postal worker, a District government employee, or even a storefront minister making up for deficiencies in the collection plate.

Washington has a unique zone fare system. Although the fares have traditionally been unfairly low, the zone system itself appears to have helped both the driver and the rider. The zone system tends to keep out large corporate fleet owners since without meters they are unable to keep tabs on the drivers. For the rider the use of zones sets a premium on getting to the destination the fastest way and not by the route that will produce the greatest total on the meter. In recent years there have been increasing complaints about cabs refusing to go to certain parts of town or to pick up blacks, especially young black males, but Washington still has one of the nation's better cab systems. Besides, it is about the only place where it is possible to hail a Mercedes diesel, Citroen, or Volvo cab (there is at least one of each). The drivers choose their own cabs, which often double as the family car, so it is not unusual to find a DC cab far from the city on a weekend outing. DC cabs are among the most efficiently used vehicles in the country. But like everyone else, they must fight the traffic.

For those in the city and surrounding suburbs, driving is one of the worst miseries of the place. In his original plan, L'Enfant had proposed that 3,606 acres out of a total of 6,111 be devoted to roads. In the *City in History*, Lewis Mumford remarks: "Only a modern highway engineer, with his extravagant intersections, could compete with L'Enfant in this reckless wastage of precious urban land." George Washington and Thomas Jefferson would have agreed; they cut back heavily on the road-building program.

In the last few decades, highway engineers, congressmen with close ties to the highway lobby, and commercial and transportation interests have been making up for lost time. Washington has been subjected to one of the most intensive urban freeway efforts in the country, helping to give it the dubious distinction of having America's greatest density of automobiles. Said Mumford:

> Washington has proved a classic testing station for the question of whether a city dedicated wholeheartedly to traffic could sufficiently survive for any other purpose.
> Already it is plain in Washington—and will become plainer as the city receives the inundation of new expressways, which recklessly spoil every view and defile every approach to its finest urban prospects—that when traffic takes precedence over all other urban functions, it can no longer perform its own role, that of facilitating meeting and intercourse. The assumed right of the private motor car to go to any place in the city and park anywhere is nothing less than a license to destroy the city. L'Enfant's plan, by its very invitation to traffic, has now proved its own worst enemy.

The invasion of the automobile, while worse than in most places, produced effects with which every urban dweller is painfully familiar. There was, however, an added insult related to DC's impotent status: by 1972 the city was losing nearly $4 million a year because 178,000 suburbanites and 240,000 tourists from other states did not pay their parking tickets.

Although the city of Washington bears the brunt of the automobile, it is not the major contributor to traffic. Only 37 percent of DC workers use their cars to get to work, and many of the remaining don't own one. In the suburbs, however, 69 percent of the workers get to their jobs by their car. Some go to the 270,000 jobs held by suburbanites in the city. In addition, some 236,000 suburbanites hold jobs outside the city and outside their own county, adding to the increasingly frequent traffic jams on the Capital Beltway. Eighty-five percent of the auto commuter traffic in the area comes from suburbanites.

To the city resident, the car is an intruder. The automania of three decades has slowly strangled every form of mass transit. The streetcars are gone. The bus system was run into the ground by a private entrepreneur more interested in real estate spinoffs than in providing service; and the buses couldn't provide decent service anyway because of all the cars on the street. Taxicabs, while cheaper and more numerous than in most major cities, have become increasingly disinterested in serving low-income neighborhoods or riders. And the planned subway system was long delayed by Congress to force completion of a hated freeway system.

The most obvious symbol of the automobile's status, other than the mass of vehicles, is air pollution. The city lacks industry and most of its pollution comes from the automobile. A few days before the 1973 Inauguration, the city experienced its first midwinter smog alert; the local environment chief thought seriously of recommending that people not come to the ceremony in order to reduce the pollution count.

When the smog lifts—especially, it seems, on Sundays when automobile traffic is light—you can rediscover Washington the beautiful. The white office buildings leap out from the brilliant blue backdrop of the sky. If it's springtime, tens of thousands of tulips planted by the National Park Service provide a pointillist ground cover to downtown squares and circles. Along Rock Creek Parkway, daffodils proclaim the beginning of Washington's favorite season. The city lives for spring and fall, periods separated by muggy summer and by an unpredictable yet dull winter. In the fall, the gauze of noxious gas that stretches over the city all summer is peeled away, permitting the sun a rare chance to lounge unimpeded against the sides of buildings or ricochet off spires. The air conditioner's monotone is finally silenced and the hint of chill is repulsed by a friendly jacket. But the spring is even better; you quickly forget the snow that didn't come, or that did come but all in one blizzard, and you luxuriate in a few months of unadulterated color and life.

Summer is awful and in winter it is best to heed the words of Mark Twain:

> When you arrived it was snowing. When you reached the hotel it was sleeting. When you went to bed it was raining. During the night it froze hard, and the wind blew some chimneys down. When you got up in the morning it was foggy. When you finished your breakfast at ten o'clock and went out, the sunshine was brilliant, the weather balmy and delicious, and the mud and slush deep and all pervading. You will like the climate—when you get used to it. . . . Take an umbrella, an overcoat, and a fan, and so forth.

Would that all critiques of the city be as valid. No other American city has so much written and spoken about it by people who have no organic connection with it and who expend so little effort on its behalf. From presidents to *Time* reporters, the city is what they wish (or have time) to see, and the resulting reports veer from descriptions of a Grossinger's for megalomaniacs to a Tolkien-like netherworld inhabited by orcs, goblins, brigands, and things that go bump in the night and take all your money.

The Washingtonian finds few friends among those who pass through. Jack Kennedy called it a place of "northern charm and southern efficiency." Liberal senator and momentary vice presidential candidate Thomas Eagleton, while serving as the chairman of the Senate District committee, responded to a complaint that a proposed home rule bill would leave Congress with a veto over all local actions by saying, "The Lord giveth and the Lord taketh away." Congressmen with impeccable liberal credentials curry favor with their conservative constituents and financial backers by supporting freeways, developers, and 'law and order' schemes for the District. And the *New York Times Guide* to the city focused its chapter about the future of Washington on a glowing description of the foolish, pretentious, and destructive Pennsylvania Avenue plan.

Such are our friends. Piled on top are a legion of race-baiters, demagogues, and legislators using the District to make deals, political and business, that would be a scandal if they occurred in their home districts, and others who use their power over the city to make sure they get cheap liquor and cheap taxi rides.

The denigration of Washington as a place follows other paths as well. The Washingtonian, told that the town is a federal city, grows up believing that this somehow prohibits the District from seeking political equality or even other sources of income (such as a commuter tax). Washingtonians have been taught to rely on the national government until they have lost much of their will for self-initiative. One of the hardest problems faced by anyone seeking change in Washington is what has become known as the "colonial mentality," a fatalistic acceptance of powerlessness.

The attitude long extended to cultural life. For years, the repeated declaration by visitors and temporary residents that Washington was a hick town devoid of cultural merit operated as a self-fullfilling description. But then, in the sixties and early seventies, Washington went into cultural therapy, shucked its inferiority complex, turned away from New York–promulgated cultural values, and struck out on its own. By 1972, Washington was attending more theatre performances than was Philadelphia, a much larger city. Leading the way in drama was the innovative Arena Stage, whose performances were preferred by many to the drivel that treked through the National Theatre on its way to Broadway.

In art, the long-excellent National Gallery and Phillips Collection and the old Washington color school were complimented by a growing number of fine artists, including blacks like Sam Gilliam, Lou Stovall, and Lloyd McNeil. In music, the National Symphony came to life under the baton of Antol Dorati; and Roberta Flack moved from a bar on Capitol Hill called Mr. Henry's to national prominence. Even the dowager princess of Washington's intellectual life, the Smithsonian Institution, regenerated itself with new galleries and an annual folk life festival on the Mall that attracted a million people in 1973.

But it was the neighborhoods that offered the best evidence of Washington's refusal to continue to accept the label of cultural inferiority. In DC you could find eleven symphony orchestras, including the DC Youth Orchestra, which in 1972 was one of two American groups chosen to take part in the Herbert Von Karajan International Festival of Young Orchestras. Black theater took root at Howard University and in Robert Hooks' Black Repertory Company. Arts workshops led by Topper Carew and his New Thing Art and Architecture Center not only brought the arts to the people but brought people into the arts. An African dance and drum troupe performed everywhere from church basements to meetings of the city council. Neighborhood antipoverty centers formed their own companies and held classes in the arts.

Despite a measly $67,000 appropriation by the city government in support of the arts, despite a monumental disinterest in the arts by the local business community, and despite the lack of an artist community like those in other large cities, Washington was becoming culturally alive. In a sense, the opening of the John F. Kennedy Center for the Performing Arts, with its three stages and plush appointments, symbolized the change; but in another more important sense it obscured it. The Kennedy Center was designed for tourists and suburbanites who feared to go downtown to the old theaters and night-places; it was inaccessible physically and psychologically to most of the city. The growth of the arts within the city seemed to owe more to a belief by those involved, particularly the black artists, that art should be a part of everyday life, not just vicarious recreation for the educated and the affluent. The Kennedy Center and the New Thing were not only geographically separated; they were miles away in the mind.

The contrast was a familiar one to Washington. It is a city of dichotomies, contrasts, and striking inequalities. It is the capital of a major democracy that lacks local democracy. It is a citadel of power whose residents lack power. It is a city with an excess of multimillion dollar office buildings and a shortage of housing. It is a city that is wealthier than most in which a sizable minority lives in great poverty. It has a 70 percent black population but the major decisions are still made by whites. It is a city in which the American dream and the American tragedy pass each other on the street and do not speak.

It is, finally, a city that has suffered a form of deprivation known primarily to the poor and the imprisoned, a psychological deprivation born of the constant suppression and denial of one's identity, worth, or purpose by those in control. Washington to those in power is not a place but a hall to rent. The people of Washington are the custodial staff. And the renters are as likely to visit the world in which this staff lives as a parishioner is to inspect the boiler room of the church.

The purpose of Washington's community is to serve,

not to be. Its school children are not taught the history of their city; they are told little of its significant men and women. There is no city festival or parade. In fact, this repository of national history doesn't even have a local history museum. The city's present is suppressed, its future is a hostage, and its past is ignored.

2 / *Low Budget Constantinople*

WASHINGTON WAS BORN TO SOLVE A NATIONAL problem between north and south; it was the issue of a political compromise. The local problems caused by the compromise, including the city's political status and the need for an adequate federal payment for services rendered the national government by the city, were left to be worked out later. It is a process that is still going on.

From the start, Washington has been a power vacuum in the nation's center of power. Unable to control its own destiny, the city has had its affairs managed by national officials who came and went, lacking, as one Washingtonian put it, "a local memory." Every new Congress and administration had its own ideas of what to do with the city that was both its host and its domain, responding with attitudes ranging from massive disinterest, even disdain, to proprietary domination. In addition, the city's black population, over 25 percent of the District's residents in 1800, 71 percent today, has been a constant issue, stated or unstated, complicating the District's fate.

Perhaps the first mistake was placing the capital at Washington. As the eighteenth century wound down, there were already a number of towns that could have handled the job well—towns with an identity, with some nongovernmental reason for existence, with a style and culture that could not be overwhelmed by a succession of transient bureaucrats and politicians tramping through their local history. With New York City, Philadelphia, or Boston as the capital, the national seat might have developed in a fashion more typical of European capitals, where the presence of the government is almost incidental to the city's function as a center of business, transportation, arts, and intellect.

But there was a deal to be made. The south was unhappy with the capital being in Philadelphia. Even before disgruntled Continental soldiers marched on Congress in 1783 to demand back pay (and forcing a temporary legislative retreat to Princeton), the complaint of the southerners was being pressed. The protest had been a mild affair, involving about 250 demonstrators and some muskets menaced at the locked windows of Independence Hall as our forefathers cowered inside. It was only in later years (particularly after the French Revolution) that the incident came, in the words of historian Constance McLaughlin Green, "to find a place in school text books as the reason for founding a new capital city out of reach of mobs and powerful local interests." What actually fueled nearly seven years of debate over the location of the nation's capital was the southern pressure. One Georgian legislator told the north that to insist on keeping the capital would "blow the coals of sedition and endanger the Union."

The north had its own problems. The sizable debt of

the Revolutionary War had been incurred primarily by the states of the north and there was a drive to have the federal government assume them, a move none too popular in the south. The deadlock was broken when Thomas Jefferson arranged with Alexander Hamilton a bit of nascent congressional logrolling. The deal was worked out over dinner between Jefferson, Hamilton, and a few key legislators. As Jefferson wrote later, the assumption bill was a pill that "would be particularly bitter to the Southern States, and that some concomitant measure should be adopted to sweeten it a little." The sweetener was a plan to move the capital to the Potomac River near Georgetown after a ten year stay in Philadelphia. Two southern members present agreed to change their votes on the assumption bill, although according to Jefferson one did so "with a revulsion of stomach almost convulsive," and Hamilton undertook to win northern approval for moving the capital in 1800 to the Potomac's banks. It was not an auspicious choice. The permanent home of the capital was little more than a swamp sandwich, a flood plain stuffed between the thin urban slices of Alexandria and Georgetown, a couple of small river ports some ninety-five miles upstream from where the Potomac flows into Chesapeake Bay.

Among the first people to come to town after Washington was chosen as the permanent capital were the land speculators. The new republic was in no financial position to buy its dreams. If a grand capital was to be built, it would require what is today known euphemistically as "a partnership between the public and private sectors." An arrangement was made for the chief land owners of the city to transfer their property to the federal government. Those areas designated for public buildings, streets, and reservations were to be donated; the United States would buy half the remaining land and the other half would go back to the original owners.

Unfortunately, an auction of the first lots brought in

little money, in part because Pierre L'Enfant, ever tinkering with his design, had failed to produce a final engraved map of the new city. In frustration, George Washington hired Baltimore surveyor Andrew Ellicott to finish the job and fired L'Enfant.

A second auction in 1792 did little better, however, even with Ellicott's map. An attempt to borrow money to build the Capitol and Executive Mansion fell through as well. At this point the private sector intervened in the persons of Robert Morris of Philadelphia (the Rockefeller of post-Revolutionary America), James Greenleaf, and James Nicholson. Writing a few years later, the French Duke de la Rochefocauld-Liancourt described their interest:

> In America, where, more than in any other country in the world, a desire for wealth is the prevailing passion, there are few schemes which are not made the means of extensive speculations; and that of erecting the Federal-City presented irresistible temptations, which were not in fact neglected.
>
> Mr. Morris was among the first to perceive the probability of immense gain in speculations in that quarter; and in conjunction with Messrs. Nicholson and Greenleaf, a very short time after the adoption of the plan purchased every lot he could lay hold on, either from the commissioners or individual proprietors; that is to say, every lot that either one or the other would sell at that period. Of the commissioners he bought six thousand lots at the price of eighty dollars per lot, each containing five thousand two hundred and sixty-five square feet.

A similar number of private lots were purchased. The conditions of the public transfer provided that Morris was to build 120 houses of brick on the lots within seven years; that no lots should be sold before January 1, 1796, or without buildings; and that payment, to be spread over seven years, would not begin until 1794.

By 1794, however, Morris et al. had already sold about a thousand of the lots, the lowest going for $293 and some running as high as $526—a three- to six-fold capital gain in a year and a half. Unfortunately for the combine, though, it went bankrupt in 1797. It was also unfortunate for the city, for the syndicate's failure discouraged other investment. Even before it became the capital, Washington's downtown was said to be dying.

By 1800, when President Adams picked up his administration and moved it to Washington, the new District was hardly ready for the event. Abigail Adams wrote to her sister a few months later:

. . . such a place as Georgetown! I felt all that Mrs. Cranch described when she was a resident there. It is the very dirtyest Hole I ever saw for a place of any trade or respectability of inhabitants. It is only one mile from me, but a quagmire after every rain. Here we are obliged to send daily for marketing. The capitol is near two miles from us. As to roads, we shall make them by the frequent passing before winter! But I am determined to be satisfied and content, to say nothing of inconvenience, etc.

Presaging W. C. Fields' epitaph, Ms. Adams remarked, "I had much rather live in . . . Philadelphia."

Adams' Secretary of the Treasury, Oliver Wolcott, was no happier. He wrote his wife:

The people are poor, and as far as I can judge, they live like fishes, by eating each other. All the ground for several miles around the city being, in the opinion of the people, too valuable to be cultivated, remains unfenced. There are few enclosures, even for gardens, and those are in bad order.

A congressman from Connecticut wrote of the avenues on the official map, ". . . not one was visible, unless we except a road, with two buildings on each side of it, called the New Jersey Avenue. The Pennsylvania

Avenue leading, as laid down on paper, from the Capitol to the Presidential Mansion, was nearly the whole distance a deep morass covered with elder bushes."

And a French diplomat asked, "My God, what have I done, to be condemned to live in such a city?"

Congress asked the same question and several times it veered towards moving the capital to some other location. The debates on the subject didn't help the economic situation any more than did the competition between Georgetown, Alexandria, and Washington—the three towns comprising the new District of Columbia.

There was yet another economic problem in store by the end of the 1820s. It had been widely assumed that the city's fortunes would be secured by completion of a canal route to the west. But when the estimates for the job came in, they far exceeded initial expectations. Although still called the Chesapeake and Ohio Canal, the plan was shortened to end the route east of the mountains, at Cumberland, Maryland. The canal, which was to have made Washington a transportation and commercial hub, was now far more modest in scope and potential effect. Ground was broken on July 4, 1828, by President John Quincy Adams. On the same day in Baltimore, Charles Carroll, the last surviving signer of the Declaration of Independence, turned the initial shovelful of dirt for the Baltimore and Ohio Railroad. Canal transportation was on the way out; the C&O Canal was to become a financial disaster.

The yellow brick road to the Emerald Capital had come to an end. The hope of self-sufficiency, and with it economic independence from the federal government, faded. As late as 1869, its only direct rail links would be to Baltimore and to the south.

All this might have been fine had the federal government been willing to pay for the pageant it wanted to create of Washington. But from the start, it clearly did not wish to do so.

Low Budget Constantinople

Not only had the public property required for the city plan been donated, but the purchase of lots by the government for resale had been financed out of funds advanced by the general assemblies of Virginia and Maryland, the states that had ceded land to create the District. Soon after the moving of the capital, the 350 taxpayers of Washington City (that portion of the District bounded roughly by the Potomac, Rock Creek, Florida Avenue, and the Anacostia) found themselves faced with an extraordinary local expense: the grading and graveling of streets 80 feet wide and avenues 160 feet wide. Fearing that the capital might be moved, the taxpayers kept quiet, even when nearly half the local budget had to go for roads and bridges.

There were other special burdens. Elsewhere, the care of the transient poor was a state problem. In Washington, however, Congress refused to assume responsibility, even though many who had come to the city to work on federal buildings or to angle for government jobs were reduced to pauper status by bad weather or lack of appropriations. When public schools were built in the territories, the federal government provided grants of land to support them. In Washington, it did not. By 1833, the city had a debt of $1.7 million and was in serious financial trouble. Most of the debt resulted from the ill-fated canal scheme, which Congress had blithely encouraged but failed to finance. In 1835, Senator Samuel Southard, in a report analysing the city's fiscal affairs, noted that under the arrangement for the establishment of the capital the government had paid $36,099 for land now worth $2.5 million. A year later the Congress finally assumed the canal debt.

When the cornerstone of Washington's city hall was laid in 1820, John Law contrasted the miserliness of Congress towards the city with the generosity of Constantine in rebuilding Byzantium into Constantinople. It was an apt comparison, for what the federal government was seeking was a bargain-basement capital, grandeur with little or no money down and years to pay.

Congress not only denied the city funds, but also the special considerations residents thought the city deserved as the capital of the nation. In the early 1800s an angry resident wrote to his newspaper: "If a national bank is created, the head is fixed elsewhere. If a military school is to be founded, some other situation is sought. If a national university is proposed, the earnest recommendation of every successive president in its favor . . . is disregarded. . . . Every member takes care of his constituents, but we are the constituents of no one."

While Congress was increasingly forced to pay the price of its pretensions, it didn't like it. It blamed local residents for rising expenses, ignoring the fact that budget items like more than a half-million dollars for the Capitol dome, a patent office, support for victims of federal construction layoffs, and maintenance of monumental avenues were hardly a local responsibility.

"I know very well that most people in the cities of Washington and Georgetown live from the drippings of the Treasury," said a Pennsylvania senator in 1856. A Georgia senator that same year complained that before long "the federal treasure will have to feed and clothe the citizens."

Between 1790 and 1870, however, only $9 million of the $44 million spent in Washington by the federal government was for local functions. Meanwhile the value of the originally donated land rose to $100 million.

When Congress granted territorial status to the District in 1870, the appointed commissioner of public works, Alexander Shepherd, took it upon himself to make up for decades of federal indifference.

Postwar Washington had become a grim sight, with slums, beggars, filth, hundreds of truant school children roaming the streets, and, according to one senator, "the infinite abominable nuisance of cows and horses, and sheep and goats, running through all of the streets of this city." He added, "Whenever we appropriate money to set up a shade tree, there comes along a cow or a horse or a goat, and tears it down the next day, and then we appropriate again." Even major streets were unpaved and sewers were minimal. Operating with more enthusiasm and speed than discretion and skill, "Boss" Shepherd proceeded to remake the city of Washington, paving streets, laying sewers, installing gas lamps, and planting trees. Coincidentally, the Board of Public Works ran up a bill that neared $19 million rather than the $6.2 million originally projected. Shepherd's plans also lacked the precision of Pierre L'Enfant or Andrew Ellicott. When two of his sewers were to be joined, workmen found that one lay ten feet below the other. Changing the street grades without aid of an accurate survey left houses perched high above the street making it impossible to drive carriages to stables in the rear. And the handling of funds was equally careless. Monies were spent without vouchers; expenses got out of hand.

In its report to the President in 1872, the Board of Public Works defended itself against its critics. It pointed out that, including streets, avenues, reservations, and lots, the federal government had acquired title to about four-fifths of the entire area of the city of Washington without any cost whatever to the people of the United States. It noted the city had been laid out "on a plan whose magnificent proportions could not fail to impoverish the most opulent city," and that if the lots donated to the federal government were now in the possession of the city, "they would afford ample means for every local improvement desired, and at the same time provide a fund sufficient to maintain the streets and avenues permanently in repair." And the board pointed out that the per-capita debt of the District was less than that in New York, Boston, Brooklyn, Jersey City, Elizabeth, Portland, or Rochester.

But Congress was not impressed by such arguments. After two congressional investigations, Shepherd found himself in Mexico and the city found itself no longer a partially self-governing territory. Having tried giving the city power without adequate funds, Congress decided to provide the funds but take away the power. For the first time in its history, the District became an unadulterated colony of the United States.

The territorial form of government was revoked and power placed in an appointed board of commissioners while Congress attempted to come up with a permanent solution. The new appointees had been in office only a short time when Congress discovered to its dismay that the city's debt had risen another $5 million. In 1878 it approved a formula under which the federal government would pay 50 percent of local expenditures (based on the relative worth of the taxable and nontaxable land) while power would be permanently vested in a three-member board of appointed commissioners.

Although the lack of local suffrage would remain fixed in the decades that followed, the fifty-fifty formula would not. By 1913 it was already down to about a third of total appropriations. Congress helped keep its share down by cutting the city's total budget, including that portion financed by local funds. For six years it refused to permit expenditures in excess of $12.8 million. Writes Constance Green, "While working on schemes to shift to the District the entire cost of street maintenance, the House dug into thirty-year-old records and exacted some $1,800,000 from local taxpayers for such items as interest on bonds of 1877 and 1878 and deficiencies in payments for services for which no bill had ever been rendered." And when Washington asked for money for public playgrounds, a congressman from Michigan opposed them on the grounds that they were socialistic.

In 1925 Congress set a $9 million ceiling on the federal contribution. Ever since, the city has provided over 70 percent of its operating budget out of local funds, exclusive of federal grants given to all states and the

District. By 1946 the federal share had dropped to 9.2 percent.

But while Congress was steadily reducing its equity in the city, it was in no way relinquishing its control. Congress's priorities controlled the local budget. It took twenty years and a death-bed plea from President Wilson's wife to provoke passage of an act to deal with the city's abominable alley dwellings. It was another two decades before the law was acted upon. While President Franklin Roosevelt spent millions on new buildings, the city's budget, based primarily on local money, was tightly reined—so much so that between 1930 and 1940 the city's appropriations rose only 20 percent while the city's population increased 36 percent. It was during this period that Elwood Street, the city's welfare head, asked Congress for help for destitute single young black women coming from the south and was told by Rep. Ross Collins, chairman of the House Subcommittee on District Appropriations, "If I went along with your ideas, Mr. Street, I'd never keep my seat in Congress. My constituents wouldn't stand for spending all that money on niggers."

Then in 1955, the federal payment was nearly doubled. What was to become known as "the urban crisis"—in large part just a belated recognition of long chronic problems in American cities—was becoming too apparent to conceal further. Congress, having committed itself to a dual role as national legislature and city council, could no longer successfully evade the responsibilities of the latter function. It spent increasingly large sums of money, but neither wisely nor ungrudgingly, and it rejected all suggestions that it was incompetent as a local government.

From Jefferson to Johnson

The city's financial problems were clear indication that the District's political system didn't work and that

Congress, whatever its claim as the "world's greatest deliberative body," could not cut it as a city council. The writers of the Constitution should have known better, but they had treated the matter of DC's political status with what now looks like benign neglect. They seemed to assume that everything would work out fairly. Madison suggested in the *Federalist Papers* that a "municipal legislature for local purposes, derived from their own suffrages, will of course be allowed them." Says Constance Green, ". . . before 1800 few contemporaries apparently had thought at all about the local problem in the making." The underlying purpose was to create a national seat free of the intramural politics of the states that composed the fragile alliance. When President Adams delivered his State of the Union address in the new capital he stated, "In this city may . . . self-government which adorned the great character whose name it bears be forever held in veneration." He then told Congress, "It is with you, gentlemen, to consider whether the local powers over the District of Columbia vested by the Constitution in the Congress of the United States, shall be immediately exercised."

Congress considered the matter and laid the ground-work for years of confusion, debate, and the ultimate denial of complete suffrage to the residents of the capital. It was proposed initially that the powers of the incorporated parts of the District, principally Alexandria and Georgetown, would be unimpaired but that the rest would be without self-government. District-wide officials would be appointed. No one within the District would vote for President, senator, or congressman. Further, the laws of Virginia would apply in that section of the District which had been ceded by Virginia; Maryland law would apply elsewhere. Its parts inconsistent with each other, its whole falling far short of the self-determination that had been widely expected, the plan came under immediate attack. Augustus Woodward, who had just moved from Alexandria to Washington, wrote to the *National Intelligencer* calling for a territorial government with an elected legislature, claiming, "It will impair the dignity of the national legislative, executive, and judicial authorities to be occupied with all the local concerns of the Territory of Columbia."

The dispute could not be resolved in time for the inauguration of Thomas Jefferson, however, and only one measure was passed. It established a presidentially-appointed judicial system including a single circuit court that had to base its decisions on the applicable Maryland or Virginia law depending upon which part of the District a case was tried. As its first exercise of "exclusive jurisdiction," Congress had established a dual legal system under one court for an area ten miles square.

While some favored territorial status, others favored retroceding the District back to Maryland and Virginia, a proposal tightly intertwined with arguments that the capital should be returned to Philadelphia.

Even as the District gained self-government—with an elected council and council-selected mayor in 1812 and a directly elected mayor in 1820, talk of territorial status or retrocession to the ceding states continued intermittently as possible solutions to the city's peculiar problem. President Monroe suggested territorial status in 1818 and those opposed simultaneously raised the retrocession issue. According to a self-described "old inhabitant," the largest proprietors in the District disapproved the idea of a union between the various jurisdictions. And although there was strong support in Alexandria and Georgetown to return to their separate former states through retrocession, still fear was widespread that this would mean the removal of the capital and the end of the city's only economic base.

Then in 1846, Congress suddenly agreed to a request that Alexandria be retroceded to Virginia. The request had been made before, but this time it came with the approval of the Virginia Assembly whose planter members were glad to obtain two pro-slavery votes they badly needed in the state legislature. As Constance Green points out, "A Republican Congress in 1861 would regret the act that relinquished federal control over the heights across the Potomac," but in May 1846 there was little concern over the decision.

Following the Civil War, Washington's problems mounted. The city's powers were insufficient to deal with the demands for new improvements in a city that grew from 61,000 to 109,000 in one decade. Even the considerable efforts of Mayor Sayles J. Bowen, a liberal white Republican of modern perspective and pro-black sympathies who used the municipal payroll to provide work for the unemployed and improvements for the city, was unable to attract either local or federal support. He was voted out of office and matters continued to deteriorate.

In an effort to meet the economic and political problems of the District, the Senate in 1870 passed a measure that would have established a territorial government with an elected governor and council, a nonvoting delegate in Congress, protection of the charters of Georgetown and Washington, and financing by the federal government proportionate to its interest.

The House, however, severely watered down the bill, which emerged from Congress providing for an appointed governor, an appointed upper chamber, an elected lower one, and a presidentially appointed board of public works with autonomous assessing powers. Further, the provision that federal property would be included in tax valuations was dropped. Blacks could vote but women, as elsewhere, couldn't. And Congress could cancel the whole deal at any time.

Even with its drawbacks, it looked good to many Washingtonians. The city held a three-day celebration. It then began to discover what it had. Democrats were particularly unhappy. President Grant had named his favorites to the appointed posts, including Alexander Shepherd as Commissioner of Public Works and noted black abolitionist Frederick Douglass as a member of the upper council. In phrases not unlike those heard at a Democratic national convention a hundred years later, the *Georgetown Courier* bemoaned that in the upper council there sat "not an old resident, nor a Democrat, nor a Catholic, nor an Irishman, and yet we have three darkies, Douglass, Gray and Hall, a German, two natives of Maine and one of Massachusetts."

But blacks also were disappointed. They had held as many as seven seats on Washington's old city council; under the combined government of the territory they only managed to elect two out of the twenty-two members of the House of Delegates. Much as regional metropolitan government today threatens black urban power, the consolidation of the District under the territorial system had diluted black political strength.

The free-wheeling, free-spending Board of Public Works also was a surprise. Tax assessments rose rapidly and in one month there were sixteen pages of ads in a local paper for properties up at tax auctions. The costs of the Shepherd regime had hit local citizens as well as the congressional purse. In 1874, the District's territorial status was revoked. And while the major local failing had been the actions of a presidentially-appointed board of public works, many whites were quick to blame what the *Georgetown Courier* called the "curse" of black suffrage.

When news of the territory's end reached them, several members of the elected House of Delegates rushed to their erstwhile chamber and liberated various souvenirs; one was caught with a feather duster in his trouser leg. In later years, the memory of the "feather dusters" was to be evoked frequently to warn citizens of the hazards of suffrage in a city with a substantial black population. Washington was, after all, a city that only ten years before the territorial government had voted overwhelmingly against black enfranchisement. The referendum vote in Washington City had been 6,591 against, 35 for. In Georgetown, it was 465 against, 0 for. To the present day, fear of the black vote remains a major stumbling block to full enfranchisement of the District's citizens.

The territorial government was replaced by a three-member board of commissioners. Two were appointed directly by the President, the other was selected by the Corps of Engineers. This system of government continued until 1967 when Lyndon Johnson reorganized the city government and placed it under a single appointed commissioner and a nine-member appointed council.

At first, the commissioner system was well received. Washington became widely viewed as an extremely well-run city. The little matter of self-determination was glossed over much in the manner of Commissioner Henry McFarland who declared in 1900 that Washington's "greatest virtue is that it is distinctly a government by public opinion. The unusually high intelligence of the citizens of the District, and their remarkable interest and activity in the conduct of its affairs, make them its real rulers, under the constitutional authority of the President and Congress." Whatever public opinion was, it certainly didn't include the 87,000 blacks in the city—31 percent of the population—and it certainly did include, out of all proportion to their numbers, members of the Board of Trade and those whose activities made it possible for a congressman to congratulate an incoming commissioner by assuring him he could net $1 million during his term of office.

Still, the commissioners, whatever side bets they might place, were reasonably honest and efficient, and blacks found themselves faced with a quandary: was it better to live in a relatively benign colony or in a democracy two-thirds white and hostile?

There were other problems. Was it better to seek home rule or national representation first? That question has divided and complicated the self-determination battle right up to the present. From the start the representation first (or only) campaign has been pressed by the conservatives and business community, while liberals have emphasized home rule. In 1938 the Suffrage League held an unofficial referendum in which over 95,000 people voted. The tally showed representation in Congress was favored 13 to 1 and home rule 7 to 1. There could no longer be any question where Washington stood on either issue.

Not that it made any difference. The matter would be repeatedly hashed over in Congress without result and meanwhile the commissioners ran the show. Some tried to do a good job; others didn't bother. The civilian commissionerships were sought after, not because of their power but because they provided a ticket to some of the more glamorous sides of Washington. The city's commissioners have always been among Washington's most ubiquitous party-goers. For the engineer commissioner, there was power as well. Said one local official in the fifties, "Don't let anyone tell you that city government is divided into thirds. It's divided into sixths —four-sixths for the engineer commissioner and one-sixth for each of the others. He makes the big decisions —on urban renewal, streets, freeways, and so on. He can do anything he wants to."

The engineer commissioner had a unique position for a District official. He received an automatic promotion to brigadier general upon appointment and was a potential chief of the Corps of Engineers. Thus, alone among all the different functionaries who have run the District over the years, he commanded respect on the Hill. As a possible future chief of the corps with control over the location of federal public works projects, legislators were solicitous of him. Washington's extensive freeway and urban renewal programs, their patterns set under the old three-commissioner system, are tributes to the influence of the engineer commissioner. As Robert McLaughlin, a civilian commissioner in the fifties, put it, "The Army and tradition and the Board of Trade—put this all together, and it's pretty difficult for the other blokes."

In the end, the commissioner system proved undemocratic and unresponsive. Like the other solutions to DC's status problem it foundered on a point that Augustus Woodward had noted in 1800. "No policy can be worse than to mingle great and small concerns. The latter become absorbed in the former; are neglected and forgotten."

One need not blame venality, greed, racism, and stupidity for this, although they all played their role. The fact is that even under the best of circumstances the system designed for Washington was intrinsically unworkable for it was actually no system but a series of temporary arrangements made by those with more important matters on their minds. Those who made the decisions about the city benefited little from the past because they did not remember it.

In recent years there has hardly been a president who has not at the outset of his term promised to make a model for the rest of the nation. For a while the promises arouse hope in the less cynical of local hearts, but then disillusionment sets in and Washingtonians settle down to wait for the next administration's flurry of local concern. Power, said Henry Kissinger, is the ultimate aphrodisiac; but Washingtonians also know from long experience that an impending change in administration is the ultimate menopause.

We move in epicycloid motion around the circumference of national politics. There is an ebb and flow to all change, but in other cities it is heavily a function of local influences. In Washington the cycles need bear no relationship to local requirements or desires.

There needn't be any consistency between national policy and local policy, either. Washington may find itself at one moment the log that gets rolled or the special concern of a president at another. President Grant was not one of our more noble chief executives but it was under his administration that the District enjoyed briefly its greatest political freedom. Lyndon Johnson fought for self-determination in the District while bombing Vietnam with abandon. And Franklin Roosevelt dedicated his administration to remaking America while treating the District with curious indifference. He appointed as one of the city's commissioners George E. Allen, a man who gained the reputation of the court jester of the administration. When Allen resigned, a small off-the-record farewell dinner was given for him by some fifty persons, including prominent New Dealers. Allen regaled the audience by proudly reporting that both the death and destitution rates had climbed during his four-and-a-half years in office. Washington was a joke.

In general, the city has fared better under earthy administrations—the Jacksonians, the Grant Administration, and the Great Society—and less well under conservatives or aristocratic liberals like Wilson and Roosevelt. But the one thing that Washington could count on was that its fortunes would change and that it would have nothing to say about when or why.

The Black City

Within this captive capital, hostage to national politicians with power over its destiny but without the responsibility that accompanies power, there was another city. Constance Green wrote a book about it, *The Secret*

55

City. This city has been even more isolated from power and self-determination than the larger whole, for it was composed of Washington's black population.

As early as 1800, more than a quarter of the population was black and nearly 20 percent of the blacks were free. While slaves were being used extensively for work on the Capitol, slavery ill-served a city economy. While slaves in the city had nearly doubled by 1820 the numbers thereafter began to decline. By the same year, free blacks comprised more than 10 percent of the total population.

But being free and black was quite a different matter from being free and white. In 1808 the first of several "black codes" were adopted. In 1812 the codes were strengthened to include a twenty dollar fine for blacks out after 10 P.M., forty lashes for slaves caught at disorderly meetings, a requirement that freedmen carry a certificate of liberty, and a ten dollar fine for blacks playing cards or dice. The codes however, brutal as they were, were less severe than in the adjoining states.

With Maryland and Virginia the two largest slave-owning states, the District became a major slave trading center and increasing local objections to the practice were heard, especially with the slave pens located right in the heart of L'Enfant's monumental design, across from what is now the site of the Smithsonian Institution.

The abolitionist movement and opposition to slave trading grew within the city, but so did the suppression of blacks, spurred by white fears of increasing migrations from slave states. By 1828 every black family had to post a peace bond of $500 signed by two white men, and blacks were barred from the Capitol grounds except on "business."

In the wake of Nat Turner's rebellion in 1831, things took a further turn for the worse. In an atmosphere of growing fear of abolitionism, the District Emancipation Society stopped meeting and a slave's attempt to murder a white woman in 1835, blamed on abolitionists, set off a white riot called the "Snow Storm." The black codes were stiffened again; the peace bond was raised to $1,000, with five white co-signers required; and business licenses were forbidden to blacks for anything but driving carts and carriages.

Still, Washington attracted blacks. Outside the north, it was the best place to come and northern congressmen offered some protection against further excesses. There was a one-third increase in the free black population in the 1830s, and a quarter increase in the 1840s.

In 1849 Congressman Abraham Lincoln introduced a bill abolishing slavery in the District, which was compromised a year later to exclude trading but not slavery itself. Meanwhile, the local city council redesigned the black codes to make them more effective in blocking black immigration. The peace bond was lowered to fifty dollars but every black immigrant had to report within five days of coming to Washington. The black influx slowed and white fears waned.

By 1860, a uniquely strong and cohesive free black community (though with internal class distinctions based on employment and darkness of skin) had developed despite such adversities as the black codes and the Dred Scott decision. It was possible for a black to lead a comfortable and even, for some, prosperous life in the District. Blacks had founded schools and churches early in the District's history and in the face of oppression had developed their own mechanisms for survival.

Before 1860, black newcomers had come slowly enough to be absorbed into the Washington black community. But the 40,000 emancipated slaves who deluged the city between 1862 and 1865 quadrupled the city's black population. Conditions for blacks deteriorated rapidly, as did local black cohesiveness. There was resentment among the older black residents, largely involved in a house servant economy, to the influx of ex–field hands from the south. The in-migration also frightened and irritated whites who saw their taxes rising with the increase in a penniless population. When the issue of black suffrage came before the City Council it was defeated, reflecting the overwhelming opposition of District whites expressed in the referendum of 1865. But radical Republicans in Congress, propelled by what they considered to be the prosouthern sentiments of local whites during the Civil War, were ready to teach the city a lesson. Acting as much out of malice towards the District's "rebels" as out of a sense of equity towards blacks, a universal manhood suffrage bill was passed for DC, nineteen months before the Fourteenth Amendment sanctioned the same result elsewhere.

Living conditions, meanwhile, continued to decline. The area now occupied by the Commerce and Labor Departments became a slum called "Murder Bay."

Showing more recognition of the social causes of crime than Police Chief Jerry Wilson who stated in 1973, "I don't consider these things to be a priority from my point of view," the then Superintendent of Metropolitan Police reported:

> Here crime, filth and poverty seem to vie with each other in a career of degradation and death. Whole families . . . are crowded into mere apologies for shanties. . . . During storms of rain or snow their roofs afford but slight protection, while from beneath a few rough boards used for floors, the miasmatic effluvia from the most disgustingly filthy and stagnant water . . . renders the atmosphere within these hovels stifling and sickening in the extreme. . . . In a space about fifty yards square I found about one hundred families, composed of from three to ten persons each . . . living in shanties one story high. . . . There are no proper privy accommodations. . . . Nor can the sanitary laws be properly enforced against delinquents, for they have no means wherewith to pay

fines and a commitment to the workhouse is no punishment.

The 1860s did not only bring in blacks. A census in 1867 found that 40 percent of the white population had come to Washington since the war. Most of them were northerners and, as the first years of black suffrage failed to produce the expected political revolution, the racial atmosphere of the city changed. In 1869 the city council passed a bill against racial discrimination in places of public entertainment. This was expanded the following year to include restaurants, bars, and hotels.

During the post-bellum years, Frederick Douglass, Washington's black abolitionist, newspaper editor, and public official, was a clear and forceful voice for local blacks. Formidable in appearance and speech, Douglass established himself as perhaps the preeminent figure of District history. He combined conviction and political acumen with a relentless yet graceful tongue. On one Fourth of July he told a crowd:

What, to the American slave, is your Fourth of July? I answer: a day that reveals to him more than all the other days of the year, the gross injustices and cruelty to which he is the constant victim. To him your celebration is a sham. To him your sounds of rejoicing are empty and heartless, your denunciation of tyrants, impudence; your shouts of liberty and equality, mockery. Your prayers and hymns, our sermons and thanksgivings, with all our religious pride and solemnity, are to him mere bombast, fraud, deception, impiety, and hypocrisy —a thin veil to cover up crimes which would disgrace a nation of savages.

Douglass was one of three blacks appointed in the upper chamber of the territorial government formed in 1871 and he joined in helping to pass in 1872 and 1873 an expansion of the antidiscrimination laws. Although the civil rights legislation would disappear behind the covers of dusty law books in post-Reconstruction Washington, it would be resurrected successfully in the early 1950s as the basis for a suit desegregating District public facilities well in advance of the rest of the south.

The territorial board of public works at first provided jobs for blacks but, as time went on, Shepherd's ventures sorely taxed black property owners and increasingly the jobs went to white laborers. But at least Washington had recognized the existence of a black community with a claim on the power of the territory. While some blacks during the postterritorial period felt comfortable as wards of Congress rather than as one-third of an electoral minority, they soon found themselves entering an era in the last quarter of the century in which they were no longer a problem to the whites—for all practical purposes they had ceased to exist. The intercourse between the races engendered by politics wilted. The newspapers acted as though the city had no black population at all. The many black government jobs of the early 1880s dried up so much that by 1891 there were only twenty-five blacks in the city government above the lowest ranks. Black professionals found business difficult (in part because of a lack of black patronage) and workers found entrance into unions barred. The government employment situation further deteriorated under the Taft, Theodore Roosevelt, and Wilson administrations. Blacks who had joined the Board of Trade at the outset resigned in the face of the white members' hostility, and white citizen associations closed their doors to blacks. The civil rights laws of the city were widely ignored, the Supreme Court threw out the federal civil rights law of 1875, the theatres had 'nigger heavens' and the railroads and interstate buses were segregated as well.

Thus there was plenty of reason for blacks in Washington to be attracted to the Niagra Movement formed in 1906 by W. E. B. Dubois and William Trotter. Seven years after the NAACP was started in 1909, the District chapter was the largest in the country with more than a thousand members. Whites, meanwhile, were becoming increasingly hostile. On a weekend in July 1919, a band of more than a hundred servicemen attacked blacks in southwest Washington. The *Washington Post,* in a story the next day, wrote:

It was learned that mobilization of every available serviceman stationed in or near Washington or on leave here has been ordered for tomorrow evening near the Knights of Columbus hut, on Pennsylvania Avenue between Seventh and Eighth Streets.

The hour of assembly is 9 o'clock and the purpose is a 'clean-up' that will cause the events of the last two evenings to pale into insignificance.

Whether official cognizance of this assemblage and its intent will bring about its forestalling cannot be told.

Five days of rioting followed and there were more than a few who thought the *Post* article had been an invitation.

In the aftermath of the riots, which resulted in the deaths of thirty-nine persons, race relations remained sour. The national administrations were of little assistance; Harding made only three black appointments and, when the president of Tuskegee spoke at the dedication of the Lincoln Memorial in 1922, he was forced to sit in the black section rather than at the speaker's table.

In 1925 the Ku Klux Klan held a parade in the city and segregation had increased to the point that a black could sit next to a white only on local trollies and buses, in public library reading rooms, or at Griffith Stadium. Then in 1926 the Supreme Court upheld the legality of racial real estate covenants.

If Washington's blacks had expected the New Deal to be a boon, they were disabused of that notion within two days of Roosevelt's inauguration when a mostly black crowd of unemployed marching on the White House were repelled by police. Black business failed to prosper, unions continued to discriminate and by 1938, 90 percent of the 9,000 blacks employed by the federal government were in custodial jobs and only forty-seven men had made it into subprofessional slots. The alley dwellings still remained and the government sanctioned segregation.

Still there was some progress. In 1938 the Supreme Court refused to grant an injunction against a grocery store boycott to force black employment, a decision that would have considerable impact twenty years later as the civil rights movement took hold. Nonsegregated CIO unions were established and the Federation of Churches invited black membership.

Then in 1939 the Daughters of the American Revolution refused to let Marian Anderson sing in Constitution Hall. Interior Secretary Harold Ickes promptly made the Lincoln Memorial available and 75,000 persons showed up for what became a symbolic watershed. In 1941 the threat of a nationwide black march on Washington spurred Roosevelt to issue an order on fair employment practices. Public housing was started. Local groups fought (unsuccessfully) for black jobs on the trollies and for home rule. Secretary Ickes desegregated Rock Creek Park, though in 1945 the local board of recreation officially sanctioned the de facto segregation on the city's playgrounds.

In the wake of the Second World War, with the uncomfortable reminder of Nazi policies on race fading, and with southerners in control of the Congressional District committees, the effort to keep Washington in the South was renewed. The walls of discrimination began to close again. Southern and local business opposition to home rule stiffened. General Ulysses S. Grant III, head of the park and planning commission, announced a redevelopment plan that provided for the "colored population dispossessed by playgrounds, public buildings, parks and schools" to be relocated in the "rear of Anacostia" across the river from the central city—a policy which was to be haphazardly but cruelly carried out in the years to come. A National Capital Housing Authority official called segregation "the accepted pattern of the community."

But the flow of black progress this time was not to be dammed. In 1948, the Supreme Court ruled racial housing covenants unenforceable. In 1949 the local parochial schools were quietly desegregated. In 1953, using the civil rights laws of the 1870s, the city's privately-owned restaurants and public facilities were desegregated. And in 1954, in a case parallel to the national one issued at the same time, public schools were made bi-racial. There were still many miles to go, but Washington had made the changes without violence and with far less evasion and obstinacy than elsewhere in the south. During the fifties, prodded by the increased militancy of people like Julius Hobson, barriers still protected by law began to fall in the face of boycotts and picket lines. And in the sixties the city found itself heavily involved in what was now a national struggle for black equality and power.

The backing and filling of DC's black history echoes the cyclical quality of the city's political and fiscal past. Washington's history, for both blacks and whites, has been one of trying to swim past a line of breakers before being swept back to shore. The city has been condemned to the sisyphean task of repeatedly rolling a rock up Capitol Hill only to have it roll down again. It has perhaps given the city a certain strength; too much faith in the inevitability of progress ill-prepares you for failure.

In Washington, where it is the acceptance of failure rather than the assumption of progress that poses the greater threat, those who refuse to resign themselves swiftly learn history's fickle ways. And as the hopes of a decade shatter in the avaricious grasp of a cynical administration, residents can comfort themselves with the knowledge in a few years it too will be gone; another President will stand on a platform and promise that the nation's capital will become a model for America and the world. And Washingtonians will gather themselves for one more try at using the promise to obtain a few more inches of progress.

3 / At Home

WASHINGTON IS A CITY OF NEIGHBORHOODS. A MAP published by the National Capital Planning Commission shows more than seventy distinct neighborhoods within the city's boundaries. It is partly because Washingtonians have been unable to control the destiny of the city at large that they have naturally turned inward toward the community that extends a dozen or so blocks from their homes. It does not appear entirely an historical accident that citizens' associations sprouted in Washington following the loss of home rule in 1874, or that a local colonel (and later engineer commissioner) named Henry Robert drafted a set of rules during that period to guide new organizations in their proceedings: Robert's Rules of Order. For nearly one hundred years, these organizations functioned not merely as neighborhood groups but as a substitute, albeit a sadly ineffective one, for democratic representation.

With the inefficiency that marked a segregated way of life, the community groups were divided into all-white and all-black federations, conveniently coded so one knew that a "citizens' association" was for whites and a "civic association" was for blacks. Even after most overt racial bars in the city had fallen, the over-lapping associations continued. There were citizens' associations that admitted blacks and the civic associations welcomed whites, but because of the decline of biracial neighborhoods, it didn't mean much.

Some of these community groups, particularly the white ones, gained near-governmental powers. But much of this power was negative. The Georgetown Citizens' Association was more effective opposing freeway projects and the Capitol Hill Restoration Society was better able to stop commercial development than either was able to improve governmental services in their neighborhoods.

Some of the groups over the long run tended to become arrogant, smug defenders of narrow interests. The Capitol Hill Restoration Society, vigorously promoted by local real estate dealers as part of their campaign for a "new" Capitol Hill, kept careful watch over every zoning variance request and its decision weighed heavily at the Board of Zoning Adjustment. If the Restoration Society had been a representative town meeting, it could have been a healthy medium of decentralized democracy. In a community that was half-black and half-white, how-ever, all but a handful of the society's members were white—mostly conservative whites at that.

Events passed many organizations by. Once when I suggested to the president of a civic association that she was out of step with the community, she replied, "We are pillars of the community." At the time, the forty-year-old organization was an emaciated shadow of its former self, lucky to draw twenty persons to a meeting.

Even the power of the strongest organizations did not stay fixed. The community associations' clout declined markedly with the rise of urban renewal, mass development, the antipoverty program, black power, and local governmental reorganization.

The antipoverty program, with substantial government funds being poured into the city's poorer neighborhoods, not only created new power bases to compete with the old, but drained people and interest away from traditional groups. The neighborhood groups were not the only ones affected. A number of aggressive organizations that had been forces for substantial change found their membership drifting into the antipoverty establishment.

Urban renewal had much the same effect. It became increasingly difficult for volunteer organizations to compete against well-funded, well-staffed and well-connected groups such as the Model Inner City Community Organization of the Reverend (later Delegate) Walter Fauntroy. Similarly, the arrival of real local politics—with elections for nonvoting delegate and school board—shifted the foci of power.

A serious fight could destroy an organization as well, as was the case with the biracial Capitol Hill Community Council which tore itself apart on the issue of whether a group of restored houses should be condemned to make way for the replacement of a junior high school known as "Horrible Hine." Liberals favored the move; conservatives opposed it and by a paper-thin margin carried the vote. The new school was built anyway and the Community Council, which had once published a monthly tabloid with 10,000 free circulation, never recovered from the battle. Fewer and fewer people showed up for its meetings and fewer and fewer officials cared what it thought.

Even powerful white groups like the Georgetown Citizens' Association and the Capitol Hill Restoration Society slipped. As the urban land-grab of the fifties and sixties grew in intensity, as the city was put on the block to the highest bidder, they became hard-pressed.

When the Georgetown Citizens' Association found itself confronted with Zoning Commission approval of high-rise, high density development of the Georgetown waterfront, it marked a dramatic low in community power. If the Georgetown Citizens' Association could not stop the developers, how could other weaker neighborhood groups hope to hold the line?

At its best, attempting to use the network of community organizations as a substitute for a local political system was frustrating and ineffective. Few things demonstrated the need for political democracy in Washington more strongly than did the failures of the ad hoc system developed to fill the vacuum. It made representatives of the community vulnerable to charges from government or competing representatives that they were "self-appointed," "lacked an organization," or only had a "paper group." Since the illusion of a constituency was more important than the fact, community organizations constantly exaggerated the size of their membership and refused to join in more effective coalitions for fear of having their image of importance shattered by something that could create an even larger illusion. Government officials and agencies constantly played one group off against the next, and excused indifference to, and inaction on, citizen demands with an attitude of how-do-we-know-you-really-represent-the community?

It was a supremely presumptuous attitude for colonial administrators, representative of nothing but the whims of a national administration, but it was one difficult to combat, especially since the local media tended to support the government's view.

Most people in Washington, however, are involved in no community organization. A *Washington Post* reporter, after several years on the local beat, remarked that his impression of the city was "200 people moving from room to room." When the antipoverty zealots dragged hapless citizens to meetings night after night, they were celebrating the delusion that the poor for some reason liked haggling over by-laws, voting pointless resolutions, and listening to turgid talks. The sort of grass-roots organizing they were attempting would have failed among the affluent of Montgomery County; there was little cause to suspect that it might work in Shaw. It was one of the great tactical errors of poverty workers, New Leftists, black militants, and assorted agitators to assume that deep down everyone was a potential poverty worker, New Leftist, black militant, or assorted agitator. If they had been attempting to create the Roman Catholic Church, they would have insisted that all parishioners be celibates and that women wear a habit and the men a collar.

Nonetheless, many of the community organizations were vitally important, even to those who took no part in them. The Emergency Committee on the Transportation Crisis helped shift the city's emphasis from freeways to mass transit. The Black United Front and other groups kept the issue of police brutality in the foreground. CORE, under Julius Hobson, tore down one discriminatory barrier after another. And the less aggressive groups, such as the urban renewal and antipoverty organizations, helped build new communities from the bottom up. When President Nixon announced in 1973 the dismemberment of the antipoverty program it was for Washington not just another federal program down the drain. It represented an attack on the city's poorer communities, the ones that had been slowly reconstructing themselves with antipoverty centers serving as nascent surrogate neighborhood governments. In one area, the Near Southeast served by Friendship House, it meant among many other things the potential loss of service to:

• The thousands of customers who used the Martin Luther King Coop Store as an alternative to walking many blocks to a Safeway and paying more.

- The 100 a month served by a hot lunch program.
- 350 teenagers in six arts workshops.
- 80 children in a day care program.
- The 134 families in Ellen Wilson Public Housing that used the center's community center.
- The 2,000 members of the credit union that were benefiting from over a quarter of a million dollars in small loans annually.
- The thousands who had availed themselves of free legal services.

In one capricious action, the federal government threatened to destroy what had taken years to start to build: a community that worked.

The nonpolitical life of Washington, like the political life, is centered in the neighborhood. Sometimes that neighborhood can be very small. When I moved from an apartment on Fifth Avenue NE to a house a few blocks north on Sixth Street, two neighborhood youths, not yet in their teens, helped me move. Over lunch, Gerald and Henry discussed the relative merits of my old and my new neighborhood.

"I wouldn't go down D Street with the whole United States Marines," said Gerald, speaking of a street exactly two blocks north of where he lived.

"Well, it's better than Death Alley," replied Henry.

"Where's Death Alley?" I asked.

"You know, that alley out back of your old place," said Henry. He explained that the dead-end alley, which had seemed dirty but harmless to me, was a favorite trap to which kids his age were chased to be tormented by local bullies.

The more general definition of a neighborhood in Washington is larger but not very large. There is a name for every square mile or so in the city. It gets pretty subjective. Someone living on the edge of Georgetown might describe their neighborhood as Georgetown; someone living in the heart of Georgetown might say the other person lived in Burleith. Some neighborhoods, like Georgetown, are known even to people outside the city; others, like Trinidad, are mainly known even within the city as signs on the front of buses.

The affluent West-of-the-Park area luxuriates in subdivisions: Burleith, Chevy Chase, Barnaby Woods, Forest Hills, Tenley, Friendship, American University, Spring Valley, Woodley Park, Glover Park, Cleveland Park, North Cleveland Park, Wesley Heights, Foxhall Village, Palisades, Massachusetts Heights, Georgetown. And that's just for 90,000 people.

Of these, Georgetown garners the most public interest. Georgetown represents the final product of a private urban restoration project that began in the 1930s and was the forerunner of city revivals elsewhere in Washington and around the country. Eighteenth century houses, nineteenth century houses, slave quarters, intown mansions and anything that didn't move were restored, often in decorator chic, to produce a community that is both quaint and quixotic. The picturesque façades are so totally in keeping with their setting that one tends to forget that the setting is not in keeping with the rest of the city. Georgetown is like a diamond set in plastic; the jewel is appealing but the whole ring doesn't go together.

Georgetown didn't always have preciosity. When I was a child there, the contrasts of urban life were much closer at hand. I knew at an early age that there were many people who lived worse than I. They were black and they lived in ramshackle houses down the street that are now restored and selling for the going Georgetown rate. (Two-thirds of Georgetown's houses cost more than $50,000.) The parking lot on Wisconsin Avenue was a bicycle shop and Lad Mills' gas station looked like a gas station rather than like a University of Virginia field house as it does now. Down the avenue, a man sat in a hole in the middle of the street, waiting for the next street car, so he could switch its power from over-head wire to the third rails the city's planners had decreed for the monumental downtown area.

In the course of the restoration of Georgetown, most of the blacks were forced out, real estate prices soared, and homogeneity replaced diversity—at least until an unexpected invasion of youth in the sixties turned the main commercial strips into a center of Washington's free community, fostering rock joints, joint-pushers, and riot-helmeted police, and causing some of the local burghers, no doubt, to wish they had the blacks back.

The freak immigration restored an element of balance to Georgetown for a few years, forcing it to relate to at least one part of the city other than itself, but it did little consciousness-raising other than turning a few congressmen and bureaucrats into potheads. It left the picturesque façades largely unmarred. The Georgetowners bravely endured the smell of urine in their restored alleys and by 1972 even Spiro Agnew was looking at a $500,000 house in the neighborhood.

Not everyone in Georgetown, however, is either on the streets or rich. Many of the houses are rented, often to young professional singles splitting the expense of a comfortable rowhouse with roommates. The result of this phenomenon is what transportation consultants call a bimodal split: Georgetown seems primarily for the old and affluent or the young and single. There are not many kids.

It is, nonetheless, a pleasant place to live or visit. Price is what keeps or drives people out. And it is still a very pampered community. Even the Hopfenmaier rendering plant is gone now. The plant had been Georgetown's nosesore, the thing that next to hippies and the flight path of planes from National Airport that Georgetowners complained about most. A nearby firm posted a large sign to advise people that the "obnoxious odors" one smelled in the area "do not emanate from this plant." When the city finally announced that it was taking over the rendering plant, it did so on the same day that air pollution regulations passed by the City Council were vetoed. Although few noticed it, the action cleared the way for construction of a new incinerator in a decidedly unaffluent and black part of town. The haves had scored again.

Georgetown is a point of reference to the rest of the city. To blacks it is a symbol of the extent to which whites still control the town. To whites it is either a model of what should or should not be done in the rest of the city. Liberal whites point out, for example, that they don't want "Capitol Hill [or Adams-Morgan] to become another Georgetown."

At the other end of town, geographically, socially, psychologically and financially, is Anacostia. Indicative of prevailing attitudes, many refer to the entire area across the Anacostia River as Anacostia, which is as accurate as describing the whole region west of Rock Creek Park as Georgetown. In fact, Anacostia is just one of a number of communities across the river.

Anacostia is divided physically from the rest of the city by the stubby, dirty waters of the Anacostia River. Directly across from Anacostia is the Washington Navy Yard, where the presidential yacht "Sequoia" is moored. But aside from this glimpse of elegance and some of the best views of the city from its highest points, trans-Anacostian communities like Anacostia share little of the glamor and prestige commonly associated with the capital city.

Trans-Anacostia is not only forgotten by the powerful and prestigious national figures who work and talk on the other side of the river: even the city's black leadership has to be constantly reminded that a quarter of Washington lives out there—so much so that a class action suit has been instituted on behalf of all trans-

Anacostians charging discrimination in the provision of numerous local government services.

No part of Washington has undergone more demographic change over the past decade than Far Southeast, of which Anacostia is a part. Not only did the population there increase 22.6 percent between 1960 and 1970, but it has changed from a community that was 60 percent white to one 90 percent black. The school age population has leaped 78 percent. In fact, aside from the New Southwest, which was evacuated to make way for urban renewal in the fifties, the only areas of Washington that have experienced large population increases in the past ten years have been Far Northeast and Far Southeast. While the population pressures for new schools and other services were declining in the rest of the city, they were substantially growing across the Anacostia River.

Anacostia began as a suburb, one of the city's earliest. In 1854, a sizable tract of land was purchased by the Union Land Association. The head of the association, John W. Hook, built a house on top of Cedar Hill, which Frederick Douglass later bought from Hook's creditors. The rest of the land was subdivided into lots for whites only. Most of the houses from that period are gone now, although Douglass's has been refurbished as a museum. They were replaced with wood and stucco homes in the early part of this century.

Following the Second World War, trans-Anacostia underwent dramatic changes. There was a demand for new housing and much of it was constructed east of the river. The area was also turned into a refugee camp for the evacuees from urban renewal and freeway sites elsewhere in the city. A recent report on Anacostia by the District government notes that "in a relatively short period, a low density neighborhood of single-family owner-occupied homes became one of predominantly rental accommodations housing a young and transient population."

The report goes on:

The apartment construction boom left a legacy of problems with which the neighborhood must now cope. Speculative over-building, poor construction, and shoe-string management led to an accelerated deterioration and even financial collapse at several complexes. The population influx accompanying housing construction strained the capacity of schools, streets, and other publicly provided facilities and services, and contributed to the decline of adjacent enclaves of single-family homes. . . .

The hills south of Morris Road are inundated with massive, bleak apartment developments relieved only by littered vacant lots. Though many of the buildings themselves are modern and attractive, they are generally crowded against asphalt parking lots, muddy courts, and an occasional empty swimming pool. Ground floor and basement units are generally barred or boarded and frequently vacant. Many adjacent streets are narrow, bumpy and curbless. Bare earth, eroded hillsides and missing sidewalks add to the overall impression of neglect. . . .

The trans-Anacostians' problems are accentuated by their living in a colony within a colony. They are in much the same relationship to the District as the District is to the national government. People from Far Northeast or Far Southeast traditionally have been accorded only token representation on city boards and committees. Even on bodies such as the local Democratic Central Committee, trans-Anacostia was long grossly underrepresented. This is changing, but what local power the District has is still hoarded on the west side of the Anacostia River.

Some of the changes have been largely symbolic—renaming a street Martin Luther King, Jr. Avenue, opening a neighborhood branch of the Smithsonian, renovating the Frederick Douglass home. But the complaints of those across the river are also being felt in more substantial ways. The District report on Anacostia, for example, was designed to lay the groundwork for a far more serious approach to the area's housing problems than had yet been taken. And when the military proposed to create a little Pentagon on the adjacent and largely empty Bolling Base tract, the Anacostia community organized to oppose it.

Bolling occupies a 900-acre site along the Anacostia River, the largest single tract of developable open space in the city. For years, the land had been held in escrow for the military with the aid of powerful House Armed Services Committee Chairman, the late Mendel Rivers —who had turned his own congressional district into a bastion of the Pentagon and seemed determined to do the same to Anacostia. Rivers was fought by a number of planners and organizations in the city, but the issue never evoked much reaction in Anacostia itself until the "Little Pentagon" plan was unveiled.

The plan called for turning the entire tract over to the military to create a self-contained, secure, and isolated military community housing 11,500 personnel and employing 22,000. Commercial, recreational, and other services were to be constructed within its confines. The District was to build two 600-student elementary schools exclusively for military dependents and a 1,000-student high school mostly for the military. The city was also expected to improve three streets and one freeway and provide sewage facilities.

All this was in the heart of an area whose own schools in 1970 were 83 percent over capacity, 40 percent of whose population was under eighteen and which deserved much more recreation space than it had.

Larry Weston, one of those organizing the fight against the plan, described its effects:

Environmental impact would be enormous. There
would be approximately 10,000 additional automobiles
congesting the primary arteries of the area. . . . The
traffic already backed up for two miles at rush hours
would be backed up for six. . . . The complex would
generate sewage from 22,000 employees and 11,500 residents into the Blue Plains Plant, which will barely be
able to handle current capacity when expanded.

None of the land would be taxable by DC and retail
sales would be exempt from DC sales taxes. The new
civilian jobs to be provided by the proposed plan would
be few in number and service maintenance in nature.
Of the jobs intended for the Defense Office Building, over
35 percent will be GS-12 and above. In view of historic
federal policies, how many black jobs will this provide?

Not only would the city be denied tax revenue from
the huge site while assuming substantial new expenses,
not only would Anacostians be faced with bigger traffic
jams, but the plan also was neatly designed to severely
limit any access by the adjoining black community.

Far Southeast is not the only neglected community
in the city. Far Northeast shares many of the burdens of
being on the other side of the river, although it has had
about half the population increase in 1960–70 as Far
Southeast. And despite the outpouring of planning funds,
media attention, and public concern, the communities
most deeply affected by the 1968 riot—Shaw, Near
Northeast, and Upper 14th Street—remain dismal monuments to the failure of contemporary urban design and
to governmental irresponsibility.

Some 1,200 residential units and business establishments were damaged in the 1968 riots. Losses reached
$58 million. And although Congress had budgeted some
$137 million for Washington's recovery effort, five years
after 1968 there were only three housing complexes
completed and three under way with a total capacity of

600 units. And while 400 buildings had been torn down, only fifty houses had been renovated.

On the fifth anniversary of the riots, *Post* reporter Eugene Meyer wrote:

> The biggest problem in rebuilding has been this: the housing planned for all the three riot corridors was mostly for moderate-income families . . . while most of those facing displacement were the poor. . . . In Shaw, where 60 percent of the 40,000 residents are poor enough for public housing, only 54 such units were planned. No public housing was planned in the other two areas.

A resident of upper 14th Street recalled: "Yeah, I looted stores and all that stuff but it don't mean a thing. We used to think that it would make the whiteys listen to us but this has proved that it don't make a bit of difference what we do. It's like they're saying, 'You burned the street down. You fix it. We don't have time for you niggers up there.'"

In the rest of the city, there are numerous neighborhoods that bridge the chasm between Shaw and Georgetown. Some of these neighborhoods are secure, comfortable black communities such as those along the Sixteenth Street Gold Coast or in Upper Northeast.

Many of these have become increasingly black in the past decade, like the Neighbors Inc. area, named after an organization that vigorously promoted integrated living. It changed during the 1960s from a community 37 percent black to one 77 percent black. Much the same thing happened in Brookland, near Catholic University in Upper Northeast. But, contrary to the popular white conception, these neighborhoods did not decay. In 1970, Brookland resident Therese Belanger described her community:

> Brookland's trees shade large Victorian homes, small 1930-ish bungalows, undefined stucco and frame happenings, as well as typically DC rowhouses with their

welcoming front porches and never-changing floor plans. To outsiders, the trees and parks—reflect a small town; to insiders the small town feel still persists, mostly because of its sense of community, of a real and viable community.

Brookland was the fountainhead of the anti-freeway movement in the city, and the Emergency Committee on the Transportation Crisis regularly held its weekly meetings there—one of the few instances of a citywide organization favoring the often forgotten Upper Northeast. It was through Brookland's pleasant homes that the North Central Freeway was supposed to go and it was Brookland's middle-class black and white citizens who pressed a fight that was eventually to alter the course of transportation planning in the city.

Perhaps the most interesting community in Washington at present is that composed of Adams-Morgan and Mt. Pleasant, aided and abetted by the adjoining Dupont Circle area. It is the only community that can lay claim to multi-ethnicity since it includes the major concentration of the city's growing Latino population. Armando Rendon, author of the *Chicano Manifesto* and a local activist, described latino Washington:

More than two years ago a job offer in Washington prompted me to uproot myself and family from California. I felt something of an immigrant myself, moving al norte, into a different ambiente, where streets and cities, the restaurants, the familiar sights and sounds and smells of the barrios would be replaced by altogether alien forms of life. My hopes for meeting other Mexican-Americans were low, though many had invaded the capital in response to Southwest demands for more Mexican-Americans in government. My pessimism was disappointed.

I discovered that the embassies, the international

agencies, the restaurants, had attracted many latinos, that in fact, a barrio had been created here.

It was not until my oldest boy entered first grade that the size and needs of the latino people became apparent. There were several children in every grade of the school who could not learn because the teacher could not speak Spanish. I believed then, and still, that the burden of communicating in the classroom must be borne by the teacher. It was obvious that the DC schools were incapable of adjusting themselves to the needs of Spanish-speaking children.

My initial cultural trauma subsided quickly when I realized the truly serious predicament of the DC barrio. Basically, hispano people here were treated as indifferently and rudely as Mexican-Americans in the Southwest.

The concentration of Latinos in Adams-Morgan and Mt. Pleasant has begun to gain strength, strength evidenced by increased participation by latinos in local politics and symbolized perhaps by the appearance of a price list in Spanish at the McDonald's at Eighteenth and Columbia Roads.

Whites make up about 60 percent of Dupont Circle and about a third of the population of Adams-Morgan and Mt. Pleasant. They include leftovers from earlier days, zealously guarding their homes from high-rises and blacks alike; young couples restoring houses off Columbia Road; and even younger single persons congregating around Dupont Circle. The area also is the headquarters for the New Thing Art and Architecture Center, which has been a leader in the local black cultural renaissance.

As Georgetown was once, and Capitol Hill after it, Adams-Morgan can today lay claim to being the energy center of the city. Young and active whites and blacks have gravitated to it and it has so far tended to avoid the search for the fountain of eternal chic that over the years has tended to stultify Georgetown and the Hill.

About 40 percent of the city's whites live in the verdant, comfortable ghetto west of Rock Creek Park. They live in Georgetown, in the refined, triple-thermostated homes in Republican Spring Valley; in the older, larger homes of Kennedy-liberal Cleveland Park; and on the more modest, tree-lined streets of Chevy Chase. The West of the Park neighborhoods were 97 percent white in 1960 and 95 percent white in 1970, hardly a monument to open housing. The average income of the 21,000 families living there was about $23,800 in 1970 or more than a quarter above adjoining suburban Montgomery County, the richest county in the nation. The neighborhoods also comprise perhaps the richest community in the nation that still manages to pull out a 50 percent Democratic vote.

Although the area represents only about an eighth of the population of the city, it pays over one-third of the city's income and property taxes. It also has become a prime target for developers since, as Northwest attorney Peter Craig notes, it is the "choicest economic plum" in the nation. The developers are particularly eyeing the Connecticut and Wisconsin Avenue corridors into downtown.

Northwest Washington also has the highest suicide rate in the city, about three times the national average. It is the only place in the country where female suicides equal that of males, a phenomenon apparently due to the presence of 11,000 widows who make up some 10% of the population: many wives of government officials stay in Washington after their husbands die. The *Washington Post* reported that Georgetown University psychiatrist Stephen Rojcewicz, who discovered the phenomenon, "speculated that when the total number of widows in one locale passes a certain statistical point, available social services may become so overburdened that it contributes to the self-inflicted death rate."

But most Northwest Washingtonians, including widows, seem quite happy. They live in one of the most pleasant urban areas in America with many of the pleasures of single-home living usually associated with the suburbs but without the long commuting time, lack of nearby services, tedious strips of neon and plastic emporiums, and other suburban handicaps.

Further, despite the housing patterns, and the considerable economic, social, and racial chasm, Washington's whites in Northwest seem less hostile toward or paranoiac about blacks than one might expect. Undoubtedly, the paucity of lower income whites feeling directly threatened by black incursions into jobs and neighborhoods contributes to the lower level of interracial tension. The fact that the affluent whites are government bureaucrats or private lawyers rather than business executives apparently makes a difference. Also, people of racist inclination are less likely to express their opinions in a city in which they are such a small minority. While they favor local white candidates over black ones, it is also true that experience has provided those West of the Park with an important lesson: Washington has turned black and is still a pleasant place.

During the sixties, only one community other than the Southwest urban renewal area experienced a substantial increase in white population—Capitol Hill. Capitol Hill is the product of mixed motives, shrewd salesmanship, and months of plaster dust that fouled lungs and domestic tranquility. The Hill was intended to be the eastern axis of L'Enfant's vision. But the plan developed in a lopsided manner, with most of the public city stretched to the west of the Capitol. Many of the large rowhouses on the Hill were built in the post-Civil War period when the area became a fashionable neighborhood for government officials. The advent of the automobile encouraged the development of Northwest, and Capitol Hill began to decline. By the thirties it was mainly notable for having some of the worst of Washington's notorious alley dwellings, sordid slums stuck behind rowhouses where poor blacks lived without benefit of indoor plumbing, electricity, or other amenities. In the late forties the first signs of a restoration movement developed. By 1955, restoration of the Hill's row houses was still huddled around the Capitol and its outbuildings with a few exceptions, such as Philadelphia Row, eleven blocks to the east. By 1960 the restoration covered much of the area eight blocks from the Capitol, and by 1968 it had moved another three blocks.

The restoration movement was fostered by the Hill's flourishing real estate entrepreneurs and by the civic organization they formed, the Capitol Hill Restoration Society. When names of important Hill people were mentioned, they were not the names of politicians and civic leaders but of real estate dealers.

The restoration effort was most attractive to young white professionals. Where else could one buy the shell of a house at a price well below the normal rate of lodging, move in, and, with some additional cash and much sweat equity, turn it into a fine home and investment? It had the makings of what seemed an ideal city community, a place where young, smart urbanites could raise their children in an integrated environment with shops and services close at hand.

But it had its price. Most of the old shells had been inhabited by poor tenants—primarily black—who were forced out to make way for the new migration. Some real estate dealers suckered low income home owners into taking far less for their properties than they were actually worth. Others engaged in block-busting, restoring the first house or houses on a block as a magnet for further restoration.

It had another price. All the time that Capitol Hill's new residents were seeking to build a stable, pleasant community, the real estate companies were working the place for all they could get. The result was that as prices rose, new arrivals had to be increasingly affluent; and it became harder and harder for more young, not-too-affluent families to move in and pull the same trick as their predecessors. It became tempting for the old residents to take their profit and move out, especially since more and more of the newcomers came without the children they had hoped would join their young in achieving racial balance in the public schools. By the seventies this model integrated community had only one public elementary school that was even one-third white, and the local junior high school had less than a half-dozen whites.

Although what was happening on the Hill was often described as a white return to the inner city, what actually happened was far more complicated. For example, between 1960 and 1965, the two census tracts closest to the Capitol gained 1,100 whites and lost 1,100 blacks, while four other census tracts, still on Capitol Hill but further away, lost 1,400 whites and gained 300 blacks.

As middle-class whites moved in, pushing blacks out, poorer white residents were simultaneously moving away in even greater numbers, leaving by 1965 a net decrease in the number of whites on the Hill. Additionally, as the economic level of the Hill rose thanks to the new arrivals, public housing was built along what was known as the "bottom of the Hill." By 1966 the small Hill area had about 20 percent of the public housing in the city, comprising 7 percent of the Hill's population. Finally, the character of the incoming white migration was constantly shifting, changing from its early emphasis on young families to increasing numbers of couples with grown children or without children, and single persons including retirement restorationists, blocs of law students renting an expensive row house for an apartment, secretaries living behind barred windows in English basements, and a sizable portion of the city's homosexual community. By 1970 whites were in the majority.

Despite all this moving about, Capitol Hill somehow managed to thrive as a neighborhood. In fact, you didn't move to Capitol Hill. You joined. And since the image of the Hill was stronger than its component parts, it survived the transient nature of much of its population, bending to meet altered conditions but still remaining uniquely The Hill.

To describe the Hill, you must stop in time. Of the ten years I spent there, the most interesting times were the three years before the 1968 riot.

It was the years of organizations like the Emergency Recreation Council. In the days before black separatism had come down to the neighborhood level, the ERC was a biracial organization that challenged the narrow definition of the Hill by including in its domain the larger Capitol East area, of which the Hill was a part. Capitol East was 80 percent black and the restorationists riled at community boundaries that diluted white power of the Hill. But the ERC didn't care; it was constantly at loggerheads with the Capitol Hill Restoration Society anyway.

Although today recreational needs seem fairly low in urban priorities, it was not then, nor is it now, a frivolous concern. Capitol East had only a fraction of the recreational facilities of more favored parts of town.

What playgrounds there were were glass-strewn, lacking in equipment, and dilapidated. For a community of 100,000, there was only one small outdoor public swimming pool. The ERC, early in its life, sent its members treking over each of Capitol East's 400-odd blocks, surveying existing facilities, looking for empty lots and seeking ideas. The resulting report would have cost tens of thousands of dollars if it had been prepared by a consultant and it would not have been nearly as good.

It formed the basis for a continuing, and partially successful, battle for improved recreational facilities.

One of the major struggles was for the construction of an indoor-outdoor pool at Seventh and North Carolina Avenue SE. The restorationists did not want the pool in the neighborhood, especially not next to Eastern Market, the center of a developing boutique strip on Seventh Street. Eastern Market was one of the last remaining farmer's markets. There a red-faced gargantuan cherub in a straw boater sold delicious cheese, low-income blacks bought chitterlings at one counter while restored white mothers were having their rib roast rolled at another, a dour Frenchman threatened his customers with excommunication if they failed to pick up the turkey they ordered, and a small counter sold ham, pork, and roast beef sandwiches to the businessmen, laborers, and shoppers who favored Boone's Lunch over some of the higher-status eating places on the Hill.

One homeowner said he didn't want "all those colored kids running through the market in their swimming suits." Over such weighty issues a battle raged for years with the restorationists opposed and the ERC just as vehemently in favor. Unlike most civic organizations at the time, the ERC operated on the assumption that city officials would respond as much to threats as they would to dignified petitions. Sometime before the radical tactical style had inculcated itself into the American mainstream, the ERC was waking the Recreation Director out of his sleep to hear the latest ultimatum from Capitol East, arrived at over several drinks that helped deepen the community's concern.

The pool was eventually built. In the midst of the struggle over its construction, the community got wind of the news that Lady Bird Johnson was snooping around Capitol East alleys in her limousine. It turned out that while her husband was defoliating Vietnam, Ms. Johnson had determined to beautify Capitol East and thus was bringing in noted west coast landscape architect Lawrence Halprin to help her.

For those sadly familiar with the growing number of grotesque abuses perpetrated in the name of urban planning, the Halprin Plan was a delight. Its first virtue made it unique: Halprin did not propose to tear down a single building or evict a single person to accomplish his goals. The plan called for the development of recreational use of Capitol East's numerous large interior blocks. It suggested vest pocket parks, some attractive cosmetics for commercial strips, a new city park along the Anacostia River, the use of vacant buildings for recreational purposes, and the creation of new playgrounds.

The phrase "beautification" considerably understated what Halprin was about. Rare among planners, Halprin proposed to upgrade the life of the existing community rather than, in more typical fashion, move the existing community out and replace it with something else. For example, the interior blocks:

In some cases these inner blocks are as much as 150 feet across. They contain service alleys, sheds, junked cars, effluvia of various kinds, but their potential is one of the richest opportunities for neighborhood improvement we have found.

Not so long ago, the alleys of Washington were its shame, and contained the worst slums. In today's terms, they can become the saving of the city by providing useful open space, as close to home as the back door.

The essential service access can be kept open through these alleys, and by application of easements, portions of the private space developed as community plazas—with game areas, shady trees, gardens, car parking, and even swimming pools. Some interior blocks lie behind a commercial street in which an arcade can be opened and the inner block could contain coffee houses, store front museums as proposed by the Smithsonian and other small community structures as well as outdoor facilities. There are whole areas where alleys extend for many blocks, and could be developed as winding pedestrian greenways for the entire community, weaving their influence throughout.

Halprin had discovered one of Washington's secret assets: its extensive alley system. Elsewhere the report noted: "The Capitol East area has any number of tiny shopping areas woven throughout its residential neighborhoods, caused by earlier conversion of houses to stores, and these afford an outstanding opportunity to add vitality and beauty to the entire area. Often all that is needed is to weld all the block together into a handsome shopping street—improve the lighting, pave the curbs back to the building line, plant trees, add pots of flowers and benches and provide places for people to sit and pass the time of day."

The Halprin Report is one of the few such documents one will find that suggests the encouragement of loitering as public policy. Larry Halprin understood how to use a city.

One might have supposed that the restorationists would have loved the plan. But some were very unhappy. The fact that the plan included proposals suggested by the ERC didn't help. Also, Halprin had made a major gaffe by proposing to take the large front lawns of East Capitol Street's rowhouses and turn them into a wide sidewalk. The L'Enfant disease gets the best of them.

On February 9, 1967, some 400 Hill residents showed up to give their views on the Halprin Plan. They were generally favorable. But one member of the Capitol Hill Restoration Society stood up to speak of the "onerous impact that this report has had on Capitol Hill property owners." He was answered by ERC cochairman John Anthony: "I appreciate the effort of the Restoration

Society to protect their investment, but no group can be an island unto itself. There are other people here." And a few days later, Hill public housing resident Jesse Locke wrote the *Evening Star:* "Both the Capitol Hill Restoration Society and the Capitol Hill Southeast Citizens Association have refused to join other neighborhood groups that are trying to make this a better community for everyone. If these purse-proud segregationist haters of the Great Society who are against the swimming pool for our neighborhood, who have opposed a decent-sized and integrated Hine Junior High School, who don't care about the poor people whose houses are being torn down to make way for a freeway, don't want beautification— that's okay. But the rest of us—the majority—who live between the Capitol Building and the Anacostia River do want more recreation facilities for all ages and a better neighborhood in which to live."

Although little came of the Halprin Plan, Ladybird, in one of the rare cases of a national figure displaying useful local concern, kept her interest in the area. She convinced the Vincent Astor Foundation to donate a magnificent playground for the Buchanan School, which the city later sadly let fall apart. And from the Mexican president came delightful striped equipment, including a slide in the shape of a guitar and a climbable donkey cart made of steel rods. Some of it was placed in a park situated near public housing. But it also was near the home of a grumpy resident who convinced the Park Service to move the equipment to a point immediately adjacent to an entrance ramp of the Southeast Freeway. There was no fence and only a few feet between the equipment and the roadway.

The work began about 6:30 one morning. In no time, telephones were ringing in Capitol Hill homes and an emergency caucus of the Emergency Recreation Council assembled in the park before breakfast to begin a partially successful battle with the power structure.

Similarly, when the sound of power saws brought out residents bordering on spacious, tree-lined Lincoln Park one morning, the phones began ringing again. It turned out that the Park Service had decided to improve Lincoln Park. Part of the plan involved a symmetrical pattern of walkways apparently designed by an architect who had never visited the park—his walks cut through trees that were contemporaries of Pierre L'Enfant himself. A few of the residents threatened to form a ring around the remaining trees; one mother made a picnic lunch for her children since she expected to be there for the duration. Soon, several men with Smokey the Bear hats arrived and after comparing the plans with the reality agreed that perhaps the trees were worth saving. The tree boxes in odd locations along Lincoln Park's walkways are a tribute to Capitol Hill activism.

For some Capitol Hill residents activism was a way of life. One was Marguerite Kelly, who took her role as local functionary of the mostly dormant Democratic Party very seriously, attempting to make up in service what she lacked in patronage. One of her better efforts was the Great Rat Purge of Precinct 63. Ms. Kelly wrote the Travolek Laboratories of Ft. Washington, Pennsylvania, to suggest that it donate sufficient quantities of their poison, Raticate, for a precinct clean-up drive. The next thing she knew, $900 worth of the stuff had arrived at her front door. There was enough Raticate to kill 4,320 rats, half the number estimated to reside in the precinct. The District government baited alleys in a sixty-block area and Democratic block captains distributed the Raticate from door to door. Clarence Travis, director of the city's vector control program, later reported: "From the cessation of rat activity observed and from the number of rat carcasses observed following our baiting activities, it appears that Raticate did a very good job of destroying rats in the treated squares." It also was feared that it might have caused the death of a Near Northeast cat, but a District Health Department autopsy on the animal indicated that it had died of a urinary infection.

Capitol Hill refused to accept the notion that the city was dying. It fought for better schools, more recreation space, more frequent trash pickups, and an end to the discrimination in the delivery of public services. It became highly self-reliant. When the city proposed to start a code enforcement program that would have forced many low-income homeowners to sell in the face of high repair bills, the community, led by black minister Jesse Anderson, exerted enough pressure that the plan was dropped even before the first public meeting on it was held.

It was also Capitol Hill that provided one of the more unique experiments of the antipoverty program. Knowing that a major problem with public agencies was to get people to them, Jane Hardin, a young white, opened a combination laundromat and service center. The center provided the range of antipoverty services while in the next room washers and dryers rumbled. One of the first customers stuck an old quilt in the machine. It dissolved, jammed the plumbing and made major pipe surgery necessary. The mechanical problems and financial ones competed with the social and economic ones, and ultimately the center folded. But during the few years of its life, it was important and useful to the community.

The local credit union was more successful, under the careful management of Warren Morris. Begun in 1965, it had 538 members after one year of operation and over 2,000 by 1973. It was making over a quarter of a million dollars worth of loans annually—mostly small loans that enabled Capitol Hill's poorer residents to get through times of economic crisis. Morris was resourceful. When the credit union started distributing food stamps, he established two lines: one for members, the other, far longer, for nonmembers. Soon even food stamp recipients were becoming members of the credit union. And even though most of the credit union's loans were in the high risk category, the delinquency rate dipped as low as 2.1 percent.

One of the more impressive displays of community spirit came when the director of the Capitol East Community Organization, which had become the major community group, was charged with receiving stolen money. CECO was rapidly becoming a force in the city as well as the neighborhood. It was causing trouble downtown and taking direct action against the local drug trade. There was more than a hint that the prosecution, based on weak and circumstantial evidence, was being pressed for political reasons. As one local resident put it, "I don't care if he's guilty or not; they're out to get CECO."

The community produced for CECO director Linwood Chatman's defense a string of character witnesses that would have charmed the most hardened juror. There were several ministers, the ward member of the school board, and, at the end, a beautiful black nun who, since she was clutching her own Bible, had to fumble about to take the oath on the court's edition. Sometime between the masterful presentation of lawyer James Heller (later local ACLU chairman) and the final blessing of Sister Mary, the jury reached the same conclusion as the community. As the foreman walked through the door behind the judge after the deliberation, he raised a clenched fist to his chest. Linwood knew the verdict before the judge did. CECO was to be allowed to continue as a major voice of the community.

As a community newspaper editor, I sometimes found myself covering three meetings in one night. The community was as over-organized as it was over-churched. In the mile-and-a-half square that comprised Capitol East, there were a hundred churches, including ones with such exotic names as the New Hope United Free Will Baptist Church, the Tried Stone FBH Church, and the Church of the Lord Jesus Christ of the Apostolic Faith. There were as many organizations, ranging from such major ones as the Capitol Hill Restoration Society and CECO to the Southeast Businessmen for Better Community Relations, the Beautification Community Organization Club, the Community Defense Organization, and the Morse-Montello-Trinidad-Florida Square Block Club.

But as the post-riot torpor and the Nixon era settled in, the sound of angry voices attempting to halt a vote by that locally sanctioned addendum to *Robert's Rules of Order*—"I've got an unreadiness"—was heard less often. There was less happening and less to go to meetings about.

In the mid-sixties the National Capital Planning Commission had laid down its objectives for Capitol East to be completed by 1972. They included:

- A rapid transit line through Capitol East.
- A scattered-site public housing program extended throughout Capitol East with a rehabilitation and leasing program being the major effort.
- Housing inspection and strict code enforcement applied to prevent the further spread of blight.
- Public works: six new elementary schools and the expansion of eight others; two new junior high schools; the development of some ninety acres for new local parks and playgrounds; the initial development and improvement of the regional park systems along the Anacostia waterfront; the replacement of the Southeast and Northeast branch libraries; the replacement of police precinct stations No. 5 and No. 9; the development of a new comprehensive public health center in conjunction with District of Columbia General Hospital; and completion of East Leg of the Inner Loop Freeway.

By the end of 1972, the only goal met was the development of a new health center and the only ones partially met were the construction of a few new schools and playgrounds and a portion of the East Leg. Some of the goals were very undesirable, some were unnecessary, and some were good; but the thing they had in common was that they were nearly all unattained.

For Washington's neighborhoods, as for the city as a whole, change came hard.

Life Inside the Monument

Photographs by Roland Freeman

Billy Graham at "Honor America Day"

HUD

Blackboard at Eastern High

Public Housing in Southwest
Urban Renewal Area;
Private Highrise in Background

Free School in Northwest

Junkman with Typical Rowhouses

Looter, April 1968

Martin
Luther
King
Food
Co-op

Marion Barry

*Former School Supt. Hugh Scott (right)
with Jesse Jackson*

Julius Hobson (far left) with Other Protesters

Commissioner Walter Washington

Arrest

lice Chief Jerry Wilson (center)

Benjamin Spock at Peace Demonstration

4 / Black, White, and In Between

AT SOME POINT IN THE FIFTIES WASHINGTON'S BLACKS became for the first time an ethnic majority. This city, which had always had a sizable black minority—ranging from one-fifth to one-third of the total population, was 54 percent black at the time of the 1960 census. By 1970 the figure had climbed to 71 percent. One of white America's worst nightmares had come true: a major city had turned black.

To many outside the city, including thousands of white emigrants, the import was clear: crisis, failure, disaster. And evidence mounted to support the fears: declining educational quality, rising crime, a troubled center city, growing welfare costs, and, in 1968, riots. It was not just Wallacites and conservatives who viewed black predominance as an urban death warrant. As late as May 1972 Sol Linowitz, chairman of the National Urban Coalition, was still saying things like, "We have to face the total abandonment of the cities" unless the white flight to the suburbs was reversed. And he warned, "By 1980 the cities are going to be black and brown, unless action is taken to revitalize downtown."

It was a peculiar perspective for an organization that considered itself progressive. The implication that a black majority and urban progress were mutually exclusive was not far removed from earlier assumptions that black enfranchisement or equality in education and employment were a threat to society. The implication was just as false. The last twenty years of Washington's history have proved it.

To be sure, Washington has serious crime, educational, economic and interracial problems. But by any fair standard, Washington's problems leave it at worst an average American large city. In a number of respects, in fact, it has survived the "urban crisis" better than most places.

Far from being an argument against self-government, Washington's black majority makes a strong case in its favor. This is not merely a matter of equity; empirically Washington's blacks have shown that they are not only capable of running a city but of doing so in a fashion that elevates rather than depresses the spirit. As a white, I would rather be in the minority in Washington than in the majority in most major American cities. This feeling has nothing to do with conscience; it is self-serving. Despite the plethora of problems that Washington shares with other cities, it remains a remarkably warm, unhostile, and human place.

This is so partially because blacks are among the last of the unautomated Americans. They are not yet enough absorbed into the national mainstream to revere abstractions or obey the dictates of bloodless conglomerates. The voice of the individual repeatedly interrupts the Muzak. Maybe eventually they will become computerized, corporatized, and numericalized—good Americans.

But for now, the influence of black culture in a city like Washington encourages everyone, black or white, to snatch a bit of personal identity from the grasping paws of what passes these days for progress.

In a 1973 article, Atlee E. Shidler, president of the Washington Center for Metropolitan Studies, pointed out some ways in which Washington fails to match its image as a crisis-racked city:

• Between 1959 and 1969 the number of black families in the city with incomes over $8,000 (in 1969 dollars) more than doubled. There was a 5 percent decrease in the number with incomes under $8,000.

• The number of blacks in professional and technical jobs rose 80 percent during the decade; those in managerial and administrative jobs rose by 128 percent. On the other hand, laborers decreased by 22 percent; blacks employed as domestics decreased by 50 percent.

• The number of DC blacks with a high school diploma increased by 63 percent.

• While there are 35 percent more black families in Washington than in 1959, there are 8 percent fewer black children under the age of five.

• The black fertility ratio in DC is virtually the same as the white fertility ratio in the suburbs.

• While the total population of DC dropped by 7,400 during the decade, the number of District households increased by 10,500.

All this happened while Washington not only was dealing with the general flood of urban problems, but also adding a quarter million blacks and losing 300,000 whites. Even in the best of times, a migratory shift of this magnitude in a city of less than 800,000 population would cause staggering changes and problems. The wonder of Washington is that it not only has managed to absorb this shift but has benefited from it. The problems that continue to loom large are ones common to all major cities and, had DC been granted the political freedom to deal with them, even they might have been mitigated.

A number of external factors contributed heavily to Washington's ability to absorb the racial change that occurred, among them the parallel rise of the civil rights movement and black power and the presence of the federal government which, particularly under Lyndon Johnson, opened up more lower grade civil service jobs to blacks. But beyond those were the internal dynamics of a city which throughout its history has been a different sort of place for both blacks and whites.

From its first days, Washington had a sizable black population—part slave and part free. As early as 1810, 10 percent of the city consisted of free blacks; by 1850 the figure had increased to nearly 20 percent. During the same period, the percentage of residents who were slave declined from 23 percent to 7 percent.

The heritage of Washington as a biracial city, as a place where blacks have not been as isolated from change and power as in other places, as a place where blacks suffered the same indignities as blacks elsewhere yet stayed a step ahead in the struggle for progress, stood Washington in good stead in the fifties and sixties. The new black migration did not come into a vacuum; there was a black culture and a black leadership waiting. It was one of the things that attracted many in the first place. Washington was not only the first urban stop on the way north, but a city that by the standards of the day was less hostile to a black influx. It was, as it had been in the past, a special place for blacks.

With the rise of the civil rights movement touching Washington at an early moment, the existing leadership in Washington's black community moved easily into the positions of power that slowly opened. When John Duncan became the first black commissioner of the city in 1961, those Washingtonians not blinded by racial misconceptions quickly discovered that he, like Walter

Washington and Walter Fauntroy after him, took charge in a manner that while, stylistically different from his predecessors, was substantially familiar.

Not that Washington's black elite was totally hospitable to the new arrivals. Under the cover of common coloration, continued economic discrimination was concealed rather than eradicated. Those who had gotten there first were not about to be knocked off their newly won perch by a bunch of immigrants, even if they were black. But that merely served to smooth the racial transition. To many in power, the racial change could at least be tolerated as long as the economic system was not challenged.

Class distinctions within black Washington remain important. Even Judge Harry T. Alexander, a liberal black judge whose rulings have provoked racially-inspired abuse, refused to arraign several defendants because "the men were brought to court without dress shirts on." He told a *Washington Post* reporter that the "police should arrest people properly clothed or allow them to get their clothes."

Alexander was particularly offended by the T-shirts and tank shirts that are common garb on Washington's streets during the summer. When a reporter asked Alexander how someone would know in advance that he would be appearing in court as a prisoner, Alexander replied: "Young men should be in the street properly clothed and should understand that an undershirt is not a dress shirt or a polo shirt. . . . First of all it's disrespectful to ladies. Second, it's a benefit to no one."

But it was not just street dudes who felt the distinctions within DC's black community. When associate school superintendent John L. Johnson, a black non-Washingtonian, quit after a short time in DC, he complained, "The internal politics here are something. An outsider is very subtly reminded on every available occasion that he is an outsider. Longstanding associations, like 'we went to Dunbar High School together,' are very resistant to change." Dunbar is where the brightest black students had gone in the days of segregation, and the top layers of the school system are spotted with its graduates.

The increasing homage paid the concept of black capitalism with the coming of the Nixon Administration bolstered Washington's black elite. Nixon knew how to exploit the latent divisions within the black community. By early 1970 money was flowing to local black business—$550,000 in federal grants to the National Business League, $641,000 to Howard's Small Business Center, $230,000 to the National Bankers Association, and $503,000 to the Black Economic Union. When Jackie Robinson and other black businessmen joined in a combine to build a high-rise office building on Capitol Hill, they received White House support and promises. There was a quid pro quo that became due in the election of 1972, when, in marked contrast to the political views of most of Washington's blacks, local recipients of minority business contracts formed support committees for the reelection of the President. It was hard not to take advantage of the Nixon largesse, but it had to be done carefully. When a stream of black leaders arrived in town for a big thank-you fund-raising dinner for the President, a local black activist stood outside ostentatiously taking photographs of the attendees. More than a few that spotted him turned their heads or covered their faces.

Andrew Brimmer, the only black member of the Federal Reserve Board, was sceptical of black capitalism, saying, "The strategy of black capitalism offers a very limited potential for the economic advancement for the majority of the Negro population." It was, he pointed out, "founded on the premise of self-employment. Self employment is a rapidly declining factor in our modern economy." Even some of the black capitalists found that the new economics weren't all they were cracked up to be. When a leading black restaurateur tore down his establishment to construct a subsidized motel on the site, he found himself in deep financial straits as promised approvals and monies failed to materialize. He was forced to draw unemployment.

It was an old story. Leadbelly sang a song about it years ago:

> He's a bourgeois man,
> Livin' in a bourgeois town,
> I got the Bourgeois Blues,
> An I'm sure gonna spread the news.
>
> The white folks in Washington,
> They know how,
> Chunk a colored man a nickel
> Just to see him bow.

Most blacks, of course, were in no position to play the black capitalism game. For the bulk of black Washington, the problem was to find a decent job and to move ahead to something better. A large number did. In 1969 dollars, here are the percentages of black families in various income classes in 1969 compared with 1959:

	1959	1969
Less than $4,000	26%	17%
$4,000–$7,999	41%	29%
$8,000–$11,999	20%	24%
Over $12,000	14%	29%

The economic and social goals of Washington's growing black middle class and its white counterpart are similar, including moving still further up the economic ladder, better schools for its children, enjoying the freedom to consume, and avoiding crime. There are, however, a number of differences. One is that a greater percentage of middle-class blacks make it financially by having both husband and wife work. Many blacks hold down more than one job; it is not unusual to find a taxi

driver who works full time for the government or somewhere else. The $14,000 family income recorded by the
statistics may actually be two incomes. Middle-class
status can remain a tough life. Besides, in expensive
Washington, the dollars don't go so far as in many
places.

There is also the problem that employment opportunities for blacks rapidly dissipate in the higher income
levels. In the summer of 1972, the Library of Congress
found itself embroiled in black employee protests. One
reason was a job pattern not untypical of the city:

Grade	Percentage of positions held by blacks
GS1–4 (lowest grade)	72.5%
GS5–8	47.9%
GS9–11	16.6%
GS12–13	6.7%
GS14–15	2.5%
GS16–18	3.6%

Throughout the federal and District government it
was clear that the jobs that had been opened to blacks
were overwhelmingly at the lower rungs. And if you
were not only black but a woman, the rungs were even
lower.

Middle-class status does not save you from other
forms of discrimination, either. As late as the end of the
sixties, black policemen and firemen were still finding
tacit official approval of whites refusing to ride in the
patrol car with them or objecting to using the same oxy-
gen breathing apparatus. Real estate dealers circumvent
equal housing regulations by devious devices like limiting the houses shown black buyers. The press still fails
to give the same weight to black social or cultural life
that it does to white. Prominent clubs continue to ex-

clude blacks and women. Even middle-class neighborhoods, if they are black, get short-changed on government services.

There's nothing monolithic about Washington's black
middle class. There is still the lifestyle typified by James
I. Minor, a school administrator who died at 85 in 1972.
His obituary reported:

> He was a member of the Pleasant Plains Civic Associ-
> ation, the Area J Board of the DC Commissioners Youth
> Council and the board of directors of the Bureau of Re-
> habilitation.
>
> Mr. Minor was a troop committeeman with the Boy
> Scouts and served on the Model School Council, the
> Traffic Guard Committee and the Salvation Army Coun-
> cil. He was active in the YMCA, the National Education
> Association, the National Retired Teachers Association
> and the Congress of Parents and Teachers.
>
> He was a member of the 19th Street Baptist Church,
> where he belonged to the senior choir, the male chorus,
> the Men's Club and the Christian Endeavor Society.

But a life devoted to dutiful service to church and
community institutions seems to be as much on the
wane for younger urban blacks as it is for younger urban whites. The middle-class city dweller has traded
community ties for freedom, preservation for change,
peer determinants for media-merchandised ones. With
this, the varieties of lifestyles have proliferated for
blacks as much as for whites. And since Washington is
a city that seems to have a better than average tolerance
for individualistic behavior, many people of both races
enjoy the benefits of not only being able to afford to live
the way they want but being allowed to do so. An atypi-
cal but still significant manifestation of this is the number of interracial marriages in the city.

In short, within Washington's middle class you can
find just about anything. There are black and white dy-

namos, stolid bureaucrats, freaks, swingers, modish executives, eggheads, homosexuals, prayer meeting puri-
tans, back-busting overtime workers, coffee-breakers,
those who cross racial lines for friendship and those who
refuse to, Volkswagen drivers and owners of Airstream
trailers. The most conservatively dressed people in town
are black functionaries of the Muslims and white functionaries of the foreign service.

It is easy in the glow of optimistic statistics and the
signs of progress to forget that a sizable portion of black
Washington hasn't made it. Forty-six percent of the
black families earn less than $8,000 a year. Unemploy-
ment in DC, while running less than 4 percent citywide
was in the early seventies as high as 17 percent for black
males under 21 and 20 percent for black women under
21 in some parts of town. Adding those in low-paying
jobs, those working only part-time and those resigned to
exclusion from the job market, it was estimated that total underemployment in the city was 100,000 in 1972,
equivalent to nearly 30 percent of the work force.

There is a housing shortage for the poor as well. In
1972 the Metropolitan Council of Government estimated
that there were 40,000 families in DC in need of better
housing. There were 5,000 families on the waiting list
for public housing. And a study done in 1968 showed
that there were more than 20,000 DC families of five or
more persons whose incomes indicated a need for subsidized housing, yet there were only about 6,000 units
planned or available for them. This meant a gap of more
than 14,000 units. In comparison, the much larger city
of Philadelphia had a gap of only 6,700 units for the
same sort of families.

Who are these people who fail to share in Washington's progress? They are laborers and welfare mothers,
drop-outs and public school graduates, those still trying
to make it and those who have given up. Although national politicians project pictures of bums on the dole,

even those taking advantage of every morsel of welfare available barely scrape by. They live in public housing units that would be condemned were they in private hands; they stand outside banks in the cold and wet waiting to receive food stamps at the drive-in window; they suffer some of the worst crime, they get the worst health treatment, and they send their children to the worst schools. And on top of all that, they are publicly insulted by the President and congressmen up for reelection.

In *Tally's Corner,* anthropologist Elliot Liebow stepped beyond the statistics and generalizations to describe in detail the life of street corner men on a Washington block. It is one of the most perceptive and sensitive descriptions of a part of the nation's underclass. In the course of it, Liebow tells of a pickup truck moving slowly down the street, the driver asking idling men whether they wanted a day's work. He was repeatedly refused. Liebow goes on:

[The driver] has been able to recruit only two or three from each twenty or fifty he contacts. To him, it is clear that the others simply do not choose to work. Singly or in groups, belly-empty or belly-full, sullen or gregarious, drunk or sober, they confirm what he has read, heard and known from his experience: these men wouldn't take a job if it were handed to them on a platter.

Quite apart from the question of whether or not this is true of some of the men he sees on the street, it is clearly not true of all of them. If it were, he would not have come here in the first place; or having come, he would have left with an empty truck. It is not even true of most of them, for most of the men he sees on the street this weekday morning do, in fact, have jobs. But since, at the moment, they are neither working nor sleeping, and since they hate the depressing room or apartment they live in, or because there is nothing to do there, or because they want to get away from their wives or any-one else living there, they are out on the street, indis-tinguishable from those who do not have jobs or do not want them. Some, like Boley, a member of a trash-collection crew in a suburban housing development, work Saturdays and are off on this weekday. Some, like Sweets, work nights cleaning up middle-class trash, dirt, dishes and garbage, and mopping the floors of the office buildings, hotels, restaurants, toilets and other public places dirtied during the day. Some men work for retail businesses such as liquor stores which do not begin the day until ten o'clock. Some laborers, like Tally, have al-ready come back from the job because the weather was too cold for pouring concrete. Other employed men stayed off the job today for personal reasons: Clarence to go to a funeral at eleven this morning and Sea Cat to answer a subpoena as a witness in a criminal proceeding.

Also on the street, unwitting contributors to the im-pression taken away by the truck driver, are the halt and the lame. The man on the cast-iron steps strokes one gnarled arthritic hand with the other and says he doesn't know whether or not he'll live long enough to be eligible for Social Security. He pauses, then adds matter-of-factly, "Most times, I don't care whether I do or don't." Stoopy's left leg was polio-withered in childhood. Raymond, who looks as if he could tear out a fire hydrant, coughs up blood if he bends or moves suddenly. The quiet man who hangs out in front of the Saratoga apartments has a steel hook strapped onto his left elbow. And had the man in the truck been able to look into the wine-clouded eyes of the man in the green cap, he would have realized that the man did not even understand he was being offered a day's work.

Others, having had jobs and been laid off, are draw-ing unemployment compensation. . . .

Still others, like Bumdoodle the numbers man, are working hard at illegal ways of making money, hustlers who are on the street to turn a dollar any way they can: buying and selling sex, liquor, narcotics, stolen goods, or anything else that turns up.

Only a handful remains unaccounted for. There is Tonk, who cannot bring himself to take a job away from the corner, because, according to the other men, he suspects his wife will be unfaithful if given the opportunity. There is Stanton, who has not reported to work for four days now, not since Bernice disappeared. He bought a brand new knife against her return. . . .

And finally, there are those like Arthur, able-bodied men who have no visible means of support, legal or illegal, who neither have jobs nor want them. The truck driver, among others, believes the Arthurs to be representative of all the men he sees idling on the street during his own working hours. . . .

Liebow makes a number of other cogent observations about the streetcorner men and their attitude towards work. He points out that they put no lower value on a job than does the larger society around them; that they are no more ready to quit a job than their employers are ready to fire them. And he describes what it means to be an unskilled laborer—the unremitting hard work broken only by sudden layoffs or the weather—and tells of a wife hearing her husband cry out in his sleep, "No more digging! I can't do no more Goddamn digging!"

To those who feel that poor blacks are too much oriented to the present, Liebow argues that the poor and the middle class are equally future-oriented, but that they have different futures. The streetcorner man, he says, "lives in a sea of want. He does not, as a rule, have a surplus of resources, either economic or psychological. Gratification of hunger and the desire for simple creature comforts cannot be long deferred. Neither can support for one's flagging self-esteem. Living on the edge of both economic and psychological subsistence, the streetcorner man is obliged to expend all his resources on maintaining himself from moment to moment."

While the streetcorner men that Liebow describes are typical residents of Washington's core, they are not the only typical ones.

There are those whose lifestyle and goals seem closer to that considered normal by many middle-class Americans. They live side by side with the streetcorner men, the junkies and the hustlers, the crime and the rats because in part it is, after all, home, and in part because their economic situation precludes any alternative. In another anthropological look at a Washington neighborhood, *Soulside*, Ulf Hannerz calls these people "mainstreamers." He writes of them:

> It is usually not very hard to detect from the outside which houses on Winston Street are the homes of mainstreamers. The new metal screen doors, the venetian blinds, and the flower pots in the windows are usually absent from other people's houses. Yet basically the small row houses in the neighborhood all look rather much alike, whether the dark bricks have a coat of paint or not, and thus it may be quite a surprise to enter a mainstreamer's home and find that behind the drab exterior there is often a home which looks quite out of place in a predominantly low-income neighborhood. One family on Winston Street has a living room set of imitation Italian antique furniture, bought at a price of about $1,500 and encased in fitted clear plastic covers; in a couple of homes the occupant-owners have had their living rooms paneled. Some have modern although usually relatively inexpensive Scandinavian-style furniture, and there are many large table lamps, sometimes matched in pairs, one on each side of the couch. New TV and stereo sets are not unusual; although the record collections include a lot of black rock-and-roll and jazz, there is often also some white pop and, less frequently, some classical music. On

the shelves there may be some vases and rather inexpensive china figurines, as well as framed graduation or wedding pictures of the inhabitants of the house or of close relatives. Similar pictures may be on the wall, perhaps sharing the space with some picture prints. There may be a picture or a color memorial plate of the late president Kennedy, whose memory is as greatly esteemed by many mainstreamers as by most other ghetto dwellers.

The mainstreamers and the streetcorner men are only examples of inner city culture; they do not encompass it. Both Liebow and Hannerz wrote full books describing the variety of life in single blocks of Washington's poorer areas. Hannerz notes: "The diversity of lifestyles has a great impact on the ordering of ghetto social relations. People of different lifestyles have different kinds of networks, and the differences influence the quantity and quality of interaction between them. Thus there are noticeable cleavages between people following different walks of life, although one must also note that there are instances when life styles compliment each other."

It is this diversity that stands out so strikingly against the common image of the inner city. The term *ghetto* itself contributes heavily to the homogenization of what is basically diverse, complex, and resistant to easy characterization. The term may be politically or sociologically descriptive, but in popular usage it denies the heart of the city every human characteristic but those evocative of despair. But then linguists have noted that we have the most words for things that matter most to us. The eskimo has no single word for snow but many. Conversely, I suppose, white America needs only one word to describe the central city.

On April 4, 1968, Washington's core reached critical mass. I was up on T Street with the Emergency Committee on the Transportation Crisis, demonstrating in front of Commissioner Washington's house over the latest freeway fiasco, when word came of Martin Luther King's death. We went home as the police cars poured by filled with shotgun-armed and helmeted police. My wife and I lived then a few blocks south of H Street, a major black commercial strip. The next morning, however, things were still quiet enough that we went about our business as usual. I came home that afternoon to find a slow stream of people walking down the street with liberated objects: hangers full of clothes, a naugahyde hassock, a television set. There were only a few whites living on the block, but I felt little tension or hostility from those I passed. I mainly noticed the black smoke pouring down from H Street. My wife was out back working in our foot-wide strip of garden, listening to reports of looting and arson on a portable radio as the black fog settled in. We decided to go up on the roof for a better look. H Street was burning. Other areas had gone first and there were reports of a lack of fire equipment to deal with the situation a few blocks to the north. I tried to count the fires but they congealed under the curtain of smoke. A picture I had seen of blocks of burned-out buildings in Detroit came to my mind and I suggested that we better pack a few things in case we had to leave. For about ten minutes we did so but our instinctive selection—nostalgic items, favorite photos, the unvaluable but irreplacable—made us laugh. Like loyal children of our generation, we settled down in our smoky living room to watch it all on television. At six-thirty the next morning a white friend from around the corner rang our doorbell. He wasn't in trouble; he just wanted company on a tour of the area. We got into his car and drove to H, Seventh and Fourteenth Streets. As I looked at the smoldering carcass of Washington and observed the troops marching down the street past store-fronts that no longer had any backs, I thought, so this is what war is like. As we drove past a gutted store on Fourteenth Street it suddenly reignited itself and flames leaped towards the pavement.

That day and for several days thereafter, we stuck close to home. The trouble had flared again. We received anxious calls from friends and relatives in other parts of town and in other towns. We assured them we were all right, but they seemed more upset about our physical safety than we were and I did not want to alarm them by speaking what was in my mind: the feeling of helplessness, anger, and frustration at seeing it come to this. For a year-and-a-half of running a neighborhood newspaper, I had observed, and tried to report, a part of the community seething with these same emotions that much of the other part refused to recognize. Now it was worse than I had even let myself think. And I subconsciously prepared myself for it to get worse. In the middle of one of the riot nights, I awakened to a rumbling noise in the street and ran to the window expecting to see tanks rolling past our house. There were no tanks. The physical threat of the riots barely touched us. The strange ambivalences of the riots—the slashes of violence mixed indiscriminately with the sparkle of carnival, the sounds of racial war penetrating the tranquility of a white couple's home four blocks from disaster, our strangely ordinary experiences in an extraordinary situation—made the disorder a crazy amalgam that took weeks to sort out. For months afterwards, when sporadic violence hit stores in our neighborhood, I expected to find our newspaper office smashed and looted. It didn't happen, despite the inviting plate glass storefront. I was inclined, with normal self-delusion, to attribute this to having paid my dues. It was more likely, however, that our second-hand electric typewriters weren't worth the candle when there was a whole Safeway up the street and a cleaners on the corner.

After five years of massive indifference to the import of the riots, I feel the pressures slowly building up again and I suspect that if they are not relieved, the disturbances of the sixties will seem like a picnic. For me, the prototypical story of the 1968 riots was of the lady in our community who liberated a case of whiskey from a liquor store. Upon arriving home she realized that she didn't have any chaser so she went back for a case of ginger ale and was arrested. There was no Mark Essex firing wildly from rooftops in 1968. Next time it will probably be different.

You can't say for sure. Things keep changing. The past years have not only dramatically altered black attitudes several times but black–white relationships as well. A few years ago dashiki militancy was the favored style of the young black activist; separatism was new and exciting and whites were explicitly and implicitly told to shut up and get out. A few months ago, however, I was at a meeting where a teenage black involved in a marxist-oriented drugless rehabilitation program said almost casually, "The thing you've got to understand is that Washington's a nationalist city; it's a stage people go through." In the past ten years "black and white together" was swallowed up in rigid black separatism; it then began to sort itself out into a mixture of close racial identity and pragmatic interracial alliances. Today one finds blacks who are hostile towards whites because they are whites and others who are hostile to certain whites, either because they are too close to white establishment values or because they are too opposed to them. On the other hand, one finds blacks who are glad to associate with whites for a variety of reasons. Some are confident of their own identities. Others value the breadth brought by interracial contact. And others suppress inner emotions in order to deal successfully with the world as they find it. You cannot sort these attitudes by class, politics, or education. Not even with any one individual do they stay fixed. The civil rights and back power movements gave blacks the opportunity to make their own peace or war with the white national majority that engulfs them. It is still a new experience, and many are trying different approaches.

I have perhaps stressed the variety of black culture and attitudes to the point of triteness. Many blacks, to whom it is obvious, probably will think so. But one of the tragedies of our society is the difficulty of the white majority to perceive minorities in other than monolithic or stereotyped ways. It is one of the unique values of Washington that the inherent variety of black life has been permitted to surface, challenging the cliches and generalizations at every turn. When two black brothers are charged with a lurid crime and the father, a Jehovah's Witness, tells a reporter that he doesn't have bail money "and I wouldn't get them out if I had it," when black welfare mothers sit in at the office of the black director of human resources, when four black candidates for office argue vehemently in a television debate, when a 75 percent black ward votes for a white school board candidate over several black candidates, when a black human relations committee chairman accuses the police of brutality and black city officials deny it, blacks emerge not as symbols of a race but as individuals. In Washington, one doesn't have to talk about it. It is widely assumed by both whites and blacks. It helps to make Washington one of the more human cities in the country.

This is not to suggest, by any means, that Washington is an interracial mecca, only that racial conflicts are dealt with at the local level in a more sophisticated manner. Unfortunately, many who are part of federal government, either in the executive branch or on the Hill, have failed to benefit from the experience. They remain insulated, their myopia guarded by marble walls, their vision of the city limited by the parkways they travel to work, hardly more sensitive to the realities of black Washington than if they were back home where "black" is primarily an adjective butting up against the word "problem." Within Washington's white minority, one of the most obvious splits is between those who take part in the life of the local community and those who don't.

But even those who are involved have problems. Washington's whites, partially out of choice and partially for reasons over which they have no control, are concentrated in certain areas like West of the Park, or on certain blocks as in Adams-Morgan or Capitol Hill. For many that is obviously the way they like it. But even those who actively seek integrated living find it hard to achieve. Most real estate dealers at best are disinterested in biracial neighborhoods; at worst they work vigorously to prevent them. When the product of this attitude is combined with a much larger demand for black housing than for white, whites find themselves faced with two alternatives: to move into a neighborhood that is solidly white or black or to move into one that is changing one way or the other. West of the Park has remained overwhelmingly white; upper Sixteenth Street has turned increasingly black; Capitol Hill has turned increasingly white. And the future of Adams-Morgan is very much in doubt. You learn to spot the signs. An ad for a house on Capitol Hill on an "exploding block" meant block-busting for whites. Now you see ads in Adams-Morgan like that. One boasted "See first the Pioneer and Creator of this Area. We have recently SOLD . . ."—the addresses of seventeen homes in still two-thirds black Adams-Morgan follow. A resident of an area clearly across Rock Creek from Georgetown reports that the agents there are beginning to call it "Georgetown East."

There are other barriers to biracial living. The fact that middle-class whites have more options than blacks means that they will tend to migrate faster away from areas with problems like bad schools, poor services, pollution, and crime. During an era when blacks have seemed disinterested in cross-cultural neighborhood life, the value of such an experience has declined in many whites' eyes as well when weighed against other factors such as physical comfort and amenities. To white liberals nursed at the breast of guilt, this can be a troublesome matter; few notice that blacks are not reluctant to move out of a tough neighborhood if they have the chance. One of the reasons so few middle-class blacks have moved to Capitol Hill, I suspect, is because to many blacks, living in a narrow row house on a dirty inner-city street is not their idea of progress. They've been there before.

Middle-class blacks looking for a good house can get a much better deal in Brookland or Crestwood than on Capitol Hill or West of the Park. Not even many moderately affluent blacks are deep enough into the luxury economy to be attracted by houses whose prices have been inflated by speculation or an intangible aura of status. In addition, blacks can move into less expensive neighborhoods that would be the envy of most urban American whites and become part of a majority rather than the corner sop to the white liberal conscience. While the *Washington Post*, with good old liberal values, described the proliferation of black middle-class neighborhoods as a sign of "segregation," the fact is that in none of these neighborhoods is there any move to attract whites back. Whites simply aren't the *sine qua non* of black health and happiness, the Urban Coalition and Downtown Progress notwithstanding.

On the other hand, the result of this process is that middle-class blacks still get, in Washington terms, second-best. The housing and ambience of the neighborhood may be on a par with white sections but government services such as police protection and trash pickup tend not to be. The best public schools are still West of the Park and the blacks who go to them have to travel some distance to get there.

As we moved from a mostly black neighborhood ten blocks south to the heart of Capitol Hill and thence to

Cleveland Park, we found the problems of urban living declining and the pleasures increasing. We also found ourselves living in increasingly white and affluent neighborhoods. Everyone from the Post Office to the Sanitation Department to the local chain supermarket seemed to respond proportionately to the increase in our property taxes. It was nice to feel that you got something for your money, but it is a hell of a way to run a city. I felt as if I was being bribed into cultural isolation by the expectation of improved living conditions. Being an epicurean at heart, I was willing to risk the damage to my soul in exchange for room for the kids to run around, less pollution, decent schools, an expansive Giant market with fresh meat and Sunday hours, and honest to god trees—not some scraggly appendages of the Triassic Era like the tree of heaven, that urban arbor that grows only in census tracts under a certain median income.

When my friends twitted me about moving West of the Park, I quoted Willy Brandt as having said upon leaving Scandinavia after the Second World War that it was more important to be a democrat in Germany than in Norway, but I was troubled more than ever by the city's extraordinary differential in services, both private and public. The fact that I was a beneficiary did not make me grateful, for my advantage was achieved at the cost of making me someone else's grievance; I wanted to enjoy a decent community without being asked to apologize for it.

Much of the blame for this sort of differential is rightly placed on white attitudes and actions. But blacks also play a role. The present black mayor has far more power than he uses to equalize services and facilities throughout the city. And there are other blacks who pay homage to discrimination, like the black teacher in a one-third white elementary school who gave all the prizes on award day to white students. That was a devastating lesson for both whites and blacks in her class.

In one sense the congregation of whites West of the Park is a good thing. As blacks gained political power in the city, whites increasingly realized that, despite their social and economic advantages, they were subject to some of the same problems of all minorities. If they could not turn black and were not allowed to remain identifiably white, they would be nothing. It is no more desirable that Washington's white minority be assimilated into its black majority than that nationwide the reverse occur.

The presence of a nearby all-white ward provides a political structure through which whites can function without constant reference to the citywide black majority. As a member of a minority, you learn to pull your punches, play it close, and skew your opinions to the bias of the majority. It's an experience that white Americans don't often have. But in Washington, whites who are involved in the life of the city quickly discover the limits created by minority status, even favored minority status. It helps them perhaps to empathize more with the feelings of blacks as part of a larger minority. It also leads to different responses.

For example, when the black leader of a local organization decided, in the interest of what he perceived to be his political advancement, to mau mau the white members of his group, the whites, rather than going away guiltily, simply regrouped around a Ward Three organization and refused to be drummed out. It was a far cry from the days of knee-jerk liberalism and from what Stokely Carmichael and Charles Hamilton described in 1967 as the myth that "assumes that political coalitions are or can be sustained on a moral, friendly, sentimental basis; by appeals to conscience." But it was a far healthier situation for all concerned. It does little for the psychological well-being of the white community for it to suppress its own identity in the name of racial justice. It doesn't help blacks, either. It is as important for blacks to recognize that the city is 30 percent white as it is for whites to appreciate that it is 70 percent black. There is no reason why, in the great national sweep towards ethnicity, that WASPS alone should be denied the solace that comes from healthy ethnic self-conception. Despite the rhetoric laying blame for four hundred years of oppression on whatever cracker happens to be handy, there is still no evidence that human virtue has a racial characteristic. And it is also true, as Saul Alinsky pointed out, that "when the poor get power they'll be shits like anyone else."

The striking thing about Washington is that whites and blacks seem more inclined to deal with each other pragmatically than elsewhere. The city is leaving the myth of assimilationist integration behind, saying goodbye to the traditional liberal concept that to become equal blacks must first become environmentally, psychologically, and socially white. Instead, there is being slowly and painfully constructed a city where blacks can be black, whites can be white, and those who want to mix it up can do so. Far from sending the city over the precipice to chaos, the rise of Washington's blacks has lifted up the city, giving it vitality, variety, and contempt for uniformity. Washington has broken the rules of who should live in the city and who should run it. For whites as well as for blacks, it works.

5 / *The Heaviest City Government*

FOR MOST OF THE NATION, 1973 WAS NOT A VERY
good year. Yet it was during those generally dismal
months that the city of Washington, to its surprise,
found itself suddenly moving toward the greatest change
in its political status in ninety-nine years. Once again,
DC was out of step with the rest of the country, only this
time, for a change, it was getting the better of the deal.
Or at least many hoped so.

Congress had finally decided to loosen its grip on the
city and had approved a bill permitting local elections
for mayor and city council, but retaining federal control
over the budget, courts, and a number of other local
matters. To some the action, which had seemed impossible only months earlier, was cause for celebration; but
the city as a whole observed the occurrence with rampant
calm.

To an outsider, it might have seemed strange that

the city could greet the apparent advent of local democracy with so little exhilaration, stranger still that there were voices—including those of some current and past members of the school board, the only existing elected body—that actually suggested opposing the measure as a sham and political Trojan horse.

The wary attitude toward the change in the city's status stemmed in part from an understanding that suffrage did not mean power. Washington was not getting home rule, but half rule—a parliamentary placebo in place of true local autonomy.

Further, it appeared to some that the new elected government had not only been assigned responsibility without authority (a major complaint of school board members) but had been given an impossible task: to please both a voting constituency and those in Congress and the White House in whose hands the city's destiny remained. It seemed almost as if the prime requisite for public office in such circumstances would be credentials as either a schizophrenic or a liar.

At the time Congress approved the change in the city's status, Washington was being run by the heaviest city government in the world. It consisted not only of an appointed commissioner and council, numerous independent agencies, an elected school board, and some 50,000 local civil servants, but of the United States Congress (through more than a half-dozen different committees) and the President as well.

Local executive power was vested in the Commissioner and legislative power in the Council, with the Commissioner having a veto over Council actions. The school board had control over educational matters, but its budgets had to be approved by the Council and Commissioner. All changes in city tax rates (with the exception of the property tax, which could be set locally) and all spending legislation had to be approved by the Congress and the President. While the city, under its police powers, could issue and amend many local regulations without direct approval of the federal government, most major local legislation had to be funneled through Congress and the White House.

In addition, the situation was complicated by the existence of independent agencies such as the National Capital Planning Commission, Redevelopment Land Agency, and Washington Metropolitan Area Transit Authority, which had legislative power, executive power, or both. And the independent Fine Arts Commission could veto the RLA, NCPC, Council or Commissioner if what they wanted to do was going to look too ugly.

One could construct an organizational chart that would show all this. It wouldn't mean much. Not only would the lines criss-cross to the point of incomprehension, but they would fail to reveal the realities of local power relationships. How does one chart a city department head who takes his marching orders from a powerful congressman rather than from the Commissioner? Or a President of the United States who bypasses the Commissioner to take up problems directly with the local chief of police?

The city's governmental structure was as exotically complex in form as it was functionally unworkable. It was a bureaucratic jungle through which powerful Tarzans could swing easily from tree to tree while most others had to hack their way through tortuous undergrowth.

The real power over the city rested not with local functionaries but with the President and the Congress. And the President left most of the details to Congress. A program aired by Washington television station WTOP-TV described the absurdity well:

As the all-powerful landlords of the City of Washington, the members of the world's greatest deliberative body have some of the world's most trivial duties.

• Congress not only has to preside over a national budget in excess of 200 billion dollars.

• It also has to determine the size of rockfish which can be sold in the District of Columbia.

• Congress not only has to see to the proper functioning of the entire U.S. economy.

• It also has to worry with the size of the registration fee for dogs in the District of Columbia.

• Congress not only must search for the causes of decay in the nation's cities.

• It also must decide whether kites may be flown in the District of Columbia.

• Congress not only must wrestle with health care programs for the country's elderly and poor.

• It also must say whether members of the DC Fire Department can play in the DC Police Department Band.

• Congress not only must decide on the size and scope of multi-billion dollar foreign aid programs.

• It also must decide whether a wife's name may be added to that of her husband on trailer registration forms in the District of Columbia.

But while Congress was the preeminent meddler in the internal affairs of the District, everyone got into the act, creating a government worthy of a Cecil B. De Mille denouement.

The President most frequently got involved in the District when a large chunk of real estate became ripe for development, or when the peculiar circumstances of the city suggested a national theme—as DC home rule complemented Lyndon Johnson's civil rights program and DC's rising crime rate suited Richard Nixon's law and order policy. But he also had to engage in specifics. Peace or war, inflation or depression, it was still the President's responsibility to appoint one Commissioner of the District of Columbia, one assistant to the commissioner, nine members of the DC Council, the members of the

Public Service Commission, five citizen members of the National Capital Planning Commission and all ex-officio members, seven members of the Commission of Fine Arts, the Adjutant General of the National Guard, judges of the Superior Court, judges of the District Court of Appeals, judges of the U.S. District Court and Court of Appeals for the District of Columbia, the Armory Board, the U.S. Attorney for the District and his assistants, federal members of the Interstate Commission of the Potomac Basin, U.S. Marshals for the District, the DC Register of Deeds, the Board of Trustees of Howard University, the head of the Redevelopment Land Agency, the head of the National Capital Housing Authority, and a portion of the Pennsylvania Avenue Commission.

In addition, the President had to coordinate the various activities of federal agencies in the District. Two departments heavily involved in the city were Justice and Interior. Justice, especially under Nixon, did not hesitate to step into District affairs. In fact, being a police chief, U.S. Attorney, or U.S. Marshal in Washington was like being a captain at an army headquarters. You didn't have the same freedom you would in the field. You never knew when the Attorney General was going to notice what you were doing; and the chain of command could become quite short, as Police Chief Jerry Wilson found out during the notorious Mayday sweep arrests, when the local police department was under the direct control of the Justice Department.

Interior's National Park Service was responsible for much of DC's recreational and park land. The National Park Police patroled those areas in pastel green cars and on horseback. Interior was also responsible for many of the monumental buildings in Washington and was partially responsible for the development of Pennsylvania Avenue and the Union Station Visitor's Center.

Various other federal agencies stuck their noses into the District. The Executive Protective Service, with 850 men, was assigned to protect the White House, federal agencies, and embassies, and routinely to patrol nearby streets. The Corps of Engineers supervised the city's reservoirs. And departments such as HUD, HEW, and Transportation frequently provided what is politely known as "guidance" to local officials.

Meanwhile Congress divided up its constitutional prerogatives over the District among a Senate and House District Committee, appropriations subcommittees, interior committees, and public works committees. In addition, the Architect of the Capitol not only had a virtual preemptory right to all land within cannon shot of the Capitol (a right he had gradually exercised over the years) but he sat on the DC Zoning Commission as well. And if you went through a red light in the vicinity of the Capitol, you would probably be apprehended by a member of the 1,000-man Capitol Police force.

By the time matters got down to the District level, they were already fairly muddled. The local government structure followed the trend. Responsibility for local planning, for example, was shared by the city's planning office, its housing office, the National Capital Planning Commission, the Redevelopment Land Agency, the Commission on Fine Arts, the Model Cities Commission, the City Council, and god knows how many advisory groups and back door consultants. A single project in the areas burned out during the riots of 1968 had to be approved by forty different bodies.

Former Assistant to the Commissioner Thomas Fletcher described his arrival in DC as being like "walking into a very large corporation—40 departments, 120 boards and commissions." Recalled Fletcher: "One of the first things I asked for when we first got in was a list of the boards and commissions and I said, 'What are they, who appoints them, what is their function, what did they do last, and how do you get rid of them?' At the end of two years, I am happy to say that we now have 126 boards and commissions; we did not reduce them."

Martha Detrich in *City Politics in DC* described the DC governmental structure this way:

Authority in the District is certainly fragmented, but it is in other cities, too. However Washington can be distinguished from other cities with respect to the way authority is diffused. There is neither top nor bottom to the structure of government in the District. Authority does not come to a peak, in a single individual or agency, nor does it rest on the broad foundation of a voting public. It is distributed not vertically, but horizontally— among an elite that circulates in the Capitol and its offices, the White House, the District Building, and the many federal and quasi-federal agencies that have a share of authority over the District.

There were, however, some obvious bulges in the horizontal line. The President was one. The powerful House District Committee was another. Liberal Representative Michael Harrington, once a member of that body, gave a pithy description of how the committee traditionally functioned:

Do you remember those eggs with an egg inside which we played with as children? Remember how you opened one, then another, and still another in descending size?

That's how government is made in Washington, DC. Inside Congress, inside the District Committee, inside the subcommittee of the District committee chairman's choice —that is where legislation is found. Where visibility is minimal—where control is maximum. There the chairman of the District of Columbia Committee appoints his chairmen and assigns legislation to those subcommittees of his choice. His power is conclusive: his constituency— a rural district of the South.

Anyone wishing to discover why the District of Columbia was so long denied even the minimal self-government permitted under so-called "home rule" legislation must stop first at the House District Committee. From 1948 to 1972 the chairman of the committee was John McMillan, a congressman from the town of Florence, South Carolina, population 25,000. Whatever the table of organization said, few in Washington doubted that as much as anyone was, John McMillan was the mayor of the city. He ruled with courtly indifference to the demands and concerns of the city's residents. In 1961 he said, "No one seems to object to the work performed by this committee except the public." In 1972, after he had finally been beaten at the polls in his home district, McMillan attacked columnist Jack Anderson for having quoted a letter from McMillan that used the word "nigger."

"I have never used that word. He made that stuff up," said McMillan. "I have always said 'colored.' "

McMillan was long considered the main stumbling block to even limited self-government. As Rep. Michael Harrington recounted:

In 1949 hearings were held but no further action was taken in the House District Committee on the Senate-passed council-manager bill.

In 1951, the House District Committee failed to approve the Senate-passed home rule bill.

In 1953 the Senate-passed bill providing for a non-voting delegation to the House was tabled by the Committee.

In 1955 the Senate-passed home rule bill died in committee.

In 1958 the bill establishing District of Columbia territorial government was passed by the Senate but received no action in the House District Committee.

In 1959, the committee failed to report the Senate-passed home rule bill.

In 1962 a bill again died in committee.

Again in 1965 attempts to dislodge the administration home rule bill from the grasp of the District of Columbia failed.

On May 11, 1966 the House District Committee under the chairman's lead rejected an effort to set up a conference with the Senate District Committee in order to coordinate some action on a home rule bill.

That bills of this type have continuously been defeated in the House District Committee is owed to a system that allows the chairman dictatorial power with no accountability.

In the closing years of McMillan's reign, however, he had to give a little. An elected school board was approved in 1968 and a nonvoting delegate to Congress in 1970. But Chairman John retired from Congress having prevented numerous self-government bills from reaching the floor of the House after passage by the Senate.

McMillan exercised his power with exquisite perversity. Unlike most congressional committees, the subcommittees of the District Committee weren't named, but merely numbered.

Harrington described how it worked:

Subcommittee No. 2 of the House District Committee has been stacked with a disproportionate number of members who generally can be considered in opposition to the practices and philosophy of the chairman. Then Subcommittee No. 2 is passed over by the chairman when major legislation is assigned. Thus far in this session [1970] Subcommittee No. 2 has been assigned 19 pieces of legislation. By way of contrast, Subcommittee No. 3, a favorite of the chairman, has been assigned 87 pieces of legislation.

While Subcommittee No. 3 has been responsible for a good part of the District of Columbia crime bill, Subcommittee No. 2 has been assigned such legislation as a bill to create a firefighter's museum and a bill to provide additional congressional [auto] tags to members.

The District Committee was not the only thorn in the city's side. House District Appropriations Subcommittee chairman William Natcher threatened, cajoled, and ultimately blackmailed the city into proceeding with construction of the Three Sisters Bridge, under threat of losing congressional funds for the subway. The extortion attempt eventually failed, at least temporarily, when a court decision halted construction of the bridge, a prime target of freeway opponents.

And there were others. House District Subcommittee chairman John Dowdy of Texas hired an exslumlord to conduct an investigation into a local federally-subsidized housing project. Illinois Representative Kenneth Gray bullied a dubious convention center project through Congress over the objections of many of the small businessmen who would be ejected to make way for it. Louisiana Congressman John Rarick suggested on the House floor that the city's problems be solved by the resettlement of its population in vacant parts of the western states.

And powerful congressman George Mahon offered this encomium to the District in 1970 as a handful of House members debated the city's appropriation bill:

A critic might look about the House chamber and say, in view of the rather small attendance at the moment, that the members of the House are not interested in the District of Columbia; that the members of the House are not interested in what goes on in Washington, DC. But that would be inaccurate and inappropriate.

Mr. Chairman, I want to say in my opinion the members of this House have great concern for the District of Columbia. They want to see the District of Columbia run well. They want to see Washington, DC, the pride of the nation and of the world.

I find, Mr. Chairman, that people from my area, and

many of them come to Washington, are utterly surprised and amazed at what they see in the Nation's Capital. Some of them have come here with fear, wondering whether or not a visit to Washington would be safe for them and for their family.

When they come to Washington they are delighted and relieved to find that Washington is a pleasant and interesting city to visit.

Representative Mahon then went on to join his colleagues in slashing the District budget.

The congressmen most involved in city affairs are the chairmen of DC committees and subcommittees, many of whom have found the District an agreeable fiefdom whose assets they can share with political friends, lobbyists, and creditors as the occasion arises. They operate like dukes of principalities which, though small, are far enough away from the major concerns of the crown to permit considerable local feudal autonomy.

Suburban senators and congressmen also take a special interest in the District. More often than not this works to the disadvantage of the city. When Maryland's Senator Joseph Tydings found himself in deep trouble with the gun lobby for advocating antigun legislation, he leaped to the support of the DC crime bill to prove to his constituents that he could stop the criminal element at the District line. He lost the next election anyway. The most colorful, disliked, and persistent DC-baiter among the suburbanites has been a bumptious and jowly Republican congressman from the Tenth Congressional District of Virginia, Joel T. Broyhill. Joel Broyhill built longevity in Congress with a blend of diligent service to his constituents and constant harassment of the District. Broyhill probably sends out as many Christmas cards as any member of Congress.

To District residents, however, Broyhill is best known for his consistently anti-District views and colorful way of expressing them. When legislation was pending to deal with the city's considerable rat problem, Broyhill commented:

> This sets up a new bureaucracy and sets up possibly a commissioner on rats or an administrator of rats and a bunch of new bureaucrats on rats. There is no question but that there will be a great demand for a lot of rat patronage.

Broyhill had a penchant for suggesting things like stationing federal troops in DC banks in order to cut down on robberies. He tried to get local black activist Julius Hobson fired from his government job and then later suggested the same thing for the far more conservative chief executive of the city, Walter Washington. Closely allied with local parking lot magnates, he pressed for more freeways and bridges. Above all, he opposed home rule. Although merely a minority member of the House District Committee, Broyhill's vigor and style earned him even greater enmity than that accorded more powerful District tormentors.

There have been, however, a few members of Congress whose concern for the District has worked to the city's advantage. One was former Senator Wayne Morse, a leader in the fight for home rule and a crucial proponent of DC's new land grant institution, Federal City College. Robert Kennedy, who won the 1968 DC presidential primary with a promise to hold unofficial elections for local offices even before self-government was granted (and to appoint those elected), was another. Probably the two most popular national politicians in DC today are Hubert Humphrey and Ted Kennedy. Both long pressed for home rule, and Humphrey, as senator and as vice president, devoted considerable energy to DC problems.

Hawaii's Senator Daniel Inouye achieved a measure of credit in the District in a different and unlikely manner—by becoming a severe critic of the local government. Some of the best critiques of waste and inefficiency in the local colonial administration came during Inouye's stint in charge of the Senate side of DC's fiscal affairs. He uncovered the fact that the city had twenty-three officials being driven around by chauffeurs, including the Recorder of Deeds and the Civil Defense Director. Remarked Inouye: "If by eliminating two drivers at $10,000 apiece we can hire a specialist to look into the mental health of children, we'll have a better bargain." Inouye also hit the ceiling upon learning that the city maintained an expensive houseboat (with cooking and sleeping facilities) to take once-a-week water samples in the Potomac.

The city's free-spending administrators were expectably upset at Inouye's examinations and at least one top aide to Commissioner Walter Washington referred sarcastically to Inouye at a hearing as one of the city's "masters." But outside the District Building he had plenty of admirers. Inouye exploded the myth that Washington's fiscal problems were solely the result of congressional stinginess; a city administration unaccountable to a local constituency had to share the blame. Inouye wrote Commissioner Washington a letter on February 7, 1972 that summed up his concern over the city's financial plight:

> This is a critical situation. The problem we faced
> . . . in connection with last year's appropriations bill is
> no secret. The District Government's credibility is at stake
> and unless this matter is dealt with on an emergency
> basis—as a matter of highest priority—almost every
> spending program you present either to the City Council
> or to the Congress will be under a cloud—most of them
> unnecessarily so.

> I hope that I have established myself as a friend to
> the District of Columbia. As a friend, however, I must
> tell you frankly that I cannot successfully carry the con-

tinued burden of "floating figures," "balancing out," or "internal adjustments" of large year-end discrepancies, a school system that does not know how many students are attending schools, a million dollars in purchase orders "in someone's drawer," or an administrator who does not know that he is carrying hundreds of unauthorized employees on his department's rolls.

With a few exceptions, however—such as California's Ron Dellums who introduced a statehood bill—even the most liberal legislators hedged on the issue of full self-determination for the District. Further, liberals and conservatives alike have been more likely to listen to city administrators, the local business community, or the police department than they were to listen to the elected school board or representatives of community organizations.

Most congressmen spent as little time as possible on District affairs. Even those on the District committees kept a low profile out of fear of their own constituents. Service on such a committee can be a liability back home. In the 1972 election, two of the most active liberal members of the House District Committee went down to defeat, the result at least in part of their DC activities if for no other reason than that they were distracted from full attention to their constituency. Even John McMillan eventually was hurt by his DC role. As times and his constituency changed, he became increasingly vulnerable to the charge that he was shortchanging the home folks by spending so much time on DC matters. And the growing black vote in his district was disturbed by the racial implications of his DC policies. After an era of power that seemed to Washingtonians like an eon, he was defeated by his own people.

Given that the District is at best a nuisance and at worst a liability to many Congressmen, it may seem strange that the Congress has clung to its local prerogatives. The explanation can be found in a number of factors.

One of the most important has been race. Fear of black local political power in the nation's capital has long been an insurmountable obstacle in the path of self-government. Only with the civil rights revolution and the growing realization that black power in DC meant something short of revolution, has the racial factor begun to decline—although by no means to disappear.

Another reason has been Washington's role as the prostitute of American cities. In other places, a politician must win affection before he satisfies his lust; in Washington satisfaction can be purchased. A congressman may vote for construction of the Three Sisters Bridge (a project shown in referenda to be opposed by as many as 80 percent of the local electorate) and thus pay a debt to the highway lobby; but he would not dare vote for such a project in his own district in the face of such opposition.

There is considerable circumstantial evidence to suggest that certain congressmen have interests in the District that extend beyond the political, but the connections are exceedingly well covered. One exception was the case of Rep. John Dowdy, a member of the House District committee who was convicted of receiving a $25,000 bribe to help get the feds off the back of the Monarch Construction Corporation, a firm involved in defrauding low-income area homeowners. Dowdy's conviction was partially overturned in 1973 on the grounds of Congressional immunity.

A *Washingtonian Magazine* article on the Monarch case noted an irony sadly familiar to DC residents:

In U.S. District Court, on the same day [that two Monarch officials] were put on probation for cheating the poor out of millions of dollars, an 18-year-old boy was sent to Lorton for snatching a purse that contained $50;

a 24-year-old was given two to six years imprisonment for stealing a television worth $500; another youth was given three to nine years for housebreaking.

In *Governing the District*, Royce Hansen wrote:

. . . Congress may be described as incredibly inept and cantankerous as a local legislature. It rarely offers any leadership. It often vetoes or stalemates vital matters which are of basic local concern, and which do not involve any higher degree of abstract federal interest than in any other American city. It often acts irresponsibly; and it is not susceptible to any form of control, internal or external, for its actions. Power is divided among at least four committees in deciding local matters. Representation is functional and diffuse. The committees whose concurrence is necessary to provide for vital action are, in fact, representative of different constituencies external to the District; and they reflect local functional interests in a manner almost exclusive of each other.

Representative Michael Harrington put it more strongly in his speech to colleagues in 1970:

District residents pay the same federal taxes and the usual complement of local taxes that other U.S. citizens pay.

Yet we have not allowed them a voice in their government, and instead of dealing with the critical national issue that faces us we must debate property tax exemptions, congressional tags for members and parking regulations for Washington.

While the nation's capital is second only to Mississippi with the highest infant mortality rate, while gonorrhea infection is the highest in the country, while the District of Columbia General Hospital runs out of penicillin and has been out of 100 of the 685 drug items stocked at the hospital, the District of Columbia Committee of the House of Representatives has not passed one major piece of legislation this session dealing with health. . . .

The Heaviest City Government

The District of Columbia Committee has made no effort in the 91st Congress to deal with poverty among the disenfranchised citizens of the Nation's capital . . . not one bill has come in this session from the District of Columbia Committee addressing the problems of housing in the nation's capital. . . .

This is how the system works. It is our system. We, the Congress, have established the system, and we keep it going.

The executive branch has tended to take a broader view of local affairs than the Congress. Under the Johnson Administration this meant a reorganization of the local government to give it more power and an honest and vigorous effort to obtain limited self-government in the form of home rule. Under the Nixon Administration it meant a return to unabashed feudal rule.

Johnson used the presidential reorganization powers to do away with the old three-commissioner system with its absurdly divided powers and responsibilities and to replace it with an appointed mayor and city council. The action eliminated the Corps of Engineers as a major factor in local politics, added an element of rationality to DC affairs, and gave the city the form, though not the substance, of a normal urban government.

When Nixon came into office, there were some who hoped that he might at least continue the greater autonomy granted the local government. But it soon became clear that the new president expected obedience from city officials. Gilbert Hahn, an independent-minded Republican city council chairman, was eased out and replaced by a mild-mannered and ineffectual loyalist. Other Council members who spoke on issues found themselves without reappointment.

On those rare occasions when Nixon personally involved himself in District affairs it was more for the camera than out of concern. Shortly after taking office, Nixon showed up on Seventh Street to talk about rebuilding the area. He was pictured with his foot on a pile of rubble—with Sol Kaplan.

Kaplan owned a lot upon which had stood a hardware store until the 1968 trouble. According to the *Washington Post*, the Nixon Administration decided to do something about Seventh Street, and had the District Building get in touch with Kaplan to see if he would lease his property for a parklet. The price was too low for Kaplan's satisfaction, so the deal was off. Then came Nixon's urbanologist Daniel Moynihan to make further entreaties. Kaplan was invited to the White House and, reported the *Post*, "In the office of Moynihan's aides, he worked out a better deal on the lease. The city's first offer was 'multiplied sixfold.'" Later, when Nixon went up to Seventh Street, he was introduced to Kaplan and told him: "You've been very cooperative. Many times the landlord is the roadblock. I appreciate your cooperation."

The Nixon Administration's major contribution to the city was a vastly increased police presence, a welter of hard-nosed judges, a crime bill of dubious constitutionality, and a further gilding of the monumental city. Crime went down (though it still was 50 percent higher than in 1960), taxes went up, and not one of the city's intrinsic problems was more than superficially dealt with.

When Washingtonians complained about some federal decision, they could count on a Nixon appointee to slap them down, as National Capital Planning Commission member Paul Thiry did when local citizens objected to military housing being constructed on that 900-acre site long sought for community use. At a hearing on the issue, Thiry (who lives in Seattle) said, "Sometimes the local community here sort of assumes a lot of rights not particularly invested in them."

Responded Metropolitan Washington Planning and Housing Association director Ralph Fertig, "I still believe in civilian control of the military."

"That may be, but that is not necessarily what most of the people of the United States believe in," said Thiry.

And opposing a plan to expand the campus of the Washington Technical Institute in the heart of white Northwest Washington, Thiry said of the low-income black community WTI serves: "We have great deference for that class of individual. There is another class of individual we seem to disregard. This is a real mistake. If we don't do something about it, we can count on the degeneration of the community."

These were not the words of a redneck standing at the schoolhouse door, but of a presidentially-appointed official with some control over the fate of a 71 percent black city. He wasn't even doing Washington's whites a favor; only a handful of the more reactionary opposed the expansion.

By the end of the first Nixon term the stern thumb of the federal government pressed down upon the colonial city. Even the president's former mild interest in self-government waned rapidly and Justice Department officials were being sent to the Hill to block home rule in the name of law and order. It would, they told Republican congressmen, destroy the effectiveness of the 1970 crime act and federal control over local courts. The argument was, as many Washingtonians recognized, a metaphor for something else. The racism that the city had struggled so hard, long, and partially successfully to eradicate, was settling in again.

The fact that blacks were nominally in charge of the District government didn't help. The top black leadership had made its pact with the Nixon Administration and even those who were uneasy kept it to themselves. Loud voices lowered. Brave bodies stilled, and the momentum that the city had gained seemed at least temporarily stopped.

There had been a time when the City Council was one of the liveliest places in town. At the outset (following its creation by the Johnson Administration) the Council had made an effort not to appear to be the colonial legislature that it was. On many occasions, especially under the leadership of its first chairman, white businessman John Hechinger, it took the side of District residents in scraps with the Commissioner, Congress, or the White House.

But as the Soviets found the liberalization of Hungary and Czechoslovakia intolerable, so Congress and the Nixon Administration found the liberalization of Washington a threat to be put down. The results were infinitely gentler than those experienced in Eastern Europe, but the parallels remained.

The Council, which had dared to stand up to Congress on the freeway issue, soon found it couldn't appease citizen pressure for more independence. It moved from sympathy to fear. Before long, the once-open Council was holding meetings with police standing nearly man-to-man along the walls. As many as seventy policemen covered one meeting.

The Council wasn't being deliberately mean; it was just scared. When pressed to take a stand against a proposed Washington ABM site, Council chairman Gilbert Hahn sat with a frozen smile on his face as citizens bombarded him with questions he refused to answer. The other councilmen were similarly quiet for there was nothing to say. They had lost the courage to represent.

One could gauge the extent of the Council's guilt and fear by the number of police cached in the rooms and corridors of the District Building. Even without an agenda, one could walk into the Council office and judge, by the presence of helmeted officers lounging in the chairs a democratic legislature would have reserved for citizens, that on that day the Council was going to vote the wrong way.

As a final irony, while the Council prepared to vote once more on freeways and this time cave in, appointed chairman Hahn permitted the arrest during a demonstration in the chamber of two of the few elected officials in the city—school board member Julius Hobson and Democratic city chairman Bruce Terris—who had come to protest the council's capitulation.

Soon, the police were no longer necessary. People stopped trying so hard to convince the council. The body that had begun its life as an advocate had turned sullen and finally vacuous, an empty room in Washington's political labyrinth.

Under the cautious leadership of Walter Washington, the executive branch of the city government gave in even sooner. Led by a bland, obedient bureaucrat, it performed its functions dutifully. No task was too demeaning. In 1970, Walter Washington joined Attorney General John Mitchell at the Board of Trade's tribute to American white womanhood, the Cherry Blossom Princess selection, and pronounced the event "one of America's finest hours." When several hundred thousand people came to Washington in November 1969 to protest the war, the Commissioner, instead of backing their protest, drove up and down Pennsylvania Avenue in a police sidecar and congratulated the people of the District on television for their marvelous restraint.

Walter Washington's background was in public housing administration. In the sixties he had been director of Washington's housing authority and later New York City's. In November 1967 he became the first Commissioner under the government reorganization carried out by Lyndon Johnson.

With more than twenty-five years experience in government bureaucracy behind him when he took office, Walter Washington was well suited to run a city that is often regarded as just another federal agency. He knew who he worked for and what they wanted. When, under Johnson, the city was granted a bit of autonomy, Walter

Washington was the "walking mayor," spreading word of the Great Society among the people. When Nixon took over, Walter Washington took off his shoes, stayed in his office, and shut his mouth. The test was no longer progress but survival and the Commissioner was up to the task.

Commissioner Washington's rationale appeared to be one as old as black oppression. By being outwardly loyal and obedient, he could garner for the city and himself morsels that would be denied those who directly confronted those who controlled the city. It was a theory that could be justified by specific example—a budget increase here, a requested project approved there. But over the long run the city sacrificed much for these morsels and for Walter Washington's survival. Because he refused to say no; because he refused to stand up for the city on freeway, police, development, and zoning issues; because he refused to fight for self-determination, he stayed in office; but the city lost an opportunity to press its case before the government and the nation.

To be sure, the Commissioner chugged along amiably enough. He charmed his admirers, reassured the doubtful with his sincerity, and simply ignored his critics. He stayed out of public fights and, when they could not be avoided, pushed a department head or assistant forward to take the flak. When he spoke, superfluous phrases danced on the heads of ambiguities. Interviewed once on the subject of his beloved command center (used as his headquarters during disturbances and demonstrations) Walter Washington said:

> I think the way it has developed, the sophistication, and the capability that a city like Washington, the Nation's Capital where people come in great numbers, it is an essential tool in order to focus on the problems that are characteristic in nations' capitals. What that means is, what we have been able to achieve . . . is the de-

velopment of the capability to quickly assemble all of the resources and all the relative information that permits you to make good decisions. Without that input, the ready information, of course, the decisions are no better or could be no better than the information that you get. Of course it works beyond that on a day-to-day basis through its same capability keeping in touch with situations, keeping in front of them so that you can respond appropriately and. . . .

It was like that every day down at the District Building, where every thrust had its capability, there were two inputs for every outreach, and you never quite knew whether the answer was yes or no.

Commissioner Washington appeared continually enmeshed in an autoerotic fantasy that he actually ran the city. The local press and the business community, delighted with his malleability, did nothing to discourage him. They fawned over him. From the day he was appointed Commissioner, they called him "Mayor." (Washington himself was more careful. He had three sets of stationary: one headed "Mayor," another "Mayor-Commissioner," and a third "Commissioner" to be used according to the recipient's view of DC affairs.)

The press avoided criticism of the government. Based on press reports, said activist Julius Hobson sourly, "DC must have the most perfect city government in the world."

Even when facts revealed the bitter truth, Walter Washington kept his peace. When a new crop of city council appointments was due, the *Post* reported, "A White House official said in an interview that it would not have been appropriate to ask the mayor, deputy mayor, city council chairman or vice chairman for their opinions on a presidential appointment." Washington didn't offer his opinion either.

The District government survived by paying respect

to those with the real power and with optimistic statements about the future. The city government, the assistant to the commissioner boasted, "is starting to develop
a capacity for a housing program." The housing program
itself was still over the horizon, but no step was too small
to brag about.

Only when personally attacked did District officials
drop their guard. When Rep. Joel Broyhill suggested that
Walter Washington was incompetent and should be replaced, Washington's chief legal aide, Charles Duncan
responded, "I personally regarded it as a 1969 statement
of the stereotype that has been of our Negro citizens and
it conjured up in my mind a plantation image. And I can
indeed see a slave-owner standing on the veranda of the
main house of the plantation looking over the slave quarters and saying to his companions that the slaves have
rhythm and were good at singing, but that they were basically shiftless and lazy and irresponsible and could not
be expected to take a meaningful role in the important
and vital aspects of our democracy."

It was the most vigorous public defense of black people Duncan had made since becoming a top DC official.
He and Commissioner Washington had never complained of racist or plantation-like attitudes of congressmen on the freeway issue. They only mildly protested
budgetary cuts for key programs. They had not publicly
complained about the Nixon administration filling the
City Council with ineffectual members nor had they vigorously sought to prevent anti-black crime legislation. In
the District Building soul was only selectively invoked.

No one knew this better than black city workers
who continued to be discriminated against under the
new leadership. In the summer of 1970, the city's
human relations commission found rampant discrimination in the Sanitation Department. Blacks made progress
in the lower rungs of the police and fire departments
but upper level discrimination remained the standard.

The Heaviest City Government

A study of forty appointments to city bodies made by Walter Washington during a three-month period in 1970 found that 42 percent of the appointees lived in the white West of the Park area, and 10 percent lived in Maryland. And in 1969, the *DC Gazette* discovered that the city's library system was spending more for books in the nearly all-white Ward Three than in five other mostly black wards combined. In fact, Ward Three was getting twice as much money for its black literature collection as the average amount for each of the other seven wards.

To be sure, in comparison with other cities, Washington's record in eliminating discrimination in government employment and services looked good. Under Walter Washington, for example, more than 10,000 jobs opened up for blacks in four years, including on the police force which recruited a higher percentage of blacks than any big city department in the country. But the availability of jobs at the bottom was not followed by a similar development at the upper levels. A black city employee's median salary was $8,775 in 1971 while the white median was $10,685. A survey by the Nelsen Commission (a group established to study local government organization) found that over two-thirds of the city's top executives were white. Further, 59 percent of the city's bosses didn't even live in the city. According to the 1972 Nelsen Commission the typical city top-grade official was white, male, and living in the suburbs and was presiding over a workforce two-thirds black and 43 percent female. Only 8.4 percent of the top jobs in the District were held by women.

The great increase in black employment in the District was achieved by adding jobs, rather than replacing whites. Under Walter Washington, the size of the city government went up 30 percent in four years, enough to add 10,000 blacks to the payroll while increasing white employment at the same time. Given the nature of the civil service and DC's status, that may have been the easiest way to do it, but it certainly was expensive. By 1973, the District government had one civil servant for every fifteen men, women, and children in the city.

For fiscal 1974 Commissioner Washington proposed a budget that stopped just short of one billion dollars. The city's capital outlay budget clung to $150 million, a ceiling imposed by Congress after DC's capital expenditures began running at a level more than twice that of San Francisco and other comparable cities.

Even DC's problem-plagued public schools were receiving more money than most comparable cities. In the 1971–72 school year, for example, comparative per-student figures ran like this:

Milwaukee	$1,240
Baltimore	$1,121
Atlanta	$1,079
St. Louis	$1,030
Cleveland	$ 988
Boston	$ 959
DC	$1,335

And while school officials wisely argued that the school systems in other cities were also failing and that the sum committed to public education nationally was far too small, it was also apparent that other problems were at least on a par with the monetary one and that there was, as Julius Hobson put it, "no way you can finance a rathole."

The big growth in the DC government occurred in the fifteen years between 1957 and 1972. During this period local government nearly doubled its number of employees. The historic and long justifiable argument that the city's colonial status caused it to be financially starved was still being made in the seventies but it was no longer valid. Congress, with the enthusiastic support of the local bureaucracy, was creating a governmental system that only a colonial system could support. No other city in the country could contemplate spending as much per capita on police, for example, as did the District. And while Congress griped about the size of the federal payment, it approved substantial increases, so much so that a seemingly liberal federal payment formula proposed unsuccessfully by President Kennedy would have left the city worse off than it was ten years later without a formula, relying on the year-to-year whims of Congress. Of course, simultaneously, local taxes rose as well. A one cent increase in the local sales tax, for example, was swallowed up just to pay for a wage hike for the city's firemen and enormous police department. And of course, the money was not being spent on the right things—priorities were all askew.

What had happened was that Congress had impaled itself on the horns of a dilemma of its own making. It insisted on maintaining control over the city and thus was faced, in the sixties, with the terrible problems facing every urban government. As a local government, however, Congress had a financial capacity far exceeding that of localities and, unwilling to deal with the organic causes of the crises, it literally bought time. Early in the Vietnam War, the late Bernard Fall pinpointed a phenomenon which was to keep America mired in Southeast Asia for years—the financial and logistical ability to cover up any mistake made. The French had to give up after Dien Bien Phu; the Americans could recover from hundreds of little and big Dien Bien Phus by flying in helicopters to evacuate trapped troops or by saturation bombing or by other techniques of luxury-class warfare. In a smaller way Congress and the White House did the same thing in its efforts to pacify urban Washington. It bought its way out of the rise in crime; it tranquilized a restless black population with methadone and by hiring its most active spokesmen and turning them into placid bureaucrats; it attempted to solve traffic jams first by spending hundreds of millions on freeways and then approving a multi-billion dollar subway system. And it was cheered on by conservatives interested in controlling unrest and by liberals who believed that money was the root of all good.

Given the objectives of the national government—the pacification of a troubled city—the technique appeared to work in the short run. But despite the enormous amounts poured into the city, the basic problems remained. Fifty million dollars of urban renewal funds were dropped into one small section of Washington over a four-year period with only a handful of new housing units to show for it. The police force was enlarged; crime dropped, but still remained at a level high enough to suggest that it might have been cheaper to have simply provided the city's criminal population with a guaranteed annual income in return for turning in their handguns. And neither the misbegotten freeways nor the world's most expensive subway system got at the problem of moving people efficiently about the city. Too many poor remained poor, too many rich got richer. Too many badly housed remained so even as temples of corporate and bureaucratic America rose beside them or forced them to move elsewhere. The less fortunate waited for the buses inching their way along streets clogged with the automobiles of the more fortunate. And the taxes of everyone, affluent or impoverished, rose to meet the rising cost of urban failure. Washington needed money, but it needed money spent wisely; and neither Congress, the Executive, nor the local government acted with wisdom or restraint. When the revenue sharing bill was passed and the District Government got its piece, it promptly made plans to hire 2,000 more employees.

It is hard to affirm that under full self-government the District would be more efficient. There is not a major city in the country that is not administratively top-heavy. But Washington's colonial system, responsible not to a tax-paying voting constituency but to an irresponsible superior government, had at least shown that autocratic local government is no fiscal boon.

The excellent analysis of the Nelsen Commission produced some poignant evidence: "The inevitable conclusion is that the District of Columbia's personnel system is significantly less efficient than those in the 12 other cities surveyed." Washington has one personnel worker for every fifty-two employees despite the fact that, unlike other cities, the personnel examining function is largely carried out by the U.S. Civil Service Commission. In the other cities, including the heavy load of examining, the ratio of personnel workers to total employment ranged from 1/84 to 1/185.

The Commission also found that the District government writes 1.7 million letters a year, 490,000 memos, 14,000 telegrams, and 325,000 other forms of communications. In addition there were 10,280 DC and departmental forms. "The review of four departments," said the report, "revealed sixteen different routing slips, including seven in one department, despite the fact that there is a District-wide routing slip, DC Form 7, of which routing slip EDA 12 in Economic Development is an exact duplicate."

Even the elected school board found itself bogged down in the bureaucratic and fiscal swamp. The president of the board that took office in 1972 estimated that 70 percent of the meetings the board held in its first year concerned fiscal matters. Although elected, the board sent its budget through an obstacle course. The budget had to be cleared by the Commissioner for presentation to the appointed City Council, approved by the City Council, sent back to the Commissioner for approval or veto, and thence in succession to the federal Office of Management and Budget, the President, the House and Senate DC appropriations subcommittees of Congress, the parent appropriations committees, the floor of the House and the Senate, Senate–House conference, and finally back to the President. By that time, self-determination as symbolized by an elected school board was substantially watered down. Nonetheless, in its first year, the new board achieved something unheard of in local government: it cut the size of the school central administrative office by one-third.

From whatever angle one views it—fiscally, managerially, or out of concern for the simple dictates of democracy—Washington's governmental system was an absurdity. It produced an administration of city affairs that was cumbersome, unnecessarily expensive, unresponsive, and slow. It produced fifty ways of saying no, and no clear way of saying yes.

It is small wonder that many Washingtonians just gave up. If there seemed to be apathy among the populace, it stemmed not from indolence but from sad experience. Too many of those who marched hopefully to the wall of Washington's government had little to show for it but welts on their forehead. As former City Council chairman John Hechinger put it, "The idea of trying to inject the hope of effective democracy on a people who have been pistol-whipped into lethargy by an unresponsive, sometimes malicious House of Representatives committee is, indeed, a difficult one."

But in the 1972 congressional elections, time finally caught up with the head of that committee. House District Committee chairman John McMillan was defeated by a constituency, containing an increasing percentage of black voters, that had grown disenchanted with Mr. Mac's preoccupation with the District.

Following the seniority rules of the House, Charles Diggs, a black from Detroit, replaced McMillan as chairman of the District Committee. In the first months of his power, it was unclear whether Diggs would be as aggressive a friend of the city as many hoped. He expressed doubts about the prospects for home rule, hauled out the old cliches about using the city as a model for the rest of the country, and generally seemed disinclined to preside over the dismemberment of a committee he had waited so patiently and long to run.

But a number of other changes were also taking place. The speaker of the House, Carl Albert, seemed genuinely interested in achieving some sort of home rule. The District Committee's conservative wing was losing strength through attrition and was being replaced by a liberal bloc more vigorous than before. Finally, a national Coalition for Self-Determination had been formed, ably directed by Dick Clark and composed of such establishment Congress-swayers as Common Cause and the League of Women Voters.

Yet even after a status bill was reported out of the House District Committee, finally giving members of the House a chance to vote on the matter, it was hard to believe that a century of effort was going to bear fruit. But suddenly the impossible was happening: ten months after McMillan left Congress, both houses approved a measure granting limited local suffrage. It was signed by the President on Christmas Eve, 1973.

McMillan's departure, critical as it was, was just one of the factors that melded to produce the bill. Another was the hard work of the Coalition for Self-Determination, borrowing on the savvy and clout of such groups as Common Cause, as was the changing nature of Congress itself, the declining paranoia over black political power, the fear that continued resistance would increase pressure for greater self-determination (one congressman attacked the idea of statehood for the District by warning that Stokely Carmichael or Jane Fonda might be elected governor here), and perhaps a growing realization in a year of despair over economic conditions, political scandals, and energy shortages that there were more important things for Congress to do than tend to the minutiae of the District.

But the heart of the success of the bill was that it

did not provide home rule. Under its provisions, the District was granted certain improvements in its status:

- It could elect a mayor and city council with the power to approve local ordinances and resolutions.
- It could levy taxes and set rates.
- It could float bond issues.
- Several formerly federal agencies, such as the public housing authority, the redevelopment agency, and the public service commission would be transferred to local control.

On the other hand, the bill fell short of full self-determination on numerous counts. The most important was that Congress retained control over the budget. Thus the city was granted the power to tax but not the power to spend, a unique division of responsibility that led one local official, Tedson Meyers, to suggest sardonically the slogan: "No spending without representation."

While the council could initiate action and override vetoes of the mayor, the President could sustain the mayor's veto. Thus the mayor would need only one vote to overrule any action of the council—the President's.

All actions by the council would be subject to veto by Congress.

The Congress could continue to initiate any local legislation that it desired.

None of the existing congressional committees overseeing the District was abolished, despite the supposed grant of "home rule."

Judges would continue to be appointed by the President.

There would be no locally controlled district attorney's office. Rather the federal U.S. Attorney's office would continue to be the main prosecutor for the city.

The council was prohibited from passing any legislation affecting the courts; nor could it approve a tax on commuter income.

While the city would have the power to initiate local

planning, the National Capital Planning Commission could veto any plans it found to be in conflict with the "federal interest."

While the city would ostensibly have control of its own police, the President could take "emergency" command of the police department.

And the city would still have no voting representation in Congress.

Thus the city found itself confronted not with a resolution of its status dilemma, but with one more inconsistent hybrid compromise, as unworkable as those that had proceeded it. It was a government with the power to tax but not the power to spend; a government expected to lower crime but with no control over its courts; a government that could initiate but could not guarantee carrying out what it had initiated; a government expected to act but lacking the freedom to do so; a government that would have to cater to the often conflicting demands of a local constituency and its federal masters.

Even Senate District Committee chairman Thomas Eagleton admitted that the plan left something to be desired: "I'll be candid to say it's not total and complete home rule."

That was a considerable understatement. For District residents who would have the opportunity to accept or reject the proposed change (but not to amend it) in a mid-1974 referendum, the bill represented one more time that the federal government had produced a local status compromise that carried within it the seeds of serious new problems. Many DC voters would go to the polls to cast a reluctant ballot on behalf of the referendum knowing full well that the greater part of the battle for local autonomy lay ahead.

6 / Crime Pays; Education Doesn't

THE PRINCIPAL OCCUPATION OF GOVERNMENT IN A colony is control of the colonized. The normal concerns of a democratic community—better education, adequate employment, decent housing, good services and amenities—are all subject to the need to control. If a soul festival in a park will cool the tempers of a summer night, there will be a soul festival. If the jobless young threaten to vandalize or riot, the government and business community will scurry around looking for summer jobs. And if the residents complain loudly enough about the school system, new schools will be built, although the curriculum will remain unaltered lest education become too staunch a foe of acquiescence.

But above all is control, a concern prodded by the realization that when containment of the governed replaces consent of the governed, power must replace consensus. The first function of such a government is to maintain more power than the people.

Thus it is that Washington has more police officers than it does public school teachers and thus it is that when the problems of the city are discussed in federal offices, it is crime that is most often mentioned and education that is seldom discussed.

It's not a new situation. In 1858 a Senate committee report on Washington complained, "Riot and bloodshed are of daily occurrence. Innocent and unoffending persons are shot, stabbed, and otherwise shamefully maltreated, and not infrequently the offender is not even arrested."

A hundred years later, senators and congressmen were talking in similar terms. Said Rep. James C. Davis of Georgia at congressional crime hearings in 1961:

> It is tragic indeed that matters have reached a stage in Washington that decent law-abiding citizens, particularly women and girls, have come to be regarded as fair game for every brute, thug, and hoodlum who roams the streets with one purpose in mind: to steal, rob, rape and murder. . . . The situation which exists is depopulating Washington. It is causing many decent law-abiding people to move out of Washington and take up residence in other areas which afford greater protection from the class of criminals who infest this city.

Crime was rising in Washington then, although at nowhere near the rate it would over the next ten years. From the start rational discourse on the problem was muddled by conflict between the reality of the crime increase and the motives of those who made it a political issue. When Rep. Davis spoke of "decent law-abiding people" he meant whites; when he spoke of the "class of criminals who infest this city," he meant blacks.

For years, politicians have used the crime issue for

political gain, while contributing little assistance to Washingtonians who are mugged, raped or burgled. For the politicians, at least, crime was definitely a paying proposition. It has helped more than one of them achieve high position, the most prominent being Richard Nixon who on June 22, 1968, declared that Washington had become "one of the crime capitals of the nation." He promised, "I pledge that a Nixon Administration will sweep the streets of Washington clean of these marauders and criminals. . . . The war will be won." By the end of Nixon's first term, crime in Washington was indeed on the decline, but only a few noticed that about half of the decline eradicated crime increases that had occurred in the first years of his term. Crime was still disturbingly common.

Understanding the nature of urban crime—its causes, its rise and decline, is far more difficult than understanding how to exploit it politically. For one thing, the statistics we use are sorely inadequate. We know, for example, that Washington has had a higher crime rate than many cities its size. On the other hand, there were six major cities in 1971, including San Francisco and St. Louis, that had a higher crime rate than DC.

What does this tell us? Not much. In the first place, there are too many indications that crime statistics are manipulated to prove a point. But beyond this is the question of whether American cities can be fairly compared. Some cities are compact; others include communities that might properly be classified as suburbs. Is it reasonable to set DC's crime rate beside that of Houston, Texas, when DC encompasses less than one-sixth the land area of Houston? On the other hand, metropolitan-wide statistics cover so much territory that they are virtually meaningless.

Whatever geographical division one uses, the fact remains that few people experience the average crime rate. Most are affected by either more or less. For example, during the sixties the DC police divided the city into 360 sectors called Carney Blocks. In one month of 1968 taken at random, the break-down of crime by Carney Blocks was:

Frequency of Crime	Number of Carney Blocks	Percent of Total Crime
40 and over	14	3.8
30–39	13	3.6
20–29	25	6.9
10–19	80	22.2
Less than 10	228	63.5

At the time, I was living in a Carney Block that usually made it into the top category, which meant that I was exposed to three to four times as much crime as two-thirds of the residents of the city. Obviously, a city-wide statistic on per-capita crime was no more applicable to me than it was to the residents of Georgetown who usually were at the bottom of the Carney Block listings.

The crime figures fail to describe the situation in other ways: although the fear of crime centers on murder, rape, assault, and muggings, 70 percent of the crime in DC consists of crimes against property; and 70 percent of those murdered are killed by someone who knows them. Further, one's exposure to crime not only depends upon where one lives but upon what one does. Banktellers, liquor store staffs, and employees of carry-outs have much more experience with crime than do most Washingtonians. In 1971, for example, there were 202 robberies and purse snatchings at the thirty DC stores of the High's Dairy chain.

But even if one doesn't work behind the counter at High's, crime has been common enough to affect the psyche if not the purse or wallet of every Washingtonian. It is small comfort to realize that while crime rose 376 percent in DC between 1960 and 1969, it rose 395 percent in neighboring Montgomery County, 434 percent in Fairfax County, and 472 percent in Prince Georges County.

Police and political mythology blamed the rise on such factors as bail reform, societal permissiveness, weak-kneed judges, and Supreme Court decisions. It was not a convincing argument. Too many jarring changes were taking place during the period of rising crime to support such glib explanations.

Not the least of these was the massive demographic shift that occurred. Hundreds of thousands of people moved in and moved out. It was not the racial composition of the migrations that was significant but the migrations themselves. Most law enforcement comes not from the police but from the mores, stability, and cohesiveness of communities. Communities in Washington underwent radical changes. As old communities broke up, the system of nonofficial law—neighbor protecting neighbor, adults concerned about children they knew—broke up as well and could not be immediately reformed. Not only were communities dismantled by voluntary migration, but public policies like those affecting freeways and urban renewal tore up the social fabric of neighborhoods —especially the poorer ones of the city. Many affected by this could find neither jobs nor the psychological and practical support that comes from being part of a community. For more than a few, crime was an organized system of survival in a city that otherwise denied them survival. They did not engage in it as a perverted aberration of acceptable behavior but because it was one of the few forms of behavior that seemed to offer any hope. In the suburbs the man behind the wheel of the Buick Electra was a successful merchant or salesman. In the inner city the merchants and salesmen who drove a "deuce and a quarter" often did so because their product was drugs. In both areas, Buick drivers help establish community values.

It is likely that more than a small part of the decline in Washington's crime in the early seventies was due to the self-stabilization of the city's communities and to the creation of more varieties of survival for low-income residents. The typical criminal of the city was not so much an abnormal person as a normal person in an abnormal and inhuman situation. As the situation became more normal and human, so did those in it.

It was not just migration and the physical uprooting of neighborhoods that had made the situation abnormal. The war in Vietnam played an important part. For young blacks it was one more unacceptable option to look forward to, and a prospect that intensified the urge for present satisfaction. The surge of drugs into the city—to which Southeast Asia contributed—made low-income blacks slaves in urban skag fields, toiling to support an economy whose profits mostly went to whites outside the city.

The police themselves contributed to the rise in crime. Between 1959 and 1964 while crime was rising 93 percent, arrests in DC were declining 12 percent. In 1969 there were fewer arrests, as a percentage of felonies committed, than there were in 1965. The police continued to concentrate a disproportionate amount of their manpower in precincts with low crime rates, producing a striking dichotomy between the number of police per capita in a particular precinct and the number of crimes per capita. Patrolmen were taken off the streets and placed in cars. Narcotics investigations were concentrated in the small central narcotics unit, and precinct officials were discouraged from proceeding on such cases on their own—a procedure that some citizens suspected was designed more to continue the flow of drugs into the inner city than to stop it. Police were woefully undertrained. (Once, in the mid-sixties, when a friend's car was broken into outside our house, we waited over an hour along with nearly a dozen policemen until the one

precinct officer on duty able to take fingerprints arrived.)
Finally, a police chief obviously incapable of handling
the growing crime problem was kept in office out of fear
of angering the very congressmen on the Hill who were
complaining the loudest about the city's crime rate—
even though local officials admitted privately that he was
not up to the job.

Crime also rose because of a variety of small, little
considered factors. I remember standing outside the
high-rise Arthur Capper public housing project with
Private Isaac Fulwood, a black officer who was a community leader long before the white-run police department would let him make sergeant. Ike looked at the
grim brick boxes and remarked, "They never ask the
police before they build a place like that." There was the
fact that an inordinate and growing amount of police
time was spent on traffic control and the fact that the
school system was dumping increasing numbers of drop-
outs and unemployable graduates onto the streets. Finally, crime went up because—seeing no alternative—
people adapted to it. Kids were recruited into it. Adults
either were too scared to react or used the increasing
availability of fenced goods as an alternative economic
system. And then there were employers like the one cited
in *Tally's Corner,* who underpaid his workers on the
grounds that he had to compensate for what they would
steal from him.

Crime went up for all these reasons and more. Every
Washingtonian had a story to tell, and the press was
more than willing to pass them along. The Washington
Daily News ran a daily "Crime Clock" that pushed both
fear and prejudice with items such as: "10:45 A.M.:
Three Negro gunmen entered the Armory Liquor Store,
126 15th st se and took an undetermined amount of
money from owner Morris Gottlieb, 49, white." In 1969
Time magazine topped a page-long report with the
headline: "Terror in Washington." Even the liberal

Crime Pays; Education Doesn't

Washington Post, as late as 1973, was still running a column titled "Crime and Justice," which, while avoiding racial identifications, primarily listed crime in the District even though most of the paper's readership was in the suburbs.

I had my own stories to tell: four housebreak-ins; a friend's car stolen and another one broken into, both in front of our house while visiting; half the teenage circulation department of the *DC Gazette* ending up in jail on various charges; cameras, tape-recorders and typewriters disappearing from the office; dudes dropping by to try to peddle merchandise ranging from a prime steak just stolen from the Safeway up the street to an old Speed Graphic camera; heroin cooking utensils turning up behind stacks of back issues; a teenaged assistant banging on our door late one evening pleading for $200 to pay off his dealer who cruised by in his two-tone "hog." Yet I found little comfort in the reaction to my situation from the press and the government. They wished to view crime as an urban Armageddon, a battle between "them" and "us." It was not unusual for a white Capitol Hill victim to be told by the investigating officer something like "Well, what do you expect living in a neighborhood like this?"

For me it was not that simple. I had been in one neighborhood long enough to see local kids grow up to be addicts, pushers, and housebreakers. They were real people, often very likable, not faceless marauders or marauding statistics. The feelings I had were markedly different than those projected by the crime exploiters or by the Westchester liberal who gets mugged off Broadway then sells his memoirs to the *New York Times Sunday Magazine* complete with analysis of how the event affected his relationship to the civil rights movement—the sort of case where you can almost imagine the victim trying to block the holdup by saying, "I gave at the office."

My reaction was one of frustration and anger, directed not so much against "the criminal element"— although I was plenty teed off, for example, to come home late one Friday to find my front door broken down —but against a system and a government that had let crime become an everyday normality of my community by sheer indifference, prejudice, and stupidity. I knew too many "criminals" who had asked me a dozen times if I knew where any jobs were; I knew too many who had dropped out of schools so bad that parents who had the choice would not have permitted their children even to drop in to them; and I could not understand why everyone in the neighborhood except the police seemed to know who the major drug dealers were and where the trading centers were.

Although crime would not start to decline until after the turn of the decade, the groundwork was laid not by the Nixon Administration but by the reorganization of the city government, the rise of local black political power, and a change in the leadership of the police department. When Chief John Layton was finally eased out, public safety commissioner Patrick Murphy leapfrogged Jerry Wilson over several more senior officers to make him the new chief. Precinct commanders were shuffled and replaced. In our precinct, the Ninth—one of the worst run in the city—the arrival of a new commander brought an almost immediate drop in crime. Most important, there were a rapidly growing number of black officers on the force and a decline in the frequency of police brutality.

But Chief Wilson, while forceful and bright, soon showed contempt for civil liberties. The Nixon Administration had chosen a two-front assault on crime: a major increase in the size of the force and passage of a new crime law that would allow the sixty-day detention before trial of arrested persons, no-knock searches and seizures, expanded use of wiretaps and adult penalties for youth multiple-offenders. The plan struck Jerry Wilson as just fine, but Senator Sam Ervin warned that the bill was an "affront to the Bill of Rights . . . as full of unconstitutional, unjust and unwise provisions as a mangy hound dog is full of fleas . . . a garbage pail of some of the most repressive, near-sighted, intolerant, unfair and vindictive legislation that the Senate has ever been presented." Congress, however, generally hewed more closely to the view of Senator Thomas Dodd who said of the no-knock provision: "Society has the right to break in. . . . If I thought for a minute that this would mean the smashing in of my door . . . or yours, I wouldn't be up here defending it." The doors of black Washingtonians were another matter, and the bill breezed through Congress. Only forty-seven members of the House opposed it.

The extraordinary expansion of the police department was also easily approved. The department rose by 2,000 men to a total of more than 5,000 in a few years. In addition, Washington crawled with other varieties of police—which by 1972 included: 814 members of the Executive Protective Service (a federal force designed ostensibly to guard the White House and embassies, but also a force-in-being if DC's increasingly black local police got too independent); 439 Park Police, 1,000 Capitol Police, 2,000 federal office guards, 92 members of the Library of Congress Special Police, 328 officers of the Smithsonian Institution protective force; 124 DC Special Police; 55 Supreme Court Police; a 1,200-man National Guard Military Police unit; 110 regular MPs; an estimated 800-agent FBI office; an unknown number of Secret Servicemen and Alcohol, Tobacco, and Firearms agents; not to mention the 20-man Aqueduct police force and the 30 members of the Zoo police— more than 12,000 police officers in a city of 750,000 or about one for every 60 people!

With the largest per-capita police department in the

country, it was not surprising that crime started to go down. But what principle of crime prevention had the team of Nixon and Wilson enunciated? Certainly not one that other cities, unable to dip into the federal trough or hike sales taxes at will, could imitate. The crime program had only proved that if you were willing to spend millions of dollars you could reduce crime somewhat.

Besides, the huge increase in police expenditures could only be credited with a part of the reduction. Just as multiple factors caused crime to rise, so multiple phenomena caused it to fall. Among them were the increase in crime deterrent devices and procedures including alarm systems, police dogs, private security guards; exact-change requirements on buses and at night gas stations; dead bolts on doors and grills on windows; changes in court procedures; the installation of billiously bright yellow lights in high crime areas; the introduction of methadone; a decline in the number of vulnerable small businesses; the winding down of the war in Vietnam; the stabilization of Washington's newer communities; vigilante actions against drug pushers in some neighborhoods; the spirit of black puritanism that accompanied the rise of nationalism; a decline in community acceptance of crime; and a generally more cautious approach to life by the city's residents. Even soul music played a part, as more and more black artists laid down the message to "Give It Up, Brother."

We will never be able to evaluate fully the relative importance of these factors, but we do know that other cities experienced a decline in crime without the massive increase in police power that Nixon implied was responsible. In New York City, for example, the police reported that crime in 1972 fell 18 percent to the city's 1967 level. Patrick Murphy, who had taken the top police job in New York following his Washington tour, attributed the drop to improvements in operations of the city's courts, a four-fold increase in addicts being treated, and better police procedures. New York still had only 3.3 metropolitan police per 1,000 residents compared to Washington's 6.7. Unlike Jerry Wilson, however, Pat Murphy was not invited to the White House to receive public congratulations from the President.

All the statistics the police used were open to question and in Washington the press shot numerous holes in Jerry Wilson's record-keeping. But as Wilson pointed out in a "Dear Ben" letter to *Post* editor Benjamin Bradlee, even the *Post*, which had been a strong critic of the figures, listed fewer entries in its "Crime and Justice" column. Crime did appear to be on the way down.

The problem with the Nixon-Wilson approach was not that it failed to reduce crime somewhat, but that it did so at an excessively high economic and social cost. Further, the creaming off of the worst of crime still left fundamental causes untouched: poor housing, lack of jobs, poor education.

The expansion of the police department did have a number of beneficial side effects. It opened the force up to large numbers of blacks (and subsequently some women) who actually liked the city they were patrolling and who never would have made it if they had to wait for normal turnover. The increase appeared to lessen the paranoia of the police and, as they became less fearful, they seemed to treat citizens more rationally. It was easier to get good officers, and the new force placed a much higher priority on competence than had been the case in earlier years.

But the nicer, smarter, more sensitive police department of Jerry Wilson concealed a dangerous fact: it posed a far more serious threat to the freedom of the city's residents than had the force that preceded it. For as the department's size, skill, and technology expanded, so did its potential for political control. Seeing Washington under its blanket of blue one could understand what

University of Maryland political scientist Ralph Stavins meant when he said, "The country is turning into a schoolroom where everybody has to raise his hand for permission to do anything." Whereas before it had been the fact of crime that put limits on behavior, increasingly it was the fear of crime, expressed through mechanisms for its control, that altered the lifestyle of the city.

If you were white, you weren't so likely to notice, except perhaps for the increase in the number of parking tickets you got, the boost in insurance rates, the omnipresent holstered pistol, and the feeling that everything was being guarded, filmed, tapped, or barred. But in other parts of town, the air filled with short siren spurts as police supernumeraries pulled over real and imagined traffic offenders. Most likely the car would be driven by a young black male, and as you watched this familiar Washington scene it was hard to avoid the suspicion that the police considered any young black male driving a car to be prima facie evidence of crime. Many, no doubt, had run a stop sign or made a wrong turn, but many also were being stopped for what was known as a "routine traffic check," a practice little known to white Washingtonians but quite familiar to younger blacks. One youth I knew was stopped three times in a year—without getting a ticket or a warning. By the spring of 1973, the issue of traffic spot checks in Washington was before the Supreme Court. And the *Washington Post* informed its readers that reports "from citizens and policemen, as well as legal charges filed in court by civil liberties lawyers, tell of stepped-up pedestrian spot-checking with a recent emphasis on stopping individuals in the downtown business area." It sounded more like Capetown than the "Capital of the Free World."

There were other indications that the police department under Jerry Wilson considered questions of individual rights subsidiary to the pacification of the capital: illegal searches, the use of the CIA for training local police officers, and Wilson's steadfast support of unconstitutional measures like the DC crime bill. Most distressing and frightening, however, were the three days of May 1971 when the DC police department literally ran amuck. In a searing report on the police department's reaction to the anti-war Mayday protest, the American Civil Liberties wrote:

Between May 3 and May 5, more than 13,000 people were arrested in Washington, D.C.—the largest mass arrest in our country's history. The action was the government's response to anti-war demonstrations, an important component of which was the announced intention of the Mayday Coalition, organizer of the demonstrations, to block Washington rush-hour traffic.

During this three-day period, normal police procedures were abandoned. Most of the 13,000 people arrested—including law-breakers caught while attempting to impede traffic, possible potential law-breakers, war protestors engaged in entirely legal demonstrations, uninvolved passersby and spectators—were illegally detained, illegally charged, and deprived of their constitutional rights of due process, fair trial and assistance of counsel. The court system, unable to cope with this grandscale emergency caused by the police, was thrown into chaos. The scale of arrests—and of official illegality—was unprecedented in Washington. Indeed it has few equals in the 20th century history of our country.

During the Mayday police riot, people were beaten and arrested illegally, locked up by the thousands in makeshift holding pens with inadequate toilet facilities and food, or stuffed into drastically overcrowded cells. People on their way to work, patients going to see their doctor, students attending classes, reporters and lawyers were all caught up in the sweep arrests. Most of those stashed in the DC Jail exercise yard were without blankets throughout a night in which the temperatures fell below forty. And in the most symbolic display of contempt for the law, more than a thousand persons were arrested in front of the Capitol where they had assembled to hear speeches, including several from members of Congress. When Rep. Ronald Dellums tried to keep a policeman from arresting a member of his staff, saying "Hey, that's a member of my staff. Get your hands off of him. I'm a United States Congressman," the policeman replied, "I don't give a fuck who you are," then hit Dellums in the side with his nightstick and pushed him down some stairs.

It was the grimmest display of mass police power— not just selective brutality against a few—this city had seen. And it was a clear warning of the fearful danger inherent in Washington's acceptance of police power as a form of government. The fact that neither the black chief executive, Walter Washington, nor the white liberal newspaper, the *Washington Post*, could summon up either the wisdom or the courage to denounce what Wilson and his men, acting under orders of the Justice Department, had done made the affair all the more dismal. More and more the city was listening to sirens luring liberty onto the rocks of safety.

The use of police was only one of the proliferating social control techniques. The heroin substitute, methadone, provided the city and the national government another means. Whatever merits methadone may have as an aid in withdrawal from heroin addiction, its use in Washington was so prolific and careless that it appeared primarily aimed at drugging a sizable minority of the black population. The city pushed methadone not so much as a substitute for heroin, but as a substitute for dealing with the bases of crime or, in the alternative, for paying still more police.

By the early seventies, the city had spent tens of millions in its frantic efforts to control crime. Individuals and businesses had spent millions more in an effort to protect themselves from the effects of the city's failure to control crime. Civil liberties had been run over in the rush to security. And crime, while declining, remained uncomfortably high.

Would nothing work? Despite the vast expenditures, less had been attempted than met the eye. We knew that most crimes of violence involved handguns, but the city failed to outlaw the estimated 75,000 small arms in DC. We knew that most of the city's criminals were eking out economically marginal lives, but failed to provide more attractive economic alternatives. And we should have known that a society that defines such a high proportion of its members as criminals is also defining itself as a failure, and that many of those engaged in crime had calculated their options far more realistically than the community as a whole dared to admit.

Instead of creating new options to make crime less appealing, we spent large sums of money to cut off the desperate option of crime without providing an alternative. To a certain extent it was bound to work—crime leveled off; politicians won elections; and insurance, alarm, and lock companies made large profits—but when two young dudes robbed Senator John Stennis in front of his Northwest home, announced, "We're going to shoot you anyway," and left him struggling for life, it provided a reminder that to make Washington, or any American city, safe again would take more than 12,000 police. Safety simply couldn't be bought.

Good education can't be bought, either. But misplaced as was much of the money, energy, and motives in the war on crime, there at least was a concentration of energy—from the President to the precinct—on the problem. During the same years that Washington's crime was rising, its ability to educate its children was declining. Here were two problems—both terribly important to the life of the city. One crept into the speeches of national candidates and onto the cover of *U.S. News and World Report;* the other—just as much the legal responsibility of the federal government that insisted on its right to govern exclusively the District of Columbia—was ignored or passed off as a "local matter." Politically, crime paid; education didn't.

Like other southern cities, Washington had, until 1954, a segregated school system. It was desegregated by the Supreme Court at the same time as the other schools in the country—but not under the same order. Because DC's nonstate status denies it the protection of the Fourteenth Amendment, the basis of Brown v. Board of Education of Topeka, the Court used the Fifth Amendment to end the city's dual school system, in a decision handed down in the case of Bolling v. Sharpe. The city's schools were quickly brought into compliance. By November 1954, three-quarters of the city's white pupils were going to school with blacks. The Catholic schools had very quietly integrated a few years earlier.

The desegregation decision undoubtedly speeded up the white move to the suburbs, a move that brought dramatic shifts in both the racial and economic characteristics of the school system. Between 1960 and 1970 the city's black population between the ages of five and fourteen went up 38 percent while the white population in this age range dropped 58 percent. By 1970 the 146,000 student system was 95 percent black.

In 1956, a white superintendent, Carl Hansen, instituted what was known as the track system, designed to put students in curriculum streams according to ability. Far from being flexible ability groupings, Hansen's tracks were rigid educational compartments which increasingly came to be seen as a form of economic and racial discrimination as virulent as the open apartheid that had previously existed. One junior high teacher spent two years trying to get a student changed to a more advanced track.

In 1966, with virtually no financial or political support, black activist Julius Hobson filed suit against the track system, the use of optional zones that permitted certain parents to send their children to better schools, and continuing teacher segregation. In a far-reaching decision, U.S. Appeals Court Judge Skelly Wright upheld Hobson's case and directed the school system to abolish the track system, provide transportation for children in overcrowded schools who wanted to go to undercrowded ones, end the optional zone system, and integrate the faculty.

In the wake of the Wright decision, the city gained an elected school board (board members had previously been appointed by local judges) and the first in a succession of changes in the superintendency that added chaos to the underlying feeling of failure permeating public education in DC. When a young, attractive black superintendent, Hugh Scott, was named in 1970, there was hope that the city might at last have found someone who could deal with the educational problems of the city.

Scott came to power in the midst of continuing controversy. The Wright decision had not yet been fully implemented and Hobson was back in court seeking firmer action. In his original suit, Hobson had shown that the gap in per-pupil expenditure in 1965 between the most and least favored schools in the city was $411. More than two years after the Wright decree had been handed down, Hobson recomputed the figures and found that the gap had actually widened to $492. Reported Hobson:

In 1965, the highest average per pupil expenditures were in schools located in the highest income areas of the city. The latest data published by the school administration for 1968 show that areas with income ranges of $10,000 to $12,000 and over still contain the schools with highest per-pupil expenditures based on regular budget funds.

The 1965 data placed in evidence also showed that the schools with the lowest expenditures per pupil in the city were located in Southeast Washington. The latest figures published by the school administration reveal the same pattern of inequity.

In the area of special projects the school administration violated the law in the distribution of compensatory funds. The cheating by DC Public Schools in the use of [federal] funds is worse than what is happening in the south.

It is amazing to find our own school system, primarily black, still discriminates economically against the poorer schools—even with compensatory funds.

As Hugh Scott, the new black hope, rounded out his second year in office, Hobson—who had railed against white superintendent Carl Hansen for assigning children to the "economic junk heap"—was still pressing his case, but now against a black superintendent and an elected school board with a black majority. Only when threatened with being held in contempt of court did the school system finally come up with a plan designed to meet the equalization formula laid down by Judge Wright.

Following the election of a new board majority under Marion Barry in 1972, the board had ended its active opposition to the Wright decree. But the mandate got lost in a year-long crisis over the budget, a crisis precipitated by a cut in funds and aggravated by Scott's inability to get his figures straight. To the casual observer it might have appeared that under an elected board the school system was not faring much better than under the old system. The appearance, however, was deceiving. The new board wanted to change the schools, but it felt compelled first to deal with the financial morass of the system. That it took so long and that the Wright decree got lost in the shuffle was more a reflection on the superintendent than on the board. Although board president Marion Barry, reacting to Scott's still considerable popularity in the city, tried unsuccessfully to extend Scott's contract one year, he had more than once indicated that he was not happy with the school administration. In an interview with the *Evening Star* he said: "When we came aboard, about 90 percent of the information we got from the school administration was inaccurate. I got Xerox copies that were illegible. They'd try to tell you that 2 and 2 adds up to 5. . . . At my first meeting, I tore up some budget stuff and threw it in the trash can."

The board, frustrated by the failings of the administration, took matters into its own hands and reworked the budget itself. Reported the *Star-News:* "Under the leadership of Barry, the school board, for the first time in seven years, had presented a budget to the mayor before his package has gone to the council or Congress. The board has also introduced the new ploy of publicly campaigning for their budget request."

But when Barry made a major issue of funding, it appeared that he might be falling into the traditional trap of assuming that money meant progress. Unfortunately, the problems of the school system ran far deeper than that.

The most obvious evidence was that the median test scores for DC students ran behind national norms. Worse, DC students fell further behind the longer they were in DC schools. When Scott came into office in 1970 a child in the third grade was reading at slightly better than a second grade level, based on large city norms. Ninth grade students, however, were nearly two grades behind in reading. One year later, there had been some improvement in the lower grades but students in seventh to ninth grades had slipped further behind. More and more money had been spent on DC schools, but it was not producing results that anyone could be satisfied with, even discounting for the substantial biases inherent in the testing system used.

But while statistics helped reveal the problem, they didn't suggest the solution. The testimony of an Eastern High School student, Greg Taylor, was more helpful.

On January 13, 1968, the black principal of Eastern had been quoted in the *Washington Post* as saying: "The students have no right to be disappointed in the school as a whole just because the reading scores are low. They don't take into account the odds we're working against. . . . We have every kind of student at this school. Some come from fine professional homes, but we have many from other kinds, you know."

On February 7, Taylor, leader of a group of activist students at the nearly all-black Eastern, told the school board:

I, myself, come from one of the other homes, my parents are not professional so what do you do with me? Am I inferior because I am not from a professional background? I, myself, believe that it is because you do not want me to be a professional person. Last year I wrote a letter of protest to a faculty member. The faculty member responded to my letter by saying, "You need to go back to the first grade because of the misspelled words. A first grader could have presented it better than you presented it to me." My feeling about what she said was if I'm down and I want to get up, she is going to make it difficult as possible for me to get up.

I am a 19-year-old junior and too old to go back to elementary school, so what do you do? You give the so-called basic student—me—anything, just enough to get me out of the way.

I have been officially labelled basic since the first grade and I'm still considered an unofficial basic now. As an example of this, I have been trying to go to college. But this is the program they gave me at the beginning of this year: First period, gym; 2nd period, applied math; third period, lunch; 4th period, English; 5th period, US history; 6th period, cooking, and 7th period, woodshop. I have had courses like cooking and woodwork all my life. . . .

Taylor had run up against a form of discrimination as brutal as that based simply on race; the economic and social discrimination that Hobson had tried to attack in one way through his suit but which has forms immune to litigation. It is a discrimination that black students feel not merely from white teachers but from blacks as well. And as blacks assumed more of the power in the school system, the intraracial discrimination became more significant.

In a perceptive analysis of the problem, William Simons, president of the Washington Teachers Union, wrote in the union newspaper:

Our black teachers are primarily those black children who did not rebel. They accepted uncritically all the assumptions of American education and American society. They believe in rugged individualism. They believe that the individual has complete control over his own destiny and they deny the influences of class, racism, economics, etc. These attitudes were developed unconsciously by the teacher as a child. When the teachers went to a school of education they were reinforced and buttressed by educational jargon. The teacher went forth into the classroom to teach good citizenship and proper work habits, to manage and discipline his charges, to rate, classify and label them. The teacher believed in the American dream. If only he could get the children to act like white people, to deny their blackness, the badge of their and his inferiority. To stop them from being black, he had to stop them from being children. To deny his own blackness, he had to deny his own humanity. . . .

The teacher tried to teach as he understood it. He

prepared careful lesson plans, he put up attractive bulle-
tin boards. He had his supplies ready, his seat work dupli-
cated, his goals listed. When the children did not learn,
the teacher was threatened. Consciously or not he knew
that he must avoid examination of himself, the school,
and the society. If the children did not learn, they and
their families were to blame. If this were not true, the
teacher's whole world would crumble. Therefore, it must
be true, You just can't teach "these" children anything.

The children learned as soon as they went to kinder-
garten that their teachers had low opinions of them. They
learned that they were not expected to learn. They learned
that they had some serious fault that could not be eradicated. They found the school an uncaring, unfeeling
place. The school was interested in only one aspect of
them—how they could read. If they did not learn to read,
they were worthless. Some children spent 13 humiliating
years in the school system—anxious, desperate, aggressive. The system labels them "behavior problems," "discipline problems," and sometimes finds special classes for
them or suspends them or expels them. It is rather devastating to be humiliated day in and day out for 13 years.
Under these circumstances, children rebel, not only
against the school, but against everything connected with
school—teachers, middle-class blacks, authority, public
buildings, property, books, children who made it in school,
education, work and learning itself.

School Board president Barry encountered this. "I
know this woman with a brilliant little girl, 145 IQ,"
said Barry, "registered her with an aunt so she could
get her in a fairly good school—not west of the park, but
in Northeast. The principal told her, 'We haven't got
anything to offer your child here. She's very bright and
we're just not geared to deal with that.' Now that's a
hell of a thing for a principal to tell anybody. The woman
now has her kid in a Montessori school."

Barry recalled: "I used to go to parties where there were teachers in the school system and about 1 or 2 A.M., when everybody's relaxed, you'd hear these teachers talking about their kids. . . . On Sunday nights you'd hear them complaining, 'Well, I got to go back to those little niggers tomorrow' or 'those thugs'—statements like that."

And west of Rock Creek Park, a sixth grader was asked on a test: "What is it that groups of people need to live together peacefully?" He answered, "Cooperation," but his teacher crossed it out and wrote, "Rules."

At the operating level, those who followed the rules best made it to the top—as principals. There, too many of them perpetuated the worst of the values in the school system, indifferent to parent complaints and scornful of young teachers who wanted to break new ground. Many of the latter simply dropped out with the students, finding the DC school system inhospitable to skill and imagination. For the parents, especially those who had no other option, there was nothing to do but to complain and complain again. When they took stronger action, the central office stood by the principal. When the parents at a Capitol Hill school, in a final act of frustration, attempted to prevent their white principal, who had little but seniority to recommend her, from entering the school, administration officials stood by as parents were arrested. The protest worked, however; the principal did not return. At another Capitol Hill school, one with a black principal who had been the target of a five-year struggle to have her transferred, action came finally only over the dead body of a student—a youth killed in a playground accident contributed to by official negligence. Superintendent Scott, brought in to move the school system, had been too timid even to transfer principals.

Larry Cuban was a teacher who liked teaching. He had spent fifteen years, on and off, teaching. In 1970 he was director of staff development for the DC schools. When the budget for staff development was gutted by the DC Council and Congress, Cuban decided to go back to teaching. He described what happened:

When my colleagues found out, a wall of silence appeared. Except for some close associates, the response— when people chose to talk to me, was disbelief. They seemed to suggest by smile, smirk or wink that I must be waiting for a good offer. Until one came along I was covering up by saying I would teach. For the most part, I was ignored. In hallways when passing someone, eyes turned away. I began to feel like a leper. I did discover, however, that the very administrators and board members who extolled teaching couldn't understand why anyone in their right mind would want to go back to the classroom. Within two months, a series of actions, unmalicious in intent, initiated and executed in a most efficient bureaucratic manner, occurred that created within me a sense of shame and failure.

The first shock came with salary. To teach meant taking a one-third wage cut. . . .

Next there was the Board of Education's official action which transfers an employee from one position to another. I received a notice which said I was "demoted without prejudice. . . ."

Then the Board of Examiners informed me a week before school began that I could not receive a regular probationary contract because I had never taken a college course in teaching at the secondary school level. With almost 15 years of classroom experience at the senior high school level in three different cities, with five years experience in preparing teachers who work in secondary schools of the District, with a book and numerous articles on teacher education—I am told that unless I take a course on Teaching in the Secondary School within two years I will not be able to teach in DC. After a pay cut, a demotion, and then a threat, I felt like I had committed a crime.

The school system could have learned from people like Greg Taylor and Larry Cuban. But it was following different drummers. They came into town to sell textbooks, plans, and consulting contracts. A few had something to offer, but too often they were of the variety that promised that "short-term sessions in social interaction, micro-teaching, interaction analysis, non-verbal communications, diagnostic technology, positive focus games and communication will be conducted to enrich the participants' experiences, teaching and learning styles." Or like the report from the Central Atlantic Regional Education Laboratory: "It is apparent that the on-going needs of children will dictate the number of decisions made in any given segment of time. Student performance and level of aspiration, teacher percepts and adequate diagnosis-prescription and evaluation would affect the quality of the operation of the proposed schema."

Superintendent Hugh Scott's own proposal for the DC schools was in the same vein. He seemed possessed of a desire to prove that a black administrator could be as obfuscating as any white educator on the block, and his report rattled with instructional supports, noninstructional supports, Flying Squads, Red Line supplies, Holiday Skill Kits, Hot Lines, Prescriptive Learning Packets, Peer Administrators Consulting in Education (that's PACE), Mobe Teams, Functional Learning Centers, norm-reference tests, criterion-reference tests, assessment teams, Quarterly Regional Profiles, 200 student decoders, and a check list with space to note whether the checker "assumes responsibility for a feedback mechanism to disseminate information from central office."

Scattered among the diarrhetic flow from consulting firms was some solid matter. Dr. Henry Passow, for example, had argued in an important but soon-forgotten report:

. . . The teachers in Washington had been led to stress reading at the expense of everything else and to place themselves as teachers in a highly directive role. Two-thirds of the school day was typically given over to activities intending to develop language skills in each of the class schedules examined. The basic approach to the teaching of reading was to drill on the recognition of words and the factual content of the materials read. The bulk of the child's day seemed to be spent in a "read-and-recite" mode. Nothing else, not even arithmetic, looms as large or important. The child spent most of his day paying closest possible attention to his teacher, following her directions, responding to her questions, and obeying her rules. The children were not encouraged to talk to one another, either formally or informally—indeed, the principal technical criticism the observers had of the language program was that it did not seem to deal with speech. And the sad fact is that in spite of all this, the children don't really learn to read, as the test surveys have repeatedly shown. Doing the same thing, but doing it harder, would scarcely seem promising.

A few years later not many would remember who Dr. Passow was and the school system would be deep into another report—this one by Kenneth Clark, author of *Dark Ghetto* and head of the Metropolitan Applied Research Center—which recommended a reading mobilization year complete with learning goals and floors, greater teacher "accountability," and a testing program to make sure it was all working. To some, Clark appeared to be suggesting more of the same—but harder. Like the Passow Report, however, the Clark plan was never tested—only paid for.

In a sense what the school system and its advisers were attempting to prove was that a generation of the best educated, best staffed and best funded school administrators in history could teach reading, writing, and arithmetic as well as their less talented, less well staffed, and less well funded predecessors several decades earlier.

Part of their problem was attempting to achieve this by treating education essentially as a management problem. Too many administering the system viewed the teacher and the student not as the center of the system but as the bottom of a pyramid of responsibility, ideas, and action. The student was the product and the teacher was the assembler. Neither was granted much respect or independence and neither was encouraged to take initiative. While the teachers—those that stayed—adapted to the system, the students, lacking the economic motivation of their instructors, did not. Being the only part of the system with no vested interest in it, many simply clogged, slowed down, or fell off the assembly line.

As products, the students' function was to become marketable. They were to serve the system rather than vice versa, and the emphasis was upon finding how closely children could be made to react in the predictable manner of inanimate objects moved by mechanical and technological forces. In his report, Scott proposed that each teacher not only "utilize the Sequential Inventory of Reading Skills and Specific Objectives for Pupil's Performance in Mathematics" but also "develop individual profiles of children charting progress in skill in reading and mathematics and diagnose each child's learning needs in reading and mathematics and project goals for each child." To accomplish the latter task, Scott suggested a "projection of scores by date and teaching goals." Not only was the students' present status to be objectively definable but their future objectively predictable as well.

All this might have worked—almost any system might have—if in fact the students had been marketable. But they knew better than anyone that they were not.

Recent high school graduates comprised one of the groups with the highest unemployment rates in the city. Although the students were told that education was the key to jobs, the reverse came closer to the truth. If a high school diploma could have guaranteed employment, then the value of education would have increased greatly. Given a wide-spread—and not unrealistic—expectation of failure, it was not surprising that so many failed to pay attention in class. A full employment policy—one that included adequate employment for black high school graduates—might have been the best educational policy available.

Without such a policy, any educational plan was bound to suffer. The parents who lined up when their children were four to get them into prestige private schools such as St. Albans and Sidwell Friends were not acting out of sheer love of learning. They knew that beyond those schools were prestige colleges and beyond that high paying jobs. The fact that over half of Washington's adult black population had not completed high school was not only a commentary on the schools, it was also a description of the economy. Many of those blacks had dropped out when they had enough education for the jobs that were available to them.

But while racism and economic factors put insurmountable constraints on the schools, the failure of the schools to deal with the reality of the situation added still more problems. Rather than develop a strategy for helping students to deal with external obstacles, the school system simply put more obstacles in their path. Rather than teach survival and, indeed, rebellion, it fostered resignation. Rather than counter the system that promised failure to its students, it remained a part of that system, providing an early micro-society filled with the same venal discriminations and values the student would find in the larger world upon leaving school.

It was bound to do so as long as it emulated the

corporate and bureaucratic world in its administration; left its schools in the control of principals who had gained their positions by the number of hash marks on their sleeves; clung to absurdly picayune teacher credential requirements; failed to provide the logistical support that is one of the few true functions of a central school administration; and refused, after hiring teachers presumably on the basis of their competency, to give them the freedom to express that competency.

Under the new board and even under the halting leadership of superintendent Scott, the course of DC schools began to change. With the help of three hundred parent-aides and Title One federal funds, seventy-one schools got special programs in reading and math. In one year in these schools there was a 1.2- to 1.4-year improvement in reading scores. In one ward, classrooms providing special materials were able to bring their students up to national norms in two years. And Superintendent Scott moved to make it possible for any teacher with five years' experience to become a principal without rising slowly up the chain of seniority. But much more was required.

It was not that there was some alternative master plan lurking around waiting to be activated. In a system of nearly 150,000 pupils, any master plan was doomed to fail a great many. The competing theoreticians of education shared a common fault—too much faith in a system. In fact, the best educational system might well be one that is indescribable, so varied would be its contents. Many of the best educated people in the country learned under such a system, one that valued competence and ability rather than conformity to the quality-controlled mediocrity which is now the standard for Washington and other big city school systems. Under such an approach, the student might be confronted with experiences that ranged from traditionally authoritarian to radically student-centered. There would be good and there would be bad and in the variety the student could learn the difference between the good and the bad. I can tell you the names of good teachers I had as a student and I can tell you the names of the bad ones. I cannot, however, identify their common characteristics beyond sensing that the good ones were competent, possessed with their jobs, and understood my capabilities and my failings, and that the bad ones did not. There were indulgent teachers and tyrants, rote-demons and youth liberators in both groups. And none of the good ones would have been caught dead working for long under the current rules and practices of the DC school system.

Decentralization and community control would be an important part of a new approach to DC education. There is a strong constituency among both black and white Washingtonians for decentralization and community control and the first steps have been taken remarkably free of the rancor and fear that these concepts have raised elsewhere. The first steps have not been unqualified successes. But the wisest among those advocating such moves did not expect that they would. What is happening in Washington is that a generation of blacks who have achieved some measure of success in their own lives is having children and does not intend them to suffer in the same manner that they did. The collective demand of Washington's younger black middle class, freed of the acceptance of failure under which their parents were raised, is one of the strongest forces coming to bear on the DC public schools. This generation, if it can be permitted to work its will on the schools, offers infinitely more hope than a continuation of a remote, unresponsive centralized authority that has clearly failed.

Beyond the structure of the system, however, is the crux of the matter: what happens in the classroom. Until the public school teacher is given the same professional freedom and logistical support that he or she might expect to find in a college or good private school, good teachers will not be attracted to public schools.

Even more important, the students must be granted respect as well. Teachers, black or white, who regard their students as "niggers" or "thugs" are as harmful to the schools as sadistic cops are to the police. But beyond overt prejudices are unconscious discriminations which produce similar results.

Among these is language discrimination. One reason that students fail to learn to read in DC schools is because many of them—to a lesser or greater degree—speak a different language than that which they are reading.

A part of this involves subject matter. Bill Rasberry, the perceptive black columnist who writes for the *Washington Post*, quoted an excerpt from a reading comprehension text given DC students: "The thing I remember best about our summer vacation in Europe was my ride on a Telepherique, an aerial railroad which climbs right up the side of a mountain on a cable. In August we took a bus from Geneva, Switzerland, around Lake Geneva to the French city of Chamonix, which is in the valley below Mont Blanc." Dig?

More significant, however, is the language itself. In a very real sense, Washington is a bilingual city. Some Washingtonians speak what the academicians call Standard English, some speak what has been dubbed Black English and some speak both. Black English is far more than employing colorful slang and a dropping of consonants at the ends of words. It involves a different syntax that, contrary to the biased ear of the Standard English speaker, is not based on ignorance or sloppiness but upon definite rules.

As Pam and Michael Rosenthal said in a review of J. L. Dillard's *Black English,* "It is not a make-do language of people who, for one reason or another, have not caught on to the principles of our language, but it is a variant form that has developed through history, shaped and molded by influences as remote as Pidgin Portuguese, spoken by seventeenth century traders on the west coast of Africa."

Here is an example of correct and incorrect Black English taken from a course taught by William Stewart at Columbia University:

Correct	Incorrect
He be sick [all the time]	He sick [all the time]
He sick [right now]	He be sick [right now]

The difference is that "He be sick" is chronic while "He sick" is temporary, a distinction Standard English can't make without the qualifiers "all the time" or "right now."

One needn't be a linguist to know that something is going on here other than slang. If you just speak Standard English, you need only to attempt to understand a conversation with a young black Washingtonian who speaks the dialect to realize that you are not speaking quite the same language.

This is a fact. Black English exists. But its existence is either denied or passed off as improper English. White liberals don't like to talk about it for fear of seeming racist. And middle-class blacks shy away from it in part because they fear its recognition would be a reflection on blacks generally and in part because they are familiar enough with it that it sounds not different but ignorant. In fact, some of those black leaders who would most vehemently oppose recognition of Black English in the schools borrow from it when it suits their purposes—as when at a political rally on H Street or talking to a group of welfare mothers who have come to their downtown office.

To young Washingtonians—and it is among the young that Black English predominates—the refusal of the adult society to recognize their speech as something other than "bad" English adds one more item to the burdens they must carry. It is not a matter of "teaching" Black English that is at issue: it has managed to survive very well for several centuries without any teaching. The point is to teach *reading* to the black child and to do it in the same way that the white middle-class child learns it—in the language and style he or she is already familiar with. What matters almost equally is that an essential part of the young Black English speaker's being —his or her language—not be rejected as an aberration of good speech and further evidence of the speaker's intrinsic inadequacy.

The language of Washington's young blacks is notable in at least one other respect: its intensity of use and its imagery. When kids are with each other, away from an adult environment, they are highly verbal and the words often involve lively and imaginative images. That of course is true of most school age youths, but what is interesting about the young black Washingtonians is that they are children who are supposed—by their test scores ye shall know them—to be excruciatingly nonverbal. The facility with words comes out during a spate of "jonin'" or trading insults, a favorite adolescent pasttime that may actually be a form of underground education: preparation for a life in which one is frequently insulted.

Now this particular form of language facility won't get you into college, earn you a job, or attract an offer to write a book. That's not the point. The point is that the student who in class may seem inarticulate and nonverbal may in fact be almost obsessively verbal in other situations. It would seem a useful task for big city schools to find out why the students' attitude towards language changes when they walk in the school door.

Whatever the reasons, the DC school system has failed an extraordinary number of its students. There has, however, been one major effort to overcome this familiar big city phenomenon in a manner that is virtually unique in the country: the establishment of Federal City College, the city's new public college, founded under the federal land-grant system. FCC has had serious problems, not the least of which has been some corrupt administrators and mismanagement of administrative affairs. These have tended to obscure the phenomenal daring of establishing a college for students from one of the worst public school systems in the country. In a speech at Boston University in 1969, Commissioner Washington noted that FCC had "received over six thousand applications for its first freshman class just over one year ago. That figure was three times the number the college could finally admit, meaning quite simply that four thousand young men and women who desired further education were denied the opportunity to secure it. Not one in fifty could pass the standard entrance requirements for the other universities in Washington."

FCC has been mired in controversy and chaos. Its students are spread over twenty temporary buildings scattered about downtown. It has been baited by congressmen anxious to find evidence of black malfeasance, who have been aided by college officials who have provided it. It must attempt to build a higher education system on the wreckage of a bad secondary and elementary system. There is little evidence to suggest either success or failure at this point, but through the turmoil and the confusion there are signs that the student body whose average age is 26 and more of whom work full or part-time, intend to make the college work. For the first time, Washington has a college that puts itself at the disposal of Washingtonians, one that is a part of the city. It is hard to exaggerate the importance of FCC in a city that had to wait 168 years for its first public college—a dismal indication of the priority given education by Washington's federal administrators.

Crime Pays; Education Doesn't

Washington's struggle for a better educational system has not been an easy or a happy one. Unlike the war on crime, the city received little help from those who ultimately control it. In many ways this was a good thing, for it has permitted Washington in the past few years to begin to build an educational system to its own liking. It is painfully clearing away the wreckage of the past and beginning to make its own precedents. But the federal priorities remain. A policeman in 1973 was still making more than a teacher in the public schools. And while the school system got $1,400 a year to spend on each of its pupils, the government was spending over $3,000 a year to keep someone in jail.

7 / *The Urban Gang Bang*

T HERE ARE SIX MAJOR ANIMAL SPECIES IN WASHING-
ton: dogs, birds, cockroaches, termites, rats, and human beings. Of these only the last is endangered. Dogs
run wild in packs in some parts of town; starlings and
pigeons resist the most technologically advanced techniques of eradication; roaches and termites thrive despite extermination service contracts; and the rat has
responded to the best efforts of the Department of Environmental Services by producing a mutant strain resistant to all known poisons. But the human is in trouble.

One reason is that the ecology of the urban human
remains little understood. We now comprehend the
hazards of blithely pouring DDT over crops, slashing
through treelands, or fouling the air. But we still act as
though we can, without penalty, wipe out neighborhoods,
force mass migrations, rip out favorite meeting places
for people, or tear down centers of communications, cul-

ture, and commerce that are as important to a community as a marsh is to a flyway.

Those human marshes we call cities are in danger throughout America, but politically powerless Washington is particularly vulnerable. How, where, or whether a convention center, freeway, subway, or high-rise office building gets built is a matter over which Washingtonians have had minimal control. They could protest in the streets or the courts—which they have done with much frequency and less effectiveness, but such power is only the power to prevent. The power to conceive and carry out has rested with others—Congress, the White House, appointed bodies such as the Zoning Commission and Redevelopment Land Agency, and their multitudinous friends in the construction and development business.

There are a few organizations in Washington dedicated to human conservation. But they generally fall into two categories: the small and weak, and those large, slick groups whose advocacy has a hollow sound. Too often the latter bodies consist of cooks protesting the stew. There are too many vested interests within their confines. What starts out as an urban coalition turns into an urban cabal. A manufacturer of redwood homes would be unlikely to win a seat on the board of the Sierra Club. In Washington, it's different. The people who have appointed themselves to solve urban problems and the people causing the problems are too often the same.

Washington, most particularly in the last two decades, has been stripmined, cut over, polluted, depleted, desecrated, and decimated by every economic and political interest that could get its trucks and machinery into the territory. Few forests, rivers, or mineral lodes have gotten worse treatment than that accorded Washington, DC. It has been one long urban gang bang.

Road-building, construction, and power companies; real estate dealers, and development syndicates; automobile manufacturers and makers of tires; publishers of newspapers; bankers and the FHA; the Board of Trade and city planners; management consultants and parking lot magnates—all have had their piece and the city lies knocked down and knocked up. The words of Job come back:

Men remove landmarks; they seize flocks and pasture them.

They drive away the ass of the fatherless; they take the widow's ox for a pledge.

They thrust the poor off the road; the poor of the earth all hide themselves. . . .

Among the olive rows of the wicked they make oil; they tread the wine presses, but suffer thirst.

From out of the city the dying groan, and the soul of the wounded cries for help.

Once again, Pierre L'Enfant had set a precedent. When Daniel Carroll began his mansion, Duddington House, L'Enfant complained that it was right in the path of New Jersey Avenue and would destroy the city plan. L'Enfant moved to have the mansion torn down, but Carroll stopped him with a magistrate's warrant. L'Enfant responded by getting a gang of laborers to dismantle the structure brick by brick in the middle of the night. Shortly thereafter, President Washington intervened, ordering the building rebuilt, but off the avenue.

Today's planners are no less determined than L'Enfant to see that their plan is carried through. L'Enfant's passion for order was reflected in that architect's planned destruction of some 200-year-old trees because they interfered with the symmetrical walkways he had designed for Lincoln Park. It was reflected in the massive clearance of Southwest Washington for urban renewal in an act as callous and casual as wiping off a Monopoly board to begin a new game. It was reflected in the growing presumption that the right of eminent domain could be exercised not only to meet public necessity but to satisfy the designer's whim.

Few have captured the causes of the urban planning disaster better than Richard Sennett in his book, *The Uses of Disorder*. Sennett traces our contemporary planning problems historically to Baron Haussmann and psychologically to societal adolescence.

Of Haussmann, who directed the rebuilding of Paris in the 1860s, Sennett says:

> Haussmann's means of correcting the wretched housing, the difficult transport, the lack of political control are important to us now because he was the first to look on the solution of these problems as essentially interrelated. What one did with transport could also be a means of dealing with the populace when civil disorders occurred; how one removed the dilapidated housing, Haussmann believed, was also a way of defining the relations between the social classes.
>
> Haussmann began to cut, through the jumble of streets, great, long, unswervingly straight avenues, avenues that could accommodate an enormous amount of traffic, serve as an easy means of getting troops into riotous sections of the city, and act like river boundaries dividing different socioeconomic sections of the city. . . . These broad avenues connected public monument to public monument; they did not connect one group of people to another with whom they might have social relations. The working man's districts of Paris thus remained, in the wake of Haussmann's reforms, unconnected to the new centers of industry on the outskirts of town. Again, these new streets often served to put the purely social problems of poverty and petit-bourgeois deprivation out of mind by putting them out of sight behind the beautiful grand boulevards.

Baron Haussmann was, to be sure, a great creator, and his positive accomplishments cannot be ignored. Yet his legacy to the cities of our time, unintended or not, has been a group of assumptions of terrible simplicity.

The first of these is that it is desirable to treat city problems as a whole. . . .

The second assumption is that it is a good idea to plan physical space of predetermined social use: that is, instead of assuming that changes in the social structure of the city should be accomplished first in order to change the physical appearance of the city, Haussmann bequeathed the notion to us that it is somehow better, and certainly easier, to change the physical landscape in order to alter the social patterns of the metropolis.

Sennett analyzes the psychology of urban planners:

Their impulse has been to give way to that tendency, developed in adolescence, of men to control unknown threats by eliminating the possibility for experiencing surprise. . . . Buried in this hunger for preplanning along machine-like lines is the desire to avoid pain, to create a transcendent order of living that is immune to the variety, and so to the inevitable conflict, between men.

Sennett says that the adolescent attempt to eliminate surprise as a defense against unknown threats leads to a desire for what he calls a "purified community." But, he notes, "in the purification of a coherent community image, fear rather than love of men's 'otherness' prevails. Out of this fear is bred the counterfeit of experience. The 'we' feeling, which expresses a desire to be similar, is a way for men to avoid the necessity of looking deeper into each other; instead, men imagine that they know all about each other, and their knowledge becomes a vision of how they must be the same."

Thus the city master plan serves some of the same functions for the urbanite as teenage cultism and faddism do for the adolescent. In the process, essential virtues of city life—variety, surprise, and an environment permitting reasonable intercourse between inevitably competing and disputatious groupings of humans—get smothered in homogeneity, phony consensus, and increasing isolation of the various groups of "we."

Sennett's description fits Washington well. Like Haussmann's new Paris, Washington has become a city of broad avenues, some of them multilane freeways, that accommodate traffic and police and which divide the city along socioeconomic lines. The freeways, and even the subway, are not designed to improve the social interrelationships of the area but rather to avoid them. The centers of industry have moved to the suburbs and the problems of poverty remain unconquered. Row upon row of unvaried office construction fills blocks where vital urban communities once existed.

The physical planning, the urge to solve Washington's problems as a whole, has left the social problems of the city in disarray. Where they have been mitigated, it has been largely accomplished through such techniques as the forced emigration of the poor or, as in the case of crime, by spending huge sums for their partial control. Just as L'Enfant's plan for more than 100 years did not produce a result even closely matching the intent, so contemporary physical planning has not only failed to eradicate the most pressing of the city's social and economic problems, it has added to them.

Washington's planning has not always followed this pattern. "Boss" Alexander Shepherd, as head of the city's Board of Public Works in the early 1870s, engaged in massive physical planning but his priorities are interesting in retrospect. Although he—like modern planners—was indifferent to the personal hardships caused by his often botched projects, Shepherd at least concentrated on improving the quality of urban life instead of on solving community problems by intentionally removing the community. Shepherd paved 180 miles of streets, built 200 miles of sidewalks, and installed 3,000 gas lamps and 25,000 shade trees in the few years of his power. Today, in too many instances, urban reconstruction has not only meant urban removal, but a lack of urban amenities. In fact, Washington has been living on the fat of amenities introduced sixty or more years ago. In the midst of the city's great freeway and development boom, residential streets remained unrepaired for years at a time. A developer could get money to construct an office in an urban renewal area but a community group couldn't get a public trashcan placed at a crowded corner. New bridges were built and more proposed while residents of Anacostia walked along streets still without sidewalks. The city could promise millions to spur the private development of 300 acres at Ft. Lincoln while the local and federal government delayed for several years and finally reneged on a promise to provide rehabilitation loans and grants to one community's low income homeowners. And while the transit system could consider spending $5 million for two-way radios of dubious virtue for each of its buses it could only find $500,000 for badly needed bus shelters. Thus, not only was it wrong to assign physical planning precedence over social and economic renewal, it didn't even produce a satisfactory physical result. Instead of correcting obvious deficiencies—an abandoned house, an over-crowded slum, a filthy river, or the lack of service facilities—the planners determined to start all over again, not to cure the diseased parts but build a new whole. The megalomaniacal presumptuousness of the planners persisted even in the face of a growing record of failure and increasing evidence that without the years of freeways, urban renewal, and subsidized development, the city might have had more low income housing, a better distributed tax base, more blue collar jobs, less crime, less welfare, and required less time to travel within its confines.

Washington, of course, was not alone in feeling

the brutal impact of monolithic urban planning. The Washington-based Citizens Advocate Center reported that in more than twenty years of federally-funded urban renewal, only 28 percent of the housing destroyed had been replaced. CAC said that Congress had authorized "over $8 billion for urban renewal which has consequently demolished 440,000 dwellings while providing only 125,000 new units in the low and moderate income categories." But while Washington shared the misery with other cities, it also got more than its share. Between 1940 and 1965 some 142 miles of freeways were built in the metropolitan area, leaving it with more freeways per acre and per capita than any other large urban area, including Los Angeles.

The freeways provided the footing for the development that followed. They contributed to a major realignment of the city's function. Increasingly, the city became a daytime working mall for suburbanites, with the roads providing easy and safe access.

It all began quietly enough on August 17, 1937, when the first local gas tax of 2¢ per gallon was enacted, with revenue going for highway use. In 1941, the DC Highway Department completed its first long-range planning study which included a soon-forgotten caveat, "Mass transportation can and should supplant much of the individual, vehicular service into the central business areas." The plan then went on to call for a twenty-year highway program; nothing was provided for mass transit. The streetcar declined due to automobile competition and after its demise in the early sixties the city's buses soon followed with drastically falling service and ridership and rapidly rising fares.

Over twenty-five years freeways in Washington and surrounding areas proliferated. By 1965, even with 142 miles of new roads behind them, the area's freeway builders still had thirty-eight more on the drawing boards, including several that involved large-scale removal of both low- and middle-income Washingtonians, the most notorious being the North Central Freeway that would cut through the heart of middle-class biracial Brookland. The interstate system was being rapidly completed, the suburban beltway and adjoining spurs were set, but problems rose rapidly at the city's borders. Without the crosstown links through cities like Washington, interstate truckers would lose valuable time and waste expensive gas. But increasingly, city residents were becoming unwilling to sacrifice their homes and their air to the interests of the truckers.

The battle waged by the local citizenry against the new roads brought it into conflict with the most potent political forces of the nation. In no other city was a freeway program pushed not only by local officials but ordered by the Congress as well in the face of overwhelming local opposition. In the 1968 Democratic primary, with 98,000 voters going to the polls, 95 percent approved a proposal that all major transportation projects be submitted to referendum. Congress ignored the vote. In 1969, an unofficial citizens referendum found 84 percent of the 11,699 persons voting rejecting construction of the Three Sisters Bridge and associated freeways.

Congress paid no more attention to the petition of local citizens than President Nixon heeded the call of protesters against the war. Yet under the vigorous leadership of the Emergency Committee on the Transportation Crisis, the fight continued anyway. Rallies, marches, and raucous demonstrations kept the struggle alive as volunteer lawyers from the firm of Covington and Burling pressed the people's case in the courts.

In February 1968, the U.S. Court of Appeals enjoined all further freeway construction until planning laws and requirements were met. Five months later Congress passed the Federal Aid Highway Act of 1968 which included a provision mandating the building of the Three Sisters Bridge and two other freeways "notwithstanding any other provision of law, or any court decision or administrative action to the contrary."

Three congressmen, Jerome Waldie, Richard McCarthy and Fred Schwengel, had filed a dissent to the committee report on the bill that laid out in blunt terms the cost of more freeways:

> These costs, according to estimates by the District Government, are as follows:
>
> (a) Destruction of another 180 acres of land in residential use, displacing 15,000 more District residents;
>
> (b) Destruction of another 225 acres of land in commercial and industrial use, depriving thousands of workers of their present jobs;
>
> (c) Destruction of 245 acres of park, monumental, and other Government-owned land presently used daily by thousands of residents and visitors for recreational use;
>
> (d) Destruction of 24 acres of land presently used for schools and education;
>
> (e) Destruction of 17 acres of land presently used for churches, cemeteries, and other tax-exempt charitable or institutional purposes.
>
> In property taxes alone, the District would lose at least $2 million annually. Including related tax losses resulting from displacement . . . the annual loss to the depleted general fund would likely exceed $6 million each year.
>
> The committee's hearings show that the District's highway program has become a Frankenstein monster which devours far too great a proportion of the District's land and financial resources. . . .
>
> Since 1940, the central city area has lost one-third of its population. Row houses have been replaced with new highways and parking lots. The city's housing shortage is desperate. More than 60 percent of the central business district is now devoted to highways and off-street storage of motor vehicles.

Throughout the District, 30 percent of the land area is preempted by highways, while only 35 percent is privately owned, tax yielding property. The sprawl generated by past highway construction led to the loss, between 1948 and 1963, of one-fourth of the city's retail establishments. By 1960, over 44 percent of the city's wage earners resided and paid taxes outside the city.

In return for its investment, the city has received increased smog, more traffic fatalities, a drastic loss of patronage in its public transit system, an ever-worsening housing crisis, and permanent scars on residential neighborhoods and monumental areas where older highways have been widened or new highways force through to make room for more auto commuters.

Nonetheless the bill was passed and Lyndon Johnson reluctantly signed it. At the end of 1968, finding a legal loophole in the congressional mandate, the City Council and planning commission approved a modified transportation plan which excluded the Three Sisters Bridge and the North Central Freeway but which provided for an alternative route that still accomplished the truckers' main aim: a cross-town expressway. House DC appropriations subcommittee chairman William Natcher, who since the middle-sixties had been holding the planned subway as a hostage to insure completion of the freeway network, was furious. He continued to hold up funds for the subway. In August 1969, the House District Committee approved a DC revenue bill which withheld federal payment from DC until the freeway system was underway beyond recall. The plan was pushed by a coalition that included Rep. Brock Adams, a supposed liberal friend of the city, and arch-conservative Joel Broyhill. The only public opposition from a member of the House's liberal caucus, the Democratic Study Group, came from Rep. Don Edwards. Said the Emergency Committee on the Transportation Crisis: "This desertion of

The Urban Gang Bang

the District by the Democratic Study Group in favor of the highway lobby's program and tactics laid seige to DC and forced DC officials to capitulate—something Rep. Natcher has been unable to achieve since 1966. With friends like Adams (et al) who needs enemies like Broyhill?"

Three days later, the City Council met to approve the construction of the freeway system demanded by Congress and the Nixon Administration. Two hundred angry citizens were expelled from the Council chamber, fourteen of them arrested. A month later, the District government let a contract for construction of the Three Sisters Bridge. In the weeks that followed, citizen and student demonstrations at the site resulted in over 150 arrests.

But the following spring, the U.S. Court of Appeals once again came to the city's defense. As in 1968 it ruled that the established procedures for public hearings and other rules had been violated:

> Appellees argue that Congress intended to bypass the hearing process because hearings would only expose community sentiment adverse to the construction of the Bridge, and that Congress intended that the Bridge be built irrespective of the wishes of the citizens of the District of Columbia. Appellees further argue that to allow a public hearing would cause local authorities to delay the Bridge, and that Congress meant to preclude hearings for this reason as well.
>
> Such a reading of the statute would condemn it as unconstitutional. A legislature may not constitutionally disenfranchise a group of citizens because of their expected views.
>
> If we were to accept appellees' reading and interpretation, Congress would have excluded from the statutory protection only one group, a totally unrepresented and voiceless minority of citizens. Any legislative classifica-

tion which singles out for invidious treatment a small
group of citizens totally excluded from the political process
does not meet the usual deference from this court. The
usual deference which courts accord legislative and administrative judgments stems from the confidence which
courts have that these judgments are just resolutions of
competing interests.

The decision did not end the dispute. The city began
paying $500 a day to guard the bridge site while it pre-
pared its next legal moves. Meanwhile, it blithely went
ahead with plans for a new concrete absurdity, a multilane road to be tunneled under the Lincoln Memorial,
across the Mall, and under the Tidal Basin. Still there
was a growing feeling by the city that the profreeway
forces were in retreat. Hundreds of millions of dollars of
road construction had been blocked for years. In the
most politically impotent city in the nation, black and
white, poor and affluent, student "crazies" and Covington
and Burling lawyers had held out against the most powerful politicians in the country. Then in 1972, an even
more powerful force intervened on the side of the city:
a flood resulting from Hurricane Agnes tore out the
caisson that had been built at the Three Sisters site and
washed it downstream until it rested against another
bridge, a sullen monument to one of colonial Washington's rare victories.

As the freeway battle began in earnest, a new assault
on the city was taking place in Southwest Washington.
In April 1954, 551 acres of land began to be cleared
for what was then the largest urban renewal project in
the nation. The plan was hailed by planners and liberals:
a 1955 report for the District was titled "No Slums in
Ten Years." A few people were not so sanguine. In a
1959 report of the National Conference of Catholic
Charities, the Rt. Rev. Msg. John O. Grady said, "We
have had many indications of what is happening in our

huge urban renewal program. It is sad. It is not urban renewal; it is a means of making a few people rich. Instead of improving housing conditions, it is shifting people around from one slum to another." A young black minister named Walter Fauntroy—who would later become the city's nonvoting delegate to Congress and who would, as a member of the City Council vote for freeways and other urban renewal projects—described the Southwest plan as "Negro removal."

The Southwest plan had been given the go-ahead by a 1954 Supreme Court decision which upheld the DC Redevelopment Act. In one of those bitter reminders that national folk heroes of liberalism can be as indifferent to the District as anyone else, the decision was written by Justice William O. Douglas. It said in part:

> We do not sit to determine whether a particular housing project is or is not desirable. The concept of the public welfare is broad and inclusive. . . . The values it represents are spiritual as well as physical, aesthetic as well as monetary. It is within the power of the legislature to determine that the community should be beautiful as well as healthy, spacious as well as clean, well-balanced as well as carefully patrolled. . . . In the present case, Congress and its authorized agencies attack the problem of the blighted parts of the community on an area rather than on a structure-by-structure basis. . . . The experts concluded that if the community were to be healthy, if it were not to revert again to a blighted or slum area, as though possessed by a congenital disease, the area must be planned as a whole.

It was a justification that was to undergird nearly twenty years of urban renewal: faith in the "experts," trust in the master plan, and unflagging belief that the city could be disassembled like a Tinkertoy and built again.

But to those who had to move out of its path, and to

those more sensitive to its implications, the Southwest urban renewal plan had other lessons—that urban renewal was a destructive force, that it created imbalances in the social order of the city, and that it was in reality reverse land reform, a further concentration of land wealth rather than its dispersal.

Today, Southwest is pleasant enough for those who can afford to live there, although it is one of the less vibrant communities of the city. The high-rise apartment buildings cater to affluent isolation, and the poor, in almost perfect imitation of the evils Southwest was supposed to correct, live in a reconstructed ghetto at one end. In this model community, a census tract with a median income of $5,000 abuts one with a median income of $24,000. In all, the federal and local government had poured $185 million into the area by 1969 and in return was receiving some $3.6 million annually in taxes which, even ignoring the new costs to the city, was less than 2 percent of the investment. The government would have done better by opening a savings account.

The people who had lived there before moved elsewhere, adding some to the welfare rolls, some to the demand for public housing, some to the crime rate, and some to the decline in the city's small businesses. Some were relocated in Southeast Washington, only to be forced out again when a new freeway plowed through their homes.

Although urban renewal went on apace, it was not until the 1968 riots that it received its next major push. A month and a half after the uprising, Commissioner Washington had said, "We must begin our planning now. According to reports, some cities affected by civic disturbances, for one reason or the other, have not proceeded with planning and rebuilding at a very rapid pace. We cannot permit this to happen in Washington. I propose . . . that planning for the rebuilding effort be completed in 100 days from today. In this way, we can start actual rebuilding before the end of the summer." In fact, five years later, only three housing projects had been completed in the riot areas, and construction had begun on another three.

Congress had committed $137 million for the city's reconstruction. Buildings had been torn down, others had been boarded up. Vacant lots remained vacant lots. Said School Board president Marion Barry of the Fourteenth Street riot corridor, "All that's happened since 1968 is a groundbreaking for a health center. I don't see how you can say that's progress."

Some thirteen hundred acres had been designated urban renewal areas but the results were dismally familiar: urban renewal was far more effective for demolishing, vacating, and deadening a community than it was for rebuilding it. Acres of land were removed from the tax rolls for years at a time. Speculators hung on to unused buildings, waiting for the right break. And neighborhoods were debilitated by the constant reminders of failure.

The plans, mired in red tape and confusion, left much to be desired. A white-collar office building was projected for the heart of the inner city. While 70 percent of riot-hit Shaw required low to moderate income housing, only a third of the planned construction was in that price range. And there was growing suspicion that the unstated agenda for Shaw was not unlike that of Southwest: the removal of economically marginal residents so the land, situated close to downtown, could be put to more profitable uses.

Even Walter Fauntroy, the foe of Southwest, seemed more interested in serving development interests than the needs of Shaw's residents. As head of MICCO, the community's urban renewal citizen advisory arm, Fauntroy helped to sell Shaw and the city on urban renewal. But as time went on, it seemed clear that whatever would happen to Shaw, many of its residents would not be around to enjoy it. Like other urban renewal, Shaw urban renewal was for someone else. Far from humbled by the growing evidence of failure in Shaw, Fauntroy proposed to extend the city's power to plan by fiat by creating an urban development corporation, without democratic control, and with broad powers of condemnation, that could spread the new urban feudalism, government by planocracy, at will throughout the city.

Not all the available city land was taken by freeways and urban renewal. There were other techniques as well. The more than three hundred vacant acres at Ft. Lincoln were put on the block to the highest developer-bidder, and what had been promised by President Johnson to be a new town in-town was relegated to the status of government-subsidized commercial development, a Southwest without dislocation. In the course of planning Ft. Lincoln the initial goal of substantial low and moderate income housing got lost. Ft. Lincoln, still in process, will turn out, perhaps, as Southwest did, another satisfactory community for those for whom communities are built these days. For those living in unsatisfactory communities, it is just another hunk of potential land gone to someone else.

In other parts of town, rezoning provided the machinery. When the city proposed to rezone the West End, it was argued that land values were too high there to permit uses less intensive than the rezoning would have allowed. This ignored the fact that land values had risen precisely because of the expectation of rezoning. At McLean Gardens in Northwest Washington, a small pocket of moderate income housing in the affluent west of the park area, ITT, with the city's strong backing, proposed to evict some 2,000 tenants and replace their apartments with a massive office-motel-shopping-apartment complex. The District Building hailed the project as a boon to the city's tax base. But a study by Howard W. Hallman of the Center for Governmental Studies suggested this was an illusion. He found that the project would bring in $4.1 million in taxes annually but cost the city $4.174 million in services, or a deficit of $74,000, not including street and/or highway improvements that might run as high as $100 million. Residents nearby fought this project, as they fought similar projects along the Georgetown waterfront and at the prime corner of Wisconsin and Western. In a rare display of activism by middle-class whites, hundreds of Northwest residents marched up Wisconsin Avenue to protest the new developments. They realized that the curse of modern planning policy no longer enveloped only the poor. No neighborhood was immune.

Neither was downtown. During the sixties downtown became a study in contradictions. It was supposed to be dying, but there was six times as much office construction as in the previous decade. Business and government officials complained that fewer people were going downtown, but they built more parking lots for them. Although there were signs of decay, land values failed to fall with them. No one gave up property without a fight or the right price.

Actually, several phenomena were occurring at once. An old downtown aimed at a white retail market was declining. A sixteen-hour downtown was being turned into an eight-hour downtown. The building boom was taking place not on the site of the old downtown but several blocks to the west. Whether one viewed downtown as dying or growing depended on whether one stood on Fourteenth Street or Eighteenth Street, was black or white, or was there at 10:30 A.M. or 10:30 P.M.

Neither the government nor the major business groups dealt with the dichotomies of downtown. Instead they exploited or exaggerated the liabilities and then promoted a variety of schemes that accentuated them. The emphasis on office construction, with nine-to-five usage, contributed to both the rise in crime and the decline of restaurants and other night-time enterprise. The destruction of businesses for urban renewal, subway construction, and monumental projects such as the FBI building deadened downtown rather than revitalizing it.

Downtown increasingly became a daytime center for commuters rather than a full-time heart of a city. By 1960, Washington's central business district had already given up 62 percent of its land area to roads and parking. Even Los Angeles had not paid such homage to the automobile. Small businesses felt the crunch as they became increasingly isolated in clumps between large office buildings that failed to attract pedestrians past their facades. Other firms, uncertain whether they would be allowed to stay, spent no money on upgrading facilities. Added to all this was the racket, business disruptions, and traffic congestion caused by Metro construction; the fact that a city shopper had to pay 75 cents an hour to park downtown while the all-day commuter paid less than 40 cents an hour; and the fact that the pedestrian cycle of some major downtown lights lasted one-half the time required to cross the street. It was small wonder that the prophesy of downtown decay seemed destined to fulfill itself. It was not, however, the product of demographic deficiencies in the city's population, but the direct result of public policy carried out at extraordinary public expense. Yet in the end, downtown refused to die; it was too intrinsically healthy to be destroyed by the myopic visions of government planners and suburban-oriented businessmen.

Much as freeways, urban renewal, and other development had caused the city to reel in the fifties and sixties, there was more to come. Hindered in efforts to spread their plans horizontally, business and government proposed to move vertically, liberating valuable land from the city's height restrictions. A City Council commission took a look at the problems of urban renewal and suggested ways of streamlining the city's planning procedures so that development could be even more expeditiously accomplished than it had been in the past. And most of all there was Metro, the mass transit system.

As the freeways had been the loss-leader to bring people into suburbs, so Metro was to become the loss-leader to reexploit the city. The suburban boom was tapering off as the sixties came to a close. Social, economic, and environmental problems were finally catching up with the counties around the city. Benjamin Ronis and William Rucker wrote in the *Washington Post:* "There is increasing evidence that pressures surrounding land development similar to those underlying the exodus from the central cities to the suburbs are now building up in the outlying areas to a point where a mass return to the city is becoming a likelihood." They pointed out that no suburban community could ever hope to build a physical plant in 25 years that it took most center cities 150 years or more to develop.

Metro was crucial both to the continued transient use of the city by suburbanites and to the redevelopment of city land to encourage suburbanites to move back into Washington. Those who had fled the city now wanted it back.

At first, everyone loved Metro. Even the radicals in the Emergency Committee on the Transportation Crisis pressed for construction of the subway, primarily as a means of pointing out how foolish more highway construction was. But that was back in the days when Metro appeared to be a mass transit system and little else.

As construction began, however, and businesses and homes were taken for what everyone had thought was going to be an underground system, opposition to Metro cropped up. Some 800 families, 500 businesses and $10 million worth of parkland were scheduled to fall under the Metro knife. Further, it turned out that Metro was not just doing this for rights-of-way and stations. It was in the land-development business, using the Redevelopment Land Agency as a front to acquire property far in excess of transportation needs in order to encourage redevelopment around Metro stops. Near future Metro stops, strange things began happening. On Capitol Hill, the city and the White House began pressing for construction of a high-rise office building at Fourteenth and Pennsylvania SE in a residential community where office construction had been verboten for some twenty years.

Metro is designed to cost about $3 billion. This makes it, according to the *Washington Post,* the largest public works project in the history of the world—larger than the Aswan Dam or thirty years of TVA dam construction. The actual cost may run far higher.

About half of the $3 billion is coming from the federal government. Another billion is being raised out of the sale of bonds, sales that had so little potential that the Congress finally agreed to guarantee them.

Obviously, such a massive commitment is not being made merely to get people downtown faster. Metro's backers had something more in mind. Suburban congressman Lawrence Hogan (R-Md.) put his finger on it: "Metro will not only revolutionize life but it will create the biggest real estate boom we have ever seen."

That's what happened in San Francisco where the much more modest BART was started out of similar motivations. The local chamber of commerce took an ad in *Fortune Magazine* to boast: "Even without a single train running, rapid transit has made an impact. BART has triggered a building boom in the billions of dollars." And Larry Dahms, BART's director of planning told a reporter from *Science Magazine:* "The thing about a bus line is that it can be moved. But a rail transit stop will be there day after day, and this allows for development." Baron Haussmann's principals were being reiterated once again.

Beyond Metro's extraordinary costs and the questionable results of Metro-inspired development lies the question of whether Metro will really solve the area's transportation problems. It seems unlikely that it will. Even the most optimistic projections leave automobile traffic a major contributor to pollution and congestion after Metro's completion. Besides, the 98 planned miles of Metro, extensive as they are, bypass wide areas. And the whole system is not due for completion until 1979, leaving plenty of time for more traffic chaos.

Perhaps the most disturbing thing is the tremendous misallocation of resources. Washington needs a mass transit system, but it needs one right away, not in ten years, and it needs one that will serve city residents as much as suburban commuters.

In early 1973, Congress offered its solution to this problem. It authorized Metro to take over the four private bus companies in the area. Metro leaped to its new assignment with the enthusiasm and expense that had marked its subway construction operations. It immediately planned to purchase 600 new buses, projected a $13 million annual deficit (the private firms had lost about $500,000 in 1971), and studied the feasibility of installing computer ticket machines in its vehicles at the cost of thousands of dollars apiece.

A consulting study by London's mass transit system had suggested a different approach. London Transport argued that the problems of local transit centered on such factors as lack of off-peak ridership, free parking for government employees, lack of bus shelters, and adequate information. Metro's reaction was to order half as many bus shelters in the first year as LT had suggested —although, predictably, at twice the cost LT had estimated.

Some 80 percent of the local bus ridership is within the District; and some city residents ask why Metro, run by a regional board on which the District has only one-third of the votes, should be setting what is essentially city transit policy. Looking deeper, it was discovered in Metro's own projections that it intended, in the first five years of operation, to increase bus ridership dramatically in Virginia and Maryland but reduce it by 20 percent in the District. Even though the absentee owner of the old DC Transit, O. Roy Chalk, had been among the least loved public figures in DC, he at least could not cut service or raise fares without lengthy regulatory commission study and approval. Metro, DC residents found out belatedly, could do just about anything it wanted when it wanted, and four out of the six votes on the board belonged to the suburbs even though the city did have a veto on certain matters. DC had exchanged one absentee bus owner for another.

The sum of twenty years of bad planning has left its mark on Washington. Sometimes, as in the case of the freeways, the local residents have been able to mitigate the results. But sometimes, as with Metro, they did not become sophisticated enough fast enough to realize what was happening. Together, the effects of urban renewal, freeways, development, and Metro have resulted in major population shifts throughout the city. A game of demographic checkers has been played. The city has not solved its social and economic problems; it has moved them to the east, across the Anacostia River or, even better from a local official's viewpoint, into adjoining Prince Georges County. Tens of thousands of people have moved to make room for false solutions to the city's ills. The biggest crime in Washington over the past two decades was not auto theft or housebreaking but land larceny, the massive misappropriation of urban soil for profitable but essentially antisocial purposes.

Wherever people, institutions or businesses have occupied land that has a potentially more profitable use, a land grab has threatened. The city has been remade for the benefit of the federal bureaucracy, parasitic developers, combines, banks, and road-builders; and altered to maintain administrators and planners dependent upon the constant disruption of the human environment for their continued employment.

Avaricious intent and adolescent vision coalesced to mar the city. Those dedicated to profit and those dedicated to plans became partners. The myths were promulgated: freeways will save the city, urban renewal will save the city, Metro will save the city, rezoning will save the city, more density will save the city. We must have a plan. . . .

It didn't work. The eco-system of the city was much more complex than its rebuilders had imagined. They knew how to calculate floor-area ratio but not all the little factors that determine each of our relationships to our community: whether we like it or not, whether we make it or don't, whether we break or keep the law, and whether we help the community by our presence, become alienated from it, or become its ward.

We could try some other way. At a retreat held by a local planning organization, I suggested that for the hell of it we attempt to draw up a 1985 plan that did not include the construction or destruction of a single building —an exercise in nonstructural thinking. This was a liberal organization that had fought some of the major planning absurdities with which the city had been faced, but it still thought of planning in physical terms. The moderator responded to my suggestion by saying, "Well, we're all socialists here," and moved immediately back to the question of physical planning.

There are obviously many physical things that need to be done to the city—any city. But unless they are integrated into programs relieving the city's social and economic deficiencies they become mere totems of good intentions, without meaning beyond the symbolic.

This is one of the things the younger left has been trying to tell its predecessors—forget your master plans, your roads and new developments, and turn instead to the congestion, pollution, and sprawl caused by our social, political, and economic systems. The buildings will follow in turn.

How such an approach would change a city like Washington is just speculation. We have yet to begin to plan our cities so as to protect diversity, encourage freedom, accept intergroup tension and contention, and guarantee economic survival. A few years ago I made a stab at drawing up a list of alternative goals for Washington. I offer selections from the list without argument on their behalf simply to point out that there is another way of doing it, that we can break out of the heritage of overemphasis on physical planning that has done so much harm to Washington and other cities:

I. Government

1. Create elected neighborhood legislative councils and neighborhood executives for each community within the city of approximately 50,000 people. Each council member should represent approximately 2,000 people. As many government decisions as possible should be made at the neighborhood level.

II. Taxes and Finance

1. Make the income tax truly progressive including the treatment of capital gains as simple income.

2. Make the property tax progressive so that the more property one owns the higher rate one pays.

3. Institute a surtax on unearned income as a form of property tax on wealth other than real estate.

4. Eliminate the sales tax on necessary items.

5. Eliminate the tax exemption for income-producing property of nonprofit organizations.

III. Economic Improvement

1. Emphasize the recruitment of blue collar jobs to the city rather than white collar ones.

2. Provide low rent facilities for small businessmen in-

cluding open and closed stalls for artisans and craftsmen in the downtown area.

3. Construct public markets throughout the city in the tradition of farmers' markets where all varieties of goods could be offered by merchants unable to own or rent their own store.

4. Convert public utilities and banks to cooperatives.

5. Convert liquor stores and shopping centers to neighborhood cooperatives.

IV. Transportation

1. Provide democratically-controlled, subsidized public transit with emphasis on buses, jitneys and streetcars.

2. Use existing surface railroad lines for commuter routes.

3. End free parking downtown and institute a parking tax.

V. Planning and Housing

1. Prohibit the removal of usable housing from the market.

2. Establish neighborhood housing banks to provide funds for community housing programs.

3. End condemnation for convenience. Restrict eminent domain use to proven public necessity.

4. Rehabilitate all presently abandoned housing.

5. Provide downpayment loans and grants for home buyers.

6. Convert all but small apartment buildings into cooperatives or condominiums, thereby effectively eliminating the landlord, a major urban parasite.

7. Provide rehabilitation loans and grants for home owners.

Admittedly this only bites at the corner of what we need to do, but it does suggest that we can make substantial changes in how our cities are run without tearing them down block by block. In a city centered in the neighborhood, plans would flow up rather than down.

They would be directed towards specific improvements rather than vague projections of progress flying on the wing of massive redevelopment. We would know whether we were moving forward or backward for the decisions we would be making would be based on what we know best—our own community.

There would be problems: Where will you find the neighborhood that will accept public housing or a narcotics treatment center?

The answer is partially that we may not need as many public housing units and narcotics treatment centers. Beyond that, those institutions or facilities considered necessary as a generality but undesirable in one's neighborhood would have to be apportioned according to an equalization procedure. It should be remembered that under traditional liberal planning principles very few public housing units or narcotic treatment centers have shown up in white liberal neighborhoods.

A city organized along lines suggested here would not eliminate conflict, rather it would make it productive. The conflict between the wide variety of interests that make up a city would not be swept under the rug as much contemporary planning tries to do. We would not love each other, but simply get along better.

It would require a major reordering of values to permit such a change to occur, for it would mean that for our cities we valued cooperation before profit, liberty before sterile order, justice before efficiency, happiness before precision, people before institutions, and the building of communities before bureaucracies. And for Washington, of course, it would require the right to run things our own way.

Gurney Norman, writing in the *Whole Earth Catalog*, put it well:

> I think the thing we're talking about is no more or less hard to understand than the simple desire to have a home.

The Urban Gang Bang

A home, and a sense of home that can only grow out of a sense of place. Cities aren't places anymore. They're scenes, projected on screens, then bulldozed away, neighborhood by neighborhood, like canceled TV shows.

People who are tired of scenes are leaving, or wanting to, anyway, longing for a place, torn between the joy of getting out of town, and a vague despair that maybe there ain't no such a thing as place after all, that maybe all there is to do is ride around in outfitted buses, floating along the bloodless traffic arteries of the world.

8 / You Gotta Technique 'Em

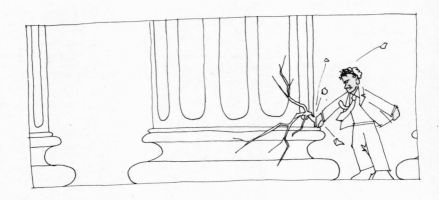

WASHINGTONIANS REACT TO THE CITY'S POLITICAL
status in varied ways. Some have resigned themselves to it; some ignore it; some are not aware of it;
some have capitalized upon it; and some have fought to
change it. To the poor of the city the matter may seem
quite irrelevant compared to their more immediate problems. To the businessman with contacts on the Hill and
at the District Building (and to those he contacts), the
present situation may be quite satisfactory. To long-time
residents, the District's status may appear as sadly inevitable as the summer humidity. And among those oriented towards the federal government—the powerful
and the wealthy who gather at cocktail parties to discuss
the latest national scandal, the political futures of their
peers, or the esoterica of their bureaucratic specialty—
the city may be seldom mentioned except as an impedi-

ment to automobile travel, a threat to their personal safety, or a dwindling source of reliable maids.

But there are still many people who throw themselves into the problems of Washington with vigor, if not always with wisdom. They have become accustomed to failure and to having their efforts ignored by the government, by the federal and suburban oriented press, and by their friends.

Many of them have adopted the city. Commissioner Walter Washington came to DC from Georgia. School Board President Marion Barry moved from Tennessee, and activist Julius Hobson was born in Alabama. Lately, I have begun to collect the names of native Washingtonians who are active in the city; the list is not growing very fast. It includes such people as school board member Charles Cassell, Delegate Walter Fauntroy, City Council aide Kirk White, *Post* editorial writer Bob Asher, and Marilyn Robinson, a black television reporter whose ancestors worked on Mount Vernon. In other cities, such a jingoistic game would quickly get out of hand; in Washington it's quite manageable.

The lack of a powerful native elite (with the exception of the Dunbar High School clique in the school system) makes it easy for concerned, impatient, or ambitious outsiders to make a mark on the city. In a town full of transients, strangers are welcome. In fact, because the newcomers have not spent their full lives in a colony, they often provide a valuable counterforce to the feeling of futility that sometimes appears to grip the city. They know it can be different.

Although there are some DC leaders who have had both national and local prominence—ADA's Joseph Rauh has been a long-time leader in the home rule fight and Stokely Carmichael headed the local Black United Front for a while—the national and local leaderships do not generally overlap. Only when national figures like Lyndon

Johnson, Robert Kennedy, or Hubert Humphrey take an interest in DC problems do their white groupies in Georgetown and Cleveland Park follow suit. And with the exception of Carmichael, no black national leader has shown much interest in the District.

Today, the local leadership for change is far more diffuse than earlier when a small core of white and black liberals carried the banner against the troglodytes of the Board of Trade and Capitol Hill. Some of the older leaders are still active. Flaxie Pinkett, a black real estate entrepreneur and former Democratic National Committeewoman, is on the Board of Higher Education. Polly Shackleton served on the first city council following the District government's reorganization in the late sixties and was one of its more effective and progressive members. Joe Rauh shows up at fund-raisers and lobbies on the Hill. But the death of black lawyer and one-time Democratic National Committeeman Frank Reeves in 1973 seemed to mark the end of an era. They hung a large sign out of a window at Pride headquarters with his name on it and the inscription, "In Deepest Respect." Reeves had been there before the phrase "black power" was coined—when everyone knew who Frank Reeves was because he had power and only a few blacks did.

But the old-style leadership was insufficient for the restless sixties and the decade spawned many new leaders, some seizing the time and others just seizing the profits of the time. Among those who rose to prominence were ministers like Walter Fauntroy and Channing Phillips, who were as different from each other as both were from the older prototypal voices of the black religious community—the ones Julius Hobson described as "ministers, preachers, deacons, deaconnesses, Eastern Stars, and other assorted heavenly bodies." Of the two, Fauntroy, the Baptist and SCLCer, understood better how to mix politics and religion, drawing on a fundamentalist constituency to propel himself into Congress as nonvoting delegate. Phillips, a suave activist who had formed a major nonprofit housing corporation, challenged Fauntroy in the 1970 Democratic primary, but was beaten badly. Phillips in 1968 had been elected Democratic National Committeeman on a slate committed to Robert Kennedy. In the wake of Kennedy's assassination, Phillips went to Chicago and emerged as the favorite son candidate of the black delegates—the first black to be nominated for president at a major party convention. But this distinction apparently pulled little weight back home. Caught between the carefully packaged "get it all together" street chutzpah of Fauntroy and the stolid conservatism of black city councilman Joseph Yeldell, Phillips ended up relying heavily on a white liberal constituency and trailing both his major opponents.

Phillips and Fauntroy were not the only ministers out front. Black Unitarian David Eaton and white Presbyterian Phillip Newell were ubiquitous activists. The Rev. Doug Moore, an affable dashiki militant, led the Black United Front in efforts to restrain the excesses of the police. In Capitol East, ministers were particularly effective with blacks like Jesse Anderson and Joshua Hutchins and whites like Tom Torosian and Ralph Dwan frequenting community meetings and demonstrations more often than the pulpit. And it was an Alinsky-oriented Presbyterian minister, Robert Smith, who laid the groundwork for what was to become the powerful Capitol East Community Organization.

Washington, blessed and cursed with a surfeit of lawyers, also found many attorneys in the sixties turning their attentions to the city. Jack Dowdy kept taking DC Transit to court and served as counsel to a growing number of perpetual litigants. Bruce Terris's efforts ran the gamut from organizing community centers to chairing the Democratic Central Committee. Florence Roisman made housing law. Jean Camper Cahn, later to head Antioch's new law school in the District, sued the city on behalf of neglected citizens east of the Anacostia River. Peter Craig helped keep the highway department and developers at bay. And, if a civil liberties case was too extreme for the not undaring local American Civil Liberties Union, there were always gutsy lawyers like David Rein.

But you didn't have to be of the cloth or of the bar to make an impact. Welfare mothers like Etta Horne and public housing residents like Mary Lanier became strong local figures. Ralph Fertig led the once timorous Metropolitan Planning and Housing Association into challenges to the city's planning policies. Reginald Booker (behind shades and in front of a group called Niggers Inc.) was a forceful leader in the battles against freeways and government employment discrimination. Chuck Stone, editor of the *Afro-American* and later aide to Adam Clayton Powell, was in the forefront of many battles. And few understood and capitalized upon the half-impatient, half-acquiescent ambivalence of the local community better than Sterling Tucker.

For all these people, the problem of producing change was complicated by the lack of local democracy. Many of the issues were hardly controversial within the local community. Washingtonians would have voted down the Three Sisters Bridge or preventive detention overwhelmingly if they had been given the chance. But they weren't. Other approaches had to be used.

Lucille Goodwin understood the problem. Ms. Goodwin, it seemed, spent all day on the phone. Long-time resident of the old Langston Terrace public housing in Near Northeast, constantly cropping up on antipoverty boards and committees, ever-present at the big fights, chairwoman of the citizens' advisory arm of the Neighborhood Legal Services program, she had plenty to talk about. A memo had come in the mail that she wanted to

read, someone was putting something over on someone
else, or perhaps she just had to report that "those folks
messed themselves up good last night" at some local
meeting. She carried out her civic functions with an
energy more typical of one half her age, and she did so
despite an ill and old husband who had to be helped in
and out of rooms and who would sit quietly in a corner
fiddling with a little plastic soldier while his wife took
on the accumulated offenses of the system. It was her
intensity and concern more than her language that carried her through, and she would toss around translit-
erated multisyllabic words like confetti. Everyone knew
just what Lucille Goodwin meant even if they hadn't
fully understood what she said.

One day she ended her call with a message that hung
around. "You know how you got to treat them people
downtown?" she asked, and then without waiting offered
the solution: "You gotta technique 'em."

The words have come back many times, watching
Washingtonians attempt to change things without waiting for the right to do it. It is one thing to use political
power; it is another thing to be denied political power
and still produce change. It was the latter talent that a
number of exceptional and unexceptional Washingtonians developed following the awakening of a local civil
rights movement. The old-line groups, like the white
liberals in the Home Rule Committee, the local NAACP,
and the black ministers would plod along with traditional lobbying, petitions, and failure, and increasingly
they would be estranged from agitators, troublemakers,
and radicals like Julius Hobson, Sammie Abbott, and
Marion Barry. The newer activists realized that without
the vote, the policymakers would be influenced only by
techniques and strategies that surprised, confounded,
aggravated, delayed, or just plain scared them.

Washington had had uppity community voices in
the past. Thomas Jefferson had once remarked of blacks:

"It appears to me that in memory they are equal to whites; in reason, they are much inferior, as I think it is impossible to find a black capable of tracing and understanding geometry; and in imagination they are dull and tasteless. . . ."

Shortly thereafter, Washington's surveyor Benjamin Banneker finished his Almanac. He sent a copy to Jefferson along with a letter that commented:

How pitiable it is that although you were so fully convinced of the goodness of the Father of mankind, you should go against His will by detaining, by fraud and violence, so many of my brothers under groaning captivity and oppression; that you should at the same time be guilty of the most criminal act which you detest in others.

A century later, Frederick Douglass would take another American hero to task as he spoke at the unveiling of a statue of a standing Lincoln, hand on a freed but still kneeling slave:

Truth is proper and beautiful at all times and in all places, and it is never more proper and beautiful in any case than when speaking of a great public man whose example is likely to be commended for honor and imitation long after his departure to the solemn shades, the silent continent of eternity. It must be admitted, truth compels me to admit, even here in the presence of the monument we have erected to his memory, Abraham Lincoln was not, in the fullest sense of the word, either our man or our model. In his interests, in his associations, in his habits of thought, and in his prejudices, he was a white man. He was preeminently the white man's President, entirely devoted to the welfare of the white man. . . .

But while scattered rebellion to the established way dotted the city's past, it was in the last two decades that it became, for more than a few Washingtonians, a way of life. Among them was Marion Barry.

You Gotta Technique 'Em

In 1963, Barry quit his $5,500-a-year post teaching chemistry at Knoxville College in Tennessee and joined the Student Nonviolent Coordinating Committee. He soon showed up in Washington to head the local SNCC office. Barry early formed an improbable and ultimately nearly explosive partnership with an erstwhile farm implements manufacturer, salesman, self-styled nutrition expert, and economic theoretician named L. D. Pratt. Barry was lean, black, soft-spoken, self-contained, and given to wearing a straw plantation style hat; Pratt was husky, white, excitable, demonstrative, and covered his baldness with a felt hat that made him appear a character out of a one-column cut in a forties edition of *Time* magazine.

Barry and Pratt's first "good shot," as L. D. liked to call things that worked out well, was a one-day boycott of the local bus system. DC Transit, whose service had declined and fares risen under the ownership of New Yorker O. Roy Chalk, was seeking another fare hike.

Using an elaborate communications system installed in the basement office of SNCC and its alter ego, the Free DC Movement, Barry and Pratt supervised a mass protest that kept thousands of Washingtonians off the buses. They stayed home, walked, rode in car pools, or used one of the many free rides provided by volunteers.

I was one of the volunteers. On the morning of January 24, 1966, I hauled myself out of bed, swallowed a cup of coffee, warmed up my '54 Chrysler, and made my way to Sixth and H Streets Northeast, one of the assembly points for volunteer jitneys. A boycott organizer filled my car with three highschool girls and a middle-aged and rather fat woman.

A bus drove by and it was empty. "They're all empty," the woman said. It was the first bus I had seen that morning and I wondered if she was right.

If both the fat lady and her husband worked, the five cent fare increase Chalk was seeking would cost them two week's worth of groceries over the course of a year.

I let my passengers off and headed back to Sixth and H. At Florida and New York, I counted five empty or near-empty buses. It wasn't even nine o'clock in the morning and the boycott was working.

"It's beautiful," the man in the slightly frayed brown overcoat said after he told me he was headed for Seventeenth Street. "It's working and it's beautiful. Hey, you see those two there. Let's try and get them."

I pulled over to the right lane by a stop where two men stood.

"Hey man, why spend thirty cents? Get in," my rider called to the pair.

"You headed downtown?"

"Yeah, get in."

"Great. It's working, huh? Great!"

At the delicatessen at Twenty-fourth and Benning, one of the assembly points, a young black who worked with SNCC greeted me: "Been waiting all morning for a car to work from here; said they were going to have one, but they didn't send it. Want a cup of coffee?"

"Thanks."

"I'm tired, man. Been up all night down at the office. We got some threats. One bunch said they were going to bomb us, but they didn't."

The SNCC worker went to the pay phone and tried to reach the office. He couldn't. "Let's go out to Thirty-fourth and Benning."

We got into my car and continued east on Benning. Lots of empty buses. "We've got to live together, man. You're white and you can't help it. I'm Negro and I can't help it. But we still can get along. That's the way I feel about it."

I agreed.

"You ever worked with SNCC before?"

"Nope," I said.

"Well, I'll tell you man, you hear a lot of things. But they're a good group. They stick together. You know, like if you get in trouble, you know they're going to be in there with you. If you get threatened they'll have people around you all the time. They stick together. That's good, man."

Later, I picked up a man at a downtown bus stop. The woman in the back seat asked him, "You weren't waiting for a bus, were you?"

"No. I just figured someone would come along and pick me up."

"That's good, 'cause if you were waiting for a bus I was going to bop you over your head."

We all laughed and the man reassured her again.

"You know," the woman in back continued, "there were some of the girls at work who said they were going to ride the bus and they really made me mad. I thought I'd go get a big stick and stand at the bus stop and bop 'em one if they got on Mr. Chalk's buses. Some people just don't know how to cooperate. And you know, you don't have nothing in this world until you get people together. . . . Hey, lookit over there, let's see if that guy's going out northeast. . . ."

People were sticking together that Monday. I carried seventy-one people, only five of them white. SNCC estimated that DC Transit lost 130,000 to 150,000 fares during the boycott. Two days later, the transit commission, in a unanimous but only temporary decision, denied DC Transit the fare hike. The commission's executive director drily told reporters that the boycott played no part in the decision. He was probably right. The commission worried about such things as cash dividends, investor's equity, rate of return, depreciated value, and company base. The boycotters worried about a nickel more a ride. And in the end, the commission was to approve the fare hike and then more; a few years later the fare was up to forty cents.

But the bus boycott was important, anyway. Never had so many Washingtonians done anything so irregular and contrary to official wishes. The assumption that DC residents would passively accept the injustices of their city was shattered. SNCC and the Free DC Movement had laid the groundwork for future action.

Although the life of the Free DC Movement would be measured in months, it seemed like years to those of us involved, so much was crammed into its short existence. Barry and Pratt both worked themselves to the marrow and it was during those months that Barry first gained the lingering reputation for always being late for appointments, news conferences, and actions. "I work on CPT—colored people's time," explained Barry, but he took a phenomenon and raised it to an art form. The press, in particular, would bitch, but since Barry was shaking up the city, they mostly waited anyhow.

Barry's subsequent moves in his drive for passage of right-to-vote legislation in Congress included an effort to get businessmen in downtown stores and along H Street (a black shopping area second only to downtown in commercial importance) to support the Free DC Movement by displaying its sticker in their windows. Hundreds of orange and black stickers with the slogan "Free DC" below a shattered chain went up in store windows; but the threat of a business boycott led other merchants to cry blackmail, and some of the more traditional civil rights and home rule leaders began to back away from Barry's tough tactics.

In the coming months, Barry and his organization would disrupt the calm of the city with increasing frequency. A number of Free DC supporters were arrested at the annual Cherry Blossom Festival. By the following fall, Barry would have been arrested three times, for failing to "move on," for disorderly conduct, and for holding a Free DC block party without official sanction.

Barry used his arrests to make points. After being arrested for failing to move on at a policeman's order, Barry said, "It is a bad law that gives policemen the sole discretion in such matters. Especially in Washington where the cops are so uneducated and awful. They use the law as a harassing device against Negroes." And he warned, less than two years before the 1968 riot, that the attitude of police might lead to an outbreak of racial violence.

While Barry was on the streets, on the tube, in court, and in jail, his associate, L. D. Pratt, was developing a reputation as the mystery man behind the operation disturbing the tranquility of the colonial capital.

Pratt refused to be interviewed by reporters and, although it was known that he was closely involved in setting up the bus boycott, few knew who he was or what he was up to.

By the time Pratt was sixteen, he had lived in Missouri, Kansas, Iowa, Virginia, and Hyattsville, Maryland, a suburb of DC. He worked for a bank in Maryland, selling farm implements in the midwest and trying to pull bankrupt businesses out of hock. At the time of the bus boycott, the 39-year-old Pratt was unemployed. His wife was supporting the family along with what money L. D. could bring by running a car pool. Meanwhile, when he wasn't involved in Free DC and SNCC business, he was at the Library of Congress where he studied food nutrition.

Pratt was fascinated by agriculture and agricultural problems. He wanted to revise the whole system and I never saw him more excited than when he developed plans, which failed, for a takeover by a civil rights and antipoverty coalition of the multimillion dollar Greenbelt Consumer Services, one of the nation's earliest and most financially successful cooperatives.

The rural and urban strains of Pratt's personality were only one of the conflicting characteristics of this extraordinary man. His talk reflected his ambivalences as he mixed street jargon with academic terms in a cacophonic lingo all of his own: "Look, man, those cats gotta implode their power base before they do anything." He was an activist and a thinker; a short-term planner and a long-term dreamer.

The pair belied their public images in person. Barry, the mortal threat to peace and order, was personally a gentle and quiet individual and Pratt, the mystery man, was, out of range of the press, an open and loquacious person.

Pratt described his relationship with Barry this way: "I am the theoretician and Marion is the practitioner. I just give suggestions and he makes the decisions. I respect his opinions more than my own."

Barry and Pratt not only upset policemen and government officials; they perturbed the established civil rights and home rule leadership in the city. While a few such leaders, Walter Fauntroy prime among them, were careful not to undercut Barry and provided as much help as they felt they could, others were plainly annoyed by the upstarts.

Tensions grew when the Free DC Movement decided to take on the White House Conference on Civil Rights that had been scheduled for May 1966. Barry planned to raise the issue of home rule at the conference and, in announcing the plans, chastised the moderate Coalition for Conscience for "wavering" in its support of the plan. Two days later the *Washington Post* reported, "Washington civil rights leaders yesterday pondered the future of the campaign for home rule in light of the growing independence on the part of Free D.C. Movement leader Marion Barry Jr. One leader said it appears that the Movement was at 'the end of its relationship with the Coalition of Conscience,' the city's loosely knit confederation of ministers and civil rights groups."

But it was not just the Free DC's militancy and independence that upset the old leaders. They also were profoundly disturbed by the rise of the black power idea; Coalition co-chairman Channing Phillips stated, "The black nationalist stand of SNCC is inconsistent with the Coalition's philosophy."

That stand, which foreshadowed a massive shift in black thought, was to affect the local scene dramatically. I felt it early. One of the last times I visited the SNCC office, we were meeting in the basement when a woman worker drew a breath and said, "Ooo, here comes the Panther." It was Stokely Carmichael. The movement was off on a new course and whites, even those angered by the paranoiac reaction to black separatism expressed by the Coalition of Conscience, began to realize that it was time to draw back and find a new course, too. Pratt continued to play a major role for some time, but his ability to work with Barry declined sharply and, feeling physically threatened in the growingly separatist atmosphere, he dropped out of the local scene.

But before that, the Free DC Movement was to play a major part in bringing the issue of self-determination further in Congress than it had been in almost a hundred years. The militancy of the Free DC Movement, so disliked by both Congressmen and civil rights moderates alike, provided the counterpressure necessary to scare more than a few legislators into thinking that maybe it was about time for a little self-government in DC. In 1967 President Johnson reorganized the local government. In 1968 the city got an elected school board.

And before it was over, Barry and Pratt had one more "shot." Hauling an odd assortment of black and white activists off to a weekend retreat, the pair organized a lecture, seminar, and planning sessions to pave the way for a massive push against slum housing. In fact, that's what it was going to be called: PUSH, People United against Slum Housing. It would be no ordinary effort. Barry theorized that the reason slumlords were invulnerable was because protests were usually directed against only a small portion of their holdings. If you could uncover the full economic interests of a slumlord, including his commercial holdings, you could organize an effective boycott against him.

From L. D.'s theoretical charts and Marion's discourse, the action moved to strange places like a hall at a Catholic woman's college where volunteers sorted out thousands of paper slips containing important information about DC eviction cases over the past two years, and the basement of the Court of General Sessions, where a friendly judge had permitted the group space to do its research closer to the source material. The little slips of paper slowly built up information concerning slumlords, lawyers, front corporations, and their interconnections. From the long tables in the basement of the Court of General Sessions, the slips went to the Recorder of Deeds office where more volunteers began arduously sifting through official records. The project never got much beyond that. Perhaps it fell of its own weight—the task of organizing all those slips of paper without a computer was staggering. Perhaps the separate directions in which various participants went was a factor. In any event, the days of the Free DC Movement were just about over.

Barry was tired, near collapse, some thought. But Marion had another plan. The plan was Pride, Inc., one that would be seen to fruition, a government-funded youth training and economic development project that was to grow despite the vicissitudes of being black, young, and contentious. It survived GAO audits and sniping from black-hating congressmen. Through its subsidiary, Pride Economic Enterprise, Inc., it operated about a half-dozen gas stations, a house painting, landscaping and gardening service, and has even taken over some apartments.

Barry also became increasingly associated with the Washington establishment. Marion Barry could speak to, and would listen to, more people in DC than most. Not that he was yet a part of the establishment, but you had to include Barry because Barry could help make things happen or help keep them from happening. So it was Marion Barry to the Urban Coalition, Marion Barry to help the Commissioner cool a disturbance, Marion Barry to help press the latest protest on freeways. And finally, Marion Barry to the school board.

It was no radical coup. Julius Hobson, a far more radical man, had sat on the school board the first time it was elected, gaining more votes than any other candidate. As early as October 1966, a *Washington Post* poll of black residents had found Barry acceptable enough to be fifth in the list of Washingtonians who had "done the most for Negro people in the area."

Barry was aided by his ability to sponge up the best that others had to offer—from the anarchical genius of populist economist Pratt, from the increasingly uptight blacks discovering logical release from the frustrating failures of the civil rights movement in Pantherism, from lawyers, from street dudes, from cautious black moderates afraid of too much change too fast, from reformed exliberals like myself.

To many, however, it also appeared that as Barry gained power, he lost interest in the things that had brought him power. The edges were getting too smooth, he was getting too slick, and the old fight seemed to drain away. When the teachers went on strike for a much-needed pay increase, Barry moved to press court action against them on advice of the city's lawyers. But two other school board members acted more as Barry would have done a few years earlier; members Charles Cassell and Hilda Mason signed up as defendants in the case.

It was not an unfamiliar story of the early seventies. Up in New York City, someone had scribbled on a subway wall, "Jerry Rubin votes." The New Left fell apart; the Black Panthers were going into the churches; the

hippies had disappeared from M Street. And Marion
Barry was on the School Board.

If Marion had joined the establishment, however,
Sammie Abbott was still on the outside. By all rights,
Sammie Abbott should have been disqualified as a DC
leader on at least three grounds: he was too white and
too old, and he lived in the suburbs. Instead, Abbott, a
short man with a nail-file voice, has been the nemesis of
public officials for years.

Abbott worked high in an office building on Connecticut Avenue as a commercial artist. Between dabs of
rubber cement, he kept on the phone tracking down witnesses for the next freeway hearing, plotting strategy
against the Highway Department, always mad as hell
about something. Occasionally his eyes would break into
an elfish twinkle, but most of the time Abbott was an angry middle-aged man showing angry young men and
women how to be angry.

One of Sammie's advantages was his voice, which
interrupted more freeway hearings than did applause.
His hoarse fury roared through a room like coal crashing
down a chute.

"The people of the District," he told a group at the
proposed site of the Three Sisters Bridge, "are fighting
not only the highway department, the Congress of the
U.S., but the media—particularly the *Star* and the *Post*
—which are not only the handmaidens [of the highway
interests] but the prostitutes." Abbott said he was prepared to die in the fight. The *Post* reported:

> Abbott seemed to warm to the crowd as the crowd
> warmed to him. A physically small man, he seemed to
> grow as he almost yelled, "Before another inch of these
> damn freeways gets laid down in the District there's gonna
> be flames, there's gonna be fighting, there's gonna be re-
> bellion! And I for one—"
> He was drowned out by cheers and clapping and
> raised his fist in salute to the crowd.

It was that kind of talk that upset government officials. Commissioner Walter Washington was reported to have listed Sammie Abbott as one of his worst headaches. Unlike Barry, Abbott never compromised, never mediated, never sought popular appeal. And when the city compromised to get Abbott and the Emergency Committee on the Transportation Crisis (of which Sammie was publicity director) off its back, Abbott was right there to show how phony the compromise was.

Being a commercial artist, Abbott appreciated the value of graphics. The ECTC's posters and flyers were distinctively lively. When the bus company sought to raise fares, ECTC put out a flyer with a masked bandit holding up bus passengers. When the ECTC got wind of a city plan to run an eight-lane freeway through the heart of black Washington, Sammie designed a three-by-four-foot poster showing in large scale bright red exactly where the freeway would go and what buildings would be taken. The poster was headlined "White Men's Roads Through Black Men's Homes" and was plastered on walls all over the affected community. Within a few days, the city was denying that there ever was such a plan, but covertly obtained highway department maps told a different story. It appeared that the poster had almost single-handedly stopped a freeway in its tracks. One summer, driving back to Washington from vacation, I observed another huge poster plastered over one of the large freeway signs marking the entrance to the city. It contained photographs of the Commissioner and two city councilmen who had supported freeway construction and was headlined, "The Three Uncle Tom Stooges Who Sold Out." I knew I was home again.

Abbott's emphasis on the graphic perhaps encouraged the ECTC to concentrate on symbols. The North Central Freeway fight centered on sixty-nine homes that were condemned and then boarded up as the struggle went on in the courts and government offices. The sixty-nine homes were talked about endlessly and finally Abbott and other ECTC members went out to them and got themselves arrested unboarding the buildings. The North Central would have taken many more homes than the sixty-nine, but it was those that made the issue come alive.

While Abbott gave the ECTC a good deal of its sense of drama, many others played important roles. The ECTC was, in the late sixties, one of the few places you could find white and black radicals getting together on an issue. Not only that, the ECTC provided a forum in which moderates and even conservatives could operate as well. The ECTC carefully avoided the exclusionary tactics of the black and white left for an approach more in the style of Saul Alinsky. It made freeways everyone's fight, not in a namby-pamby Common Cause or Urban Coalition sort of way, but by recognizing that its own radicalism was not for everybody and welcoming supporting actions from anyone who cared.

So it was that black militant Reginald Booker and white proper Georgetowner Grosvenor Chapman could share the speakers platform at an ECTC rally and that little white ladies who didn't want freeways next door would be welcomed as witnesses at hearings even though they might not wish blacks next door either.

As well as anything can work in a town denied political power, the ECTC strategy worked. The ECTC-fostered coalition of antifreewayites, a parallel struggle in the courts, and the unremitting opposition to even an inch of new roads, slowly halted freeway projects, despite both local and federal support. And the ECTC taught the people how to technique not only their own appointed administrators, but the President and Congress of the United States as well.

The Free DC Movement and the Emergency Committee on the Transportation Crisis were dramatic examples of Washingtonians learning to take power denied them. But there were smaller shifts in places that seldom got into the news.

You Gotta Technique 'Em

At Friendship House, an old-time settlement house on Capitol Hill that had become one of the city's antipoverty centers, a black coup took place. Friendship House had been run by a white director and a board dominated by persons who not only weren't black but didn't live in the community. Following a firebombing at the house and increased pressure from blacks, the old board attempted to preserve its position by nominating a more broadly based executive committee without altering the fundamental balance of power. But blacks and whites on the board and in the community refused to cooperate. To a person, they declined bids to serve, leaving the board with the potential of an executive committee totally unrepresentative of the community being served. The nominating committee returned to the board and reported it could not produce a slate. Though short of votes, the community had shown that it was not short of power. The old guard capitulated and shortly Friendship House had a black director and a black chairman of the board.

Things didn't always go that smoothly. Just north of Friendship House was Near Northeast, a community served by another antipoverty agency, the Community Improvement Corporation. Unlike Friendship House, the CIC was a creation of the war on poverty; before its birth, Near Northeast had been without a major service agency.

For several years, the CIC operated what amounted to a federally-funded school for internecine warfare. Its prime purpose, it appeared, was to self-destruct after an appropriately long period of torment. Feuding and factionalism replaced programs and, in a community where one-third of the population had less than an eighth-grade education, it was obvious that a surprising number of people knew *Robert's Rules of Order* by heart.

It was not really the community's fault. The federal government had suddenly laid a few hundred thousand dollars a year and the implication of power down on a community that had seen little money and less power and had said, "Do something."

One of the first things the community did was to fight over the money and power. By July 1967, a violent battle had erupted in which a dissident faction was claiming that incumbent officials had acted in a secret and dictatorial fashion, that scheduled elections had been delayed, that there were too many sets of conflicting bylaws for the various supervisory groups, and that minutes were missing. The director and assistant director were at loggerheads and each was rapidly developing a loyal cadre of supporters who increasingly did battle with one another.

Meetings and countermeetings were held and, as tempers rose, the parliamentary ploys became more exotic. One CIC board member commented, "If you plan to come into this group with nothing but good intentions, you're going to get your head bashed in." At one "call meeting" (a meeting held on petition of members), the chairman of the citizen's advisory committee told those present that the meeting was illegal and could not be held. Immediately, the vice chairman, the Rev. Frank Milner, stood up in the back of the room and announced that the meeting would go on and requested everyone to turn their chairs around. Most did, leaving the chairman dumbfounded in what was now the rear.

The chairman probably deserved it. He had a tendency to say things like, "I don't play politics with the poor people. I made the first effort to bring this program to Near Northeast and I can exert enough pressure to do what I want, chairman or not." He was asking for trouble.

Even the intervention of the Lord didn't help much. The Rev. Mr. Milner, a courtly black Republican, had constantly tried to soothe heated meetings by invoking the Christian spirit. And the Bishop R. H. Prince, a combination storefront preacher and cab driver, stood up at one CIC meeting, replete in clerical collar and cabbie's change maker, and intoned: "Calm the tempest, bridle tongues, and govern our thoughts." It didn't work.

The minutes of the CIC bring back the flavor, if not the purpose, of the dispute:

> The meeting was held on the above date with Mr. Swaim presiding. As a background he reviewed the Annual Assembly of Delegates which was not held because there was no quorum, and questions concerning the By-Laws, missing minutes and the fact that the Executive Committee minutes were not available.
>
> —May 25, 1967
>
> Mrs. Mayo felt that all people should be allowed to speak. Mr. Geathers stated that it was not legal for non-members to participate. Mrs. Mayo then asked, "Who are the members?" Mr. Geathers stated that we were going to establish definitely the answer to this question.
>
> —May 11, 1967

Things went from bad to worse. From the federal government and the United Planning Organization, the city's umbrella antipoverty agency, came no assistance. Asked in the summer of 1967 whether UPO was aware of the problems in CIC, the agency's acting director said, "We understand they're having discussions."

On July 13, 1967, the CIC board reelected its chairman, who had been continually at odds with the agency's director. In September, a board meeting broke up in chaos because several members objected to letting the assistant director speak. And on September 28, Elmer Geathers was ousted as chairman at a call meeting of the CIC board and replaced by Bruce Hyman, a thoughtful barber who had antagonized fewer people than most of those involved in the struggle. A dispute over the location of the meeting found the anti-Geathers bloc assembling at the CIC office at 1326 Florida Avenue NE while Geathers and his supporters met at Calvary Episcopal Church, about ten blocks away. Geathers was unable to produce a quorum for his meeting; as he made frantic phone calls, a church choir rehearsed "Lord Have Mercy on Me" on the other side of the undercroft. Geathers and his group finally decided to go to Florida Avenue, but when they got there they found that Geathers had been ousted and Hyman was firmly in charge.

The feuding, however, did not end and still no assistance came from downtown. The war on poverty offered the poor money; the ground rules did not provide for technical assistance, like accountants to help straighten out fouled-up books or lawyers to help with the complexities of getting a quarter-million-dollar-a-year organization off the ground.

Finally, in early 1968, UPO's new director, Wiley Branton, stepped into the dispute. He announced at a January 25 meeting that he was taking charge of the situation. In a speech delivered with a fervor more reminiscent of a preacher than a poverty official, Branton laid down a series of "suggestions" that were unanimously adopted by the CIC board. His comments for reorganizing the CIC were punctuated with repeated murmurs of "Tell it" and "Amen" as he lit into the failures of the Near Northeast antipoverty program and of the organization to which he had come. He told the CIC: "I cannot sit by and let any program become ineffective so that it not only hurts Near Northeast but the entire poverty program in the District. We must attempt to salvage the program. We must wash and cleanse our hands." Branton decried what he called the two extremes of philosophy among poverty workers. One is that "poor people had the God-given right to determine the most technical matters imaginable. It just ain't so." The other extreme he said was the "intellectual paternalism" among workers who not only felt they knew what was best for the poor but what the poor ought to say about their problems.

Things began to slowly resolve themselves in the following months. But for the leadership of Near Northeast, assuming power and learning to deal with those who had still more power had been a painful and halting affair. Hours had been frittered away in pointless parliamentary hassles and thousands of dollars had been wasted by a system that tended to rate progress in the war against want by the number of block clubs organized. There was the 1400 Block of Fourteenth Street Block Club, and the Near Northeast Progressive People's Association, a bolshevik-sounding organization whose major achievement was getting some free grass seed from the city government. Nevertheless, the antipoverty program in Near Northeast, for all its failings, had propelled the area into the consciousness of city officials; and in learning to fight each other, Near Northeast also learned how to fight downtown. Out of the fracas came leaders like Lola Singletary who was to end up on the city's library board of trustees, and John Anthony, a gentle but tough man who became a power in a number of civic organizations, including a term as first vice president of the Metropolitan Washington Planning and Housing Association, a group that only a few years earlier had been the preserve of white noblesse obligers. And Lucille Goodwin, the woman who said, "You gotta technique 'em," wound up as chairman of the citizen advisory arm of the Neighborhood Legal Services program.

The John Anthonys, Lola Singletarys, and Lucille Goodwins were part of a massive transfer of power in Washington that was presaged by the breakdown of segregation in the fifties and which began in earnest in mid-sixties. When Lyndon Johnson reorganized the city government in 1967 and Walter Washington took over as the appointed commissioner, blacks began to have a measure of mastery over local political affairs.

The transfer was not simple. It took several years for the Commissioner to gain enough nerve or energy to ease out major department heads carried over from the old administration. Several still remained, most notably the highway and recreation directors, but slowly the District Building became a different place. The number of blacks rose by the thousands although far more slowly in the upper than the lower ranks, and the clenched fist became a casual greeting in District Building corridors rather than a threat to local order.

Then the progress the city had made during the Johnson years started to evaporate as Richard Nixon determined to run the city once again as a tight little preserve, where executive whim could be exercised without reference to popular will. Lyndon Johnson had instructed the first appointed City Council to act as though it had been elected. For a while, the Council tried to take him seriously, but under Nixon not only the Commissioner but the City Council as well took cues from the White House, and in Washington it became increasingly clear that Nixon was the one. With a greatly expanded police department under the direction of a man who went to the Republican convention and GOP election night celebrations, with one-time activist blacks safely in well-paying but impotent government positions, and with local black businessmen and community organizations being fed grants in return for silence, Washington shifted from rebelliousness back toward compliance.

And then Julius Hobson was stricken with multiple myeloma, an incurable cancer of the spine.

Throughout the years of Washington's awakening, no one individual had changed the course and the psychology of DC more than Julius Hobson. In a city where it could be said that never had so many sold out for so little, Hobson refused to compromise. In a city where good causes were often victimized by the manipulations of hustlers, Hobson was a man of extraordinary integrity. In a city that tended to take a self-congratulatory respite following every step forward, Hobson kept pointing out the distance left to travel. And at the height of the era of black nationalism, Hobson married a white woman.

Julius Hobson was born in Alabama. His father ran a drug store and a cleaning plant; his mother was principal of a high school. They talked about education at the dinner table. Recalled Hobson: "Everybody who stayed in school learned to read. Learning to read was no big deal. Now, it was a lousy high school. They didn't teach languages—no Spanish, no German, no French, no Latin, very little history except General Lee. But out of that high school still came a group of students who were able to function in that they could read, write, spell, and communicate."

After the Second World War, where Hobson flew dozens of missions and won three bronze stars along with other medals, he attended Columbia University briefly, then ended up at Howard. There he was introduced to Marxist and radical thought, some of it from professors who would subsequently be fired during the McCarthy era.

After Howard, he got a job as a GS-5 junior professional in the Legislative Reference Service of the Library of Congress. After about six years there, he went to work for the Social Security Administration.

Slowly, Julius got more involved in civic activities. He started with the PTA, then the local civic association, then the Federation of Civic Associations (as vice president), then the NAACP.

But Julius was an angry man and the caution and propriety of such organizations could not contain his anger. As chairman of the local CORE branch, Hobson finally struck out on his own. To his detractors, his organization was just "six men and a telephone booth," but one by one old barriers began to fall.

Between 1960 and 1964, Julius Hobson ran more than 80 picket lines on approximately 120 retail stores in downtown DC, resulting in employment for some 5,000 blacks.

He initiated a campaign that resulted in the first hiring of black bus drivers by DC Transit.

Hobson and CORE forced the hiring of the first black auto salesmen and dairy employees and started a campaign to combat job discrimination by the public utilities that led to a permanent court injunction to prevent Hobson from encouraging people to paste stickers over the holes in punch-card utility bills.

Hobson directed campaigns against private apartment buildings that discriminated against blacks and led a demonstration by 4,500 people to the District Building that encouraged the District to end housing segregation.

He conducted a one man lie-in at the Washington Hospital Center that produced a jail term for himself and helped to end segregation in the hospitals.

His arrest in a sit-in at the Benjamin Franklin School in 1964 helped lead to the desegregation of private business schools.

In 1967, Julius Hobson won, after a long and very lonely court battle that left him deeply in debt, a suit that outlawed the existing rigid track system, teacher segregation, and differential distribution of books and supplies, and which led, indirectly, to the resignation of the school superintendent and first elections of a city school board.

Beyond all this, Hobson was repeatedly involved in the peace, police, and transportation issues; he filed a major suit in 1969 accusing the federal government of bias against blacks, women, and Mexican-Americans.

With such a record, one might have expected Julius Hobson to emerge as a national civil rights leader. His record of achievement was as impressive as the best of them and if he had wished to he could have drifted into the more comfortable world of semi-acceptance enjoyed by James Farmer, Whitney Young, Roy Wilkins, and even Martin Luther King in his later years—a world achieved by exchanging effectiveness for respectability and progress for power.

But Hobson eschewed power and he refused acceptability. He was equally frank about his Marxist philosophy and his atheism. He had an innate distrust of leaders, black or white, and he spoke disparagingly of the new leadership in the city government as "pasteurized Negroes."

There was no let-up in the Hobson irascibility. When he ran for nonvoting delegate in 1971, he did so for the express purpose of being permitted to raise hell on behalf of the District in the United States Congress. And if Hobson had been elected, he might have made the greatest black congressional hell-raiser, Adam Clayton Powell, look like a moderate.

Even prospect of an early death failed to chasten the man. He described the conversation he would have with the Lord, if there turned out to be one, as Hobson presenting a bill of particulars on behalf of the oppressed people still back on earth. And he concluded, "That's what I'd have to say to the Maker. And if the Maker doesn't like it, to hell with him."

In his office was a poster quoting Frederick Douglass:

> Those who profess to favor freedom, yet deprecate agitation, are men who want crops without plowing the ground; they want rain without thunder and lightning; they want the ocean without the awful roar of its many waters.

He might well have framed and set beside it some earlier words of William Lloyd Garrison:

> Tell a man whose house is on fire to give moderate alarm; tell him to moderately rescue his wife from the

hands of the ravisher; tell the mother to gradually extri-
cate her babe from the fire into which it has fallen.

It was Hobson's unflagging distaste for moderation
that led a city official to say in 1965, "He's never satisfied. He's never agreeable. You can't compromise with
him. He wants everything and refuses to barter or trade.
When the hell will he quit?"

But it was not just city officials and businessmen
who were sent up the wall by Hobson. When Julius was
in the hospital with his disease, a black woman patient
told him that she hoped he would die because he had
been nothing but trouble for black people. And if the
city's black population appreciated Hobson's years of
work on their behalf, they were more disturbed by his refusal to let things be, his atheism, and his white wife.
When he ran for delegate his strongest black support
came from younger and more radical voters rather than
from the older ones who had directly benefitted from his
efforts. One day during the campaign, Julius Hobson, on
the back of a flat bed truck, passed a bus driven by a
black driver. Through the loud-speaker, Hobson reminded the driver who had busted open DC Transit. The
bus driver gave him the finger.

But Julius was used to being alone: his aloneness
helped give him a perspective on the hustles and the
hassles around him. He remained aloof from the wave
of black nationalism that swept the city and the country
in the latter part of the sixties, and when people like
Marion Barry adopted a dashiki, he stuck to his pipe and
fedora, black tie, and conservative suits. When a white
peace leader apologized for racism in the peace movement following a public attack by a number of local
black politicians, Hobson said the man wasn't a racist
but a fool. And few things made him madder during the
delegate campaign than sniping references to his second
wife, Tina, a woman of great force and strength and an

activist in her own right. Julius remained one of the few
leaders in Washington who could lead an effective black-
white coalition. Hobson knew that nationalism and militancy were not synonymous, and he preferred militancy.

His coalitions, though never large, were given impact
by Hobson's flair for the dramatic and his sense of the
media. He knew how to get a headline and how to
frighten people. He threatened to capture rats in the poor
sections of town and release them in Georgetown, but he
knew that all he needed to do was ride around with a few
rats in a cage on top of a car to get the effect. And when
the American Civil Liberties Union gave its annual
award to Senator Joseph Tydings, Hobson copped the
coverage by leading a picket line outside the dinner to
protest an award to one who had played a leading part in
passage of the repressive DC crime bill.

The spirit of the man came out with every paragraph
that he spoke. House District Committee Chairman John
McMillan was a "rat." Joe Rauh, ADA and local home
rule leader, was a "milquetoast liberal," and J. Edgar
Hoover and the FBI were "a bunch of idiots."

When picketed businessmen told Julius Hobson,
"Bring in some people and we'll hire them," Hobson replied: "Baby, I ain't no employment agency. But I'm going to take 70 percent of your business away from you."

On delegate candidate Walter Fauntroy's constant
allusions to his work with Martin Luther King: "With all
respect to Martin Luther King, he is dead. He is not running for this seat. He will not be the man who will be on
the floor of the House." He also accused Fauntroy of
"running in the shadow of a dead man."

On a provision of the DC crime bill permitting no-
knock searches: "If anyone breaks down my door, I will
meet him with whatever I've got."

On Marxism: "Ideologically I consider myself a
Marxist. . . . I believe in socialism; I believe what we're
fighting over is the distribution of goods and services and

the production of them; and I believe that everybody on earth has the inalienable right to share in them."

On what he would do if elected to Congress: "My position is that, if elected, they can't isolate me from the House District Committee. I'll break up their goddamn meetings. What's going on up there anyway? Nothing but theft. I'd go to the floor of the House and speak until I'm tired. I wouldn't honor any procedure about my being a junior Congressman or any of that bullshit. I think for a while they need a real man up there, and if they throw me out—all right. Because then, at least, the people of the District will be forced to realize that if somebody gives you your freedom at their pleasure, they can take it away from you at their pleasure."

On democracy: "In this country, you don't have any democracy really. You have the right to elect but not to select. For example, here's two people: you get to vote for one of them. But you didn't choose in the first place either of them. That's not democracy from what I understand."

On being a politician: "Let me explain something to you. I am not a politician. A politician is someone who does things to get elected. He is a guy who says things to please the public, that he thinks the public wants to hear, and his story changes with every passing day. I want to be elected, but I am not going to say a damn thing for your benefit, or that person's benefit out there on the street, or anybody's."

On the nature of the struggle: "The struggle isn't whether you like a nigger or a nigger likes a cracker or whitey is a pig or any of that stuff. I've called people whitey and pig and the FBI never said a word. All I have to do is put on a dashiki, get a wig, go out there on Fourteenth Street, and yell, 'Whitey is a pig and I'm going to take care of him'—the FBI will stand there and laugh at me. But the moment I start to discuss the way goods and services are distributed and I start talking about the na-

ture of the political system and show that it's a corollary
of the economic system, that's when the FBI comes in
for harassment."

On capitalism: "Can black people ever win the fight
for freedom so long as they accept America's exploitive
capitalism as the economic system within which they
must wage the battle? Black leaders have not confronted
this question. Whether from a lack of understanding of
our economic and political systems or from an unwilling-
ness to challenge them, their silence is a betrayal of
trust of the black people they purport to lead."

On a local black minister: "I was asked to speak at
his church one Sunday. I went over there and when I
went there I looked over the congregation. I would say
the average person in there had on a pair of Thom McAn
shoes, that their suits cost an average of $35 apiece, that
their shirts were from Hecht's basements, and they were
very poor and very illiterate—almost illiterate—people
who were emotionally shocked, just came to the church
to let out this scream. [The minister] took up a love offering, he took up a minister's travel offering and then
he took up a regular—he took up five or six offerings. So
when he got to me to speak, I got up and said, 'God-
damnit, if this is Christianity I want no part of it,' and
'This son of a bitch is stealing from you, and the thing
is, he's not just stealing your money, he's stealing your
minds. And I refuse to be a part of this.' And I walked
off."

Julius Hobson changed the face of modern Washington as much as any single person. A statistician, he operated with a calculator and conviction. Sometimes the
changes came almost coincidentally in the churning
wake of his actions. When he filed suit against the school
system to end unequal expenditures, the rigid track system, and other inequities, he aimed the action against
the local city judges, since it was they, under a peculiar
provision of DC law, who were responsible for appoint-

ing the school board. The case was consequently bounced up to the U.S. Court of Appeals where Judge Skelley Wright issued his historic decision. It was not long after, in part because of the local judges' reluctance to get involved in the increasingly political issue of DC schools, that Congress granted the District an elected school board, the first elected local body in almost a hundred years.

But while Julius Hobson was a man as important to Washington in his way as Martin Luther King and Malcolm X were to the nation, he differed markedly from other charismatic figures in that he never developed a mass following. One local activist who worked closely with Julius for a number of years said, "He's a prophet; but he can't organize shit." Hobson's inherent suspicion of the system and its faults also occasionally enveloped his friends and coworkers as well. Remarks dropped at meetings like, "Everyone in favor of this idea say aye, the rest get the hell out of here," were only partly facetious and if you weren't pretty tough, it was easy to leave one of Julius's forays with hurt feelings. He got drummed out of CORE at one point in the midst of complaints against his dictatorial way of running the organization. He could be mercurial, be all in favor of an idea or a tactic one day, then dump on it the next.

But his irascibility was not really a personal thing. He was a loner and the pressures, frustrations, and compromises demanded of one man creating a movement left him irritated, impatient to the point that he would make a rigid decision just to keep things moving. In less public and less pressured situations, Hobson was extremely receptive to both ideas and criticisms. He both gave and received advice with a generous spirit that contrasted with his public image as an enfant terrible.

When Washington learned of his fatal illness, it reacted with the sort of reevaluation of a man's life that usually takes place after his death. The *Washington Post* ran a long interview series with Hobson. The *Evening Star and News* became solicitous. And a group of old friends and associates organized a testimonial evening that brought out 2,000 friends, enemies, and observers of Hobson from GOP City Council Chairman Jack Nevius to exstudent Stokely Carmichael. Hobson was there, sitting in a comfortable chair and smoking a cigar that helped quell the nausea created by the drugs he was taking.

Although the evening, which Julius had earlier described as "his wake," had moments of embarrassing schmaltz (Joan Baez sang "Swing Low, Sweet Chariot"), it was as moving and genuinely emotional a few hours as any of those present were likely to experience in a long time. Stokely Carmichael quoted Nkrumah: "Revolutions are made by men who think as men of action and act as men of thought," a near perfect encapsulation of Hobson. Julius's family was there, providing a dramatic reminder that he was one man who had not sacrificed his family on the altar of public service. His mother ended her strong speech with the benediction, "Go, son, go," bringing the audience to its feet. Scattered throughout the crowd were people who were important just to Julius—those unknown people who had stood with him on picket lines or joined him in other protests and who had, unlike many who share the early rise of the important, retained the loyalty and friendship of the man who was being honored. And at the end, one old friend shook the hand of another and said, "Where do we go from here, baby?"

9 / Taking Care of Business

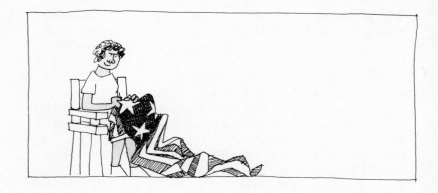

WHERE WE GO FROM HERE DEPENDS IN LARGE
measure upon whether Americans finally become
outraged by the prospect of 750,000 of their fellow citizens being denied full self-determination. In nearly 175
years of Washington's history, the cyclical peaks of the
country's social conscience have somehow neglected the
city's plight. Even today's information-glutted media
transmissions have passed Washington's status dilemma by.

Raised to believe they could not be free, Washingtonians, like residents of colonies elsewhere in the world,
have long tended to accept their proscribed limits. This acceptance has often been called apathy, but it is closer to
fatalism—a reasonable assessment of one's powerlessness to do anything about one's condition. Little in
Washington's history suggests that any but Washingtonians care about the injustices inflicted upon the city;

as far as Washingtonians can tell, presidents do not care, nor does Congress, the press, or Americans generally.

Government, schools, and the local press have tended to discourage the development of local awareness; Washingtonians are taught implicitly and explicitly that they are residents of a national capital, as opposed to a city that can be called their own. The federal symbols are revered; the local ones denigrated.

Many Washingtonians are personally hostage to federal interests. A government employee too involved in the fight for local freedom risks retribution, as Julius Hobson discovered when several congressmen expended considerable effort to get him fired from his civil service post. Other Washingtonians, representing powerful interests, find the status of the city quite to their liking. Finally, the will of the people of the District, even if it were to be vigorously pressed, is no match for the police and military might of the federal government. The political freedom that other Americans take for granted is considered a threat to the state in Washington, DC. In a democratic community equity can be sought through the accumulation of votes. In a colony one chooses between rebellion, argument, and resignation.

While the latter choice has been characteristic of the city, things are changing. The rise of black power, with its sophisticated understanding of the nature of colonialism, is speeding the change. More and more Washingtonians are unwilling to accept that being the seat of government should deny them the right to enjoy the supposed fruit of that government, freedom; and more and more Americans are coming to sympathize with their sense of injustice and with the need for self-determination.

Until 1970, it was generally assumed that there was but one way for the District to achieve self-determination: through what was known as "home rule" legislation. Further, it was assumed that representation in Congress would have to come through a constitutional amendment.

The reason for this is that the Constitution states in Article I, Section 8, that Congress shall have the power "to exercise exclusive legislation in all cases whatsoever, over such district (not exceeding ten miles square) as may, by cession of particular States, and the acceptance of Congress, become the seat of the government of the United States."

Although many members of Congress argued that this provision denied the District even the right to elect a government subject to congressional veto, this claim does not stand up under either historical or legal examination.

In Federalist Paper 43, James Madison said, in justifying the creation of the District: ". . . as the inhabitants will find sufficient inducements of interest to become willing parties to the cession; as they will have had their voice in the election of the government which is to exercise authority over them; as a municipal legislature for local purposes, derived from their own suffrages, will of course be allowed to them . . . every imaginable objection seems to be obviated."

In attempting to understand the provision for the District in the Constitution, several things should be kept in mind. The first is that the District had a population of less than 14,000 when it was created. It is unlikely that the Constitution's signers envisioned the District eventually having more population than the largest of the original states did in the eighteenth century. Further, the federal government is far more dispersed now than it was then. There are more federal buildings in each of forty-six states than there are in DC; less than .5 percent of all federal buildings are in the District. And the federal government owns more land in every state except Connecticut and Rhode Island.

Second, the provision for the District's government was a housekeeping chore for the authors of the Constitution. In retrospect, one might accuse the framers of sloppiness and lack of forethought, but you can be quite certain that they would have been among the first to fight for rectification in the light of the changing role of the national city had they survived to observe it. After all, among them were signers of the Declaration of Independence, a document that can be excerpted freely as a contemporary list of grievances against the federal government. Here are some of the complaints the Americans had against the King that have application to the District:

He has refused his assent to laws, the most wholesome and necessary for the public good.

He has forbidden his government to pass laws of immediate and pressing importance, unless suspended in their operation till his assent should be obtained; and when so suspended, he has utterly neglected to attend to them.

He has dissolved representative houses repeatedly, for opposing with manly firmness his invasions on the rights of people.

He has refused for a long time, after such dissolutions, to cause others to be elected;

He has obstructed the administration of justice. . . .

He has made judges dependent on his will alone. . . .

He has erected a multitude of new offices, and sent hither swarms of officers to harass our people and eat out their substance. . . .

He has affected to render the military [read police] independent of and superior to the civil power.

Other complaints included:

Imposing taxes on us without our consent.

Taking away our charters, abolishing our most valuable laws, and altering fundamentally the forms of our governments.

Suspending our own legislatures, and declaring themselves invested with power to legislate for us in all cases whatsoever.

Obviously, the 1973 legislation is in many ways an improvement over the previous situation. Nonetheless, this solution to Washington's status conundrum has one major catch: home rule legislation will never really provide home rule. As long as the Constitution remains unamended, Congress retains the right to veto any locally passed act. Further, it can initiate and pass any local legislation it wishes. Congress can still legislate at will by simple amendment to the home rule measure. The tendency for Congress to meddle in District affairs will be lessened, but it will certainly not be eliminated as congressional harassment of the elected but still weak school board has indicated. And if the local government really annoys Congress, it can cancel the home rule it has granted. Senator Eagleton's response to this criticism —"the Lord giveth and the Lord taketh away"—is warning enough that even Congress's supposedly liberal vanguard is not willing to relinquish its hold on the city.

From time to time, it is proposed that the city be retroceded back to Maryland, whence it came. This idea has enjoyed the support of a number of reactionary congressmen such as former District Committee Chairman McMillan. The nature of its proponents, and the fact that Maryland's officials have made it quite clear they don't want DC back again, has led the retrocession proposal to get less attention than it deserves. At the very least, however, it points up the liabilities of home rule status under ultimate federal control. The fact is that Washingtonians would be more nearly equal with other Americans if they were residents of Maryland than with "home rule." If there were some inherent advantage in not being a part of a state, then one might expect to find some agitation by residents of those parts of Virginia that were once part of the District to join it again. There is no such interest, however, for obviously the Alexandrian and Arlingtonian Virginians prefer being part of a sovereign member of the Union.

In March 1969, an important but little recognized event took place that was to open, for the first time, the way to full self-determination for the people of the District. Doug Moore, Chuck Stone, Jesse Anderson, and several other black activists held a news conference to announce the founding of the DC Statehood Committee. They issued a manifesto that declared that "statehood for the District of Columbia is a natural right which can no longer be denied and must be achieved by whatever means necessary by the people."

It turned out to be another 12-hour revolution—beginning with a morning press briefing and ending with the 11 P.M. news. It was not until more than a year later, in the fall of 1970, that statehood emerged as a prominent issue in District affairs with Julius Hobson's campaign for delegate. A few months earlier, I had written an article giving for the first time a detailed proposal and justification for statehood. The response had been underwhelming. One reader, George Shields, sent in five dollars and said it should be used whenever anything got organized. That fall, though, when a group of us gathered in a parochial school hall to plan the Hobson campaign against what seemed to us to be an undistinguished bunch of candidates, the idea was embraced as the basic platform plank. In that first delegate election, Hobson and the Statehood Party received a healthy 15,000 votes. In the second delegate election, with a less well-known candidate and a third of the campaign money, the party received 18,000 votes. Although this only amounted to 12 percent of the vote, the support for statehood as an idea grew much more rapidly than support for the Statehood Party, which was far too radical for many people's taste. Increasingly, longtime home rule supporters admitted that they could find no fault in the logic of statehood, but only doubted its potential as a cause.

Two statehood bills have been introduced in the House. The school board has two Statehood Party members on it as of 1973. The president of the board, Marion Barry, has said he is for statehood or any other form of self-government the city can get. When Republican John Nevius ran for delegate in 1971, he said he would support statehood if the people of the District wanted it. And shortly before he was defeated, House District Committee chairman John McMillan surprised even statehood supporters by stating that he might consider statehood as a second choice after his pet plan to give most of the District back to Maryland. Said McMillan: "The only way you are going to get pure, unadulterated representation is by ceding the city back to Maryland or through statehood."

The home rule lobby, however, attempted to ignore the statehood movement and Democratic congressional delegate Walter Fauntroy was openly hostile. He claimed statehood "would give us a reservation after they kill all of the buffalo and rob the land of its potential." And he drew a parallel with the Belgian Congo, which, after receiving independence had not freed itself of European business interests, although he did not make it clear whether he therefore opposed independence for the Congo. Finally, Fauntroy claimed that the city could not afford statehood economically.

The antipathy between Fauntroy and the statehood movement (Hobson called the future delegate "Little Lord Fauntroy"), played a small but interesting part in the presidential politics of 1972.

For several months following the March 1971 delegate campaign, a number of us in the Statehood Party worked with members of Senator George McGovern's staff on a statehood bill. A memo was prepared for McGovern's study. A short time later, Julius Hobson and the McGovern staffers went to make a direct pitch. As both reported, they were prepared to argue about the matter. They didn't have to. McGovern had bought the idea and desired to proceed forthwith. The bill was written and it was decided that McGovern's office would release the story for the Sunday papers on July 3, holding a news conference on July 6, the day after the long holiday weekend. As Hobson attempted to line up cosponsors, Fauntroy got wind of what was going on and got on the phone to McGovern's office. According to one of McGovern's staffers, "He was suffering from nausea." Fauntroy claimed that the March election had been a referendum on the issue of home rule vs. statehood (which was hardly the case, since the well-financed and popular Fauntroy could have actually gotten more votes had he supported statehood since it would have robbed Hobson of an important issue). He went on to use the Congo analogy. Fauntroy's protests had no apparent effect on McGovern's decision. As late as June 29, the news release was being prepared. Then that afternoon, McGovern called from out of town and told his staff to hold off. According to a staffer, "mutual friends of long standing" of Fauntroy and McGovern had gotten to the senator and, in what was to become a tradition in his campaign, McGovern began slipping off his perch of principle. On Thursday, July 1, McGovern informed his staff that the bill was off. After months of preparation, after full agreement on the need for statehood for the District, after leading the Statehood Party down to the wire, McGovern had ducked out because of phone calls from old friends.

To those familiar with the Hill's Lazy Liberal Bar and Caucus, it wasn't really too surprising. But McGovern was meant to be different—the purported alternative to the wafflings of the Muskies, et al. He had a chance to do something important for the District, to make local suffrage a national issue for once, and he blew it. It was one more reminder of how little Washingtonians can rely upon even those who are supposed to be their closest friends in national politics.

Despite the McGovern fiasco, the statehood movement had a good first few years. For the first time, the fundamental principle of self-determination has not been begged, for statehood is the only status that would make Washingtonians fully and irrevocably equal to other American citizens.

Home rule legislation with its congressional veto will not accomplish this. The local government can be free only to the extent that it does not alienate the federal government.

Statehood would avoid such pitfalls. Under statehood the District would be granted political equality with the other units of the federal system. Unlike home rule, statehood would not leave Congress or the President with a veto over District affairs. Unlike a constitutional amendment to change DC's local government or grant it national representation, statehood could not be revoked. It would, by simple majority vote of Congress, permit the three-quarter million residents of the District to join the Union as full and equal members.

Statehood could be made possible by the simple expedient of redefining the size of the District. The Constitution puts an outer limit on the size of the District—ten miles square—but indicates no minimum size. Congress could redefine the District of Columbia as it did when it retroceded the Virginia portion in 1846. The new District could consist of an unpopulated area stretching from the Supreme Court and Library of Congress to the Lincoln Memorial (including the Mall and Federal Triangle). The rest of the city could be granted statehood.

The technical procedure for obtaining statehood is relatively simple:

1. Congress would authorize and fund an elected constitutional convention to draw up a state constitution and negotiate an agreement with the federal government for an annual payment in lieu of taxes and for transitory grants to get the new state on its feet. The enabling legislation would define the area of the new state and of the remaining federal district.

2. The District would hold a constitutional convention, draw up a constitution, and submit the issue of statehood to referendum.

3. The convention, upon the approval of the people, would petition Congress for admission of the proposed state to the union.

4. Congress, by majority vote, would grant admission.

Naturally, such a proposed change in the status of Washington has aroused criticisms. One is that statehood would weaken the federal government's security in the city. Yet dozens of other stable countries, such as England, France, and West Germany, manage to grant self-government to their capital city without endangering national security. Should problems arise, the federal government has abundant power to deal with disturbances, as has been demonstrated by the use of federal troops in other cities in recent years.

It is also said that the District is too small to be a state. Yet it has a population larger than ten states and twenty independent nations. Every territory admitted since 1789, except Oklahoma, had fewer people at the time of its admission than the District does now. It is true that it is small geographically, but votes are assigned to people not acres.

Perhaps the most frequent criticism of statehood is that the new state could not support itself. Critics suggest that the present federal payment to the city, (about $190 million in 1972) would dwindle or disappear entirely, leaving Washington bankrupt. Yet DC's colonial status has in no way assured it a reliable and just federal payment. The payment over the past 100 years has varied from 9 percent to 50 percent of the local budget. This marked variance points to a major misunderstanding about the payment: it is not a function of status so much as of simple equity. The federal government absorbs a great deal of otherwise taxable land; it requires a large number of municipal services; and it consumes manpower and space that might otherwise be used in activities more profitable to the city, like industry and commercial services. These conditions will remain regardless of status, and fairness requires that the federal government offer proper compensation. This would be true if the city was in a fully colonial status, under home rule, or with statehood. The federal payment should not be regarded as a payment for servitude, as the critics of statehood seem to suggest, but as a just payment for services. Besides, if we are to be bribed into giving up freedom, surely the price comes higher than the annual $250 per capita that the present payment represents.

Actually, the importance of the federal payment to the city has been considerably exaggerated. A study done in 1967 showed that some thirteen states were receiving a higher portion of their budget in federal monies than was the District. Even Washington, while it was receiving $190 million in federal payment, was receiving $296 million in other federal assistance. Added to this in 1973 was Washington's cut of revenue sharing, which came to an amount larger than any federal payment before 1960.

But the District would not lose its federal payment under statehood. With four votes on the Hill and no congressional veto over local affairs, the city would actually be in a better position to seek a fair payment than it is now or would be under home rule. One would be hard-pressed to find examples of Congress attempting to bully a state in the way that it now does the District and will most likely continue to do under home rule. One of the basic traits of Congress is a reluctance to undercut the special interests of its members. The back-scratching tradition on local issues is based on the realization that the vote one casts today can be reclaimed tomorrow. The new city-state would benefit considerably from this new leverage. It is hard to conceive of a Congress deliberately alienating the four-member delegation from Washington in a dispute, say, over $20 million of federal payment. Congress just doesn't work that way.

The argument that the new state could not support itself is a familiar one in the history of statehood movements. It was one of the major reasons cited for opposition to Alaskan statehood. Yet it has been repeatedly true that new states have been aided towards self-sufficiency through special grants of monies and, more dramatically, immensely valuable lands. Statehood, in fact, may be considered almost a prerequisite to financial self-sufficiency for units of the federal system. In order to be financially equal, one must first be politically equal.

The two most recent states, Hawaii and Alaska, benefitted from enormous federal grants at the time they were granted statehood and for years afterwards. Hawaii got a trust of public lands to support public schools and other improvements. Alaska got 103 million acres of federal land, $28.5 million in transitional grants, 90 percent of the proceeds from government-owned mines and 70 percent of the sales of fur seal and sea otter skins.

But the economic justification for statehood does not rest on the assumption of fair compensation from the federal government; it is based on the economic potential of the city itself. Contrary to the myth of the "dying city," Washington has been and will continue to be a center of expanding economic opportunity. The great increase in black income in the city over the past decade, the decline of the percentage of the city in poverty, and the decline in the birth rate all contribute to prospects for a good economic future. DC has the highest median family income of any of the fifty largest cities in the country; the per capita income is higher, in fact, than any state. If DC can't support itself, none of us can.

When people talk about the city's eroding tax base, they are really describing the phenomenon that government expenditures have outstripped the growth in the tax base. Between 1959 and 1969 personal income originating in the District went up 78 percent according to the Nelsen Commission, compared to comparable cities where the growth ranged from 54 to 87 percent. Business earnings climbed 85 percent compared to a range of 42–78 percent in other cities. Retail sales were up 13 percent compared to a range of 3 percent decline in Newark to a 28 percent increase in New Orleans. But local government expenditures went up from $433 per capita in 1961 to $1,025 in 1969, a jump of 136 percent!

Under statehood, the city-state would be able to raise and spend revenues in a manner of its own choosing without fear of congressional veto, or worse, the possibility that the limited form of self-government granted under home rule might again be repealed entirely. Sources for the increased revenues might include:

• Property Tax Reform: Property taxes are a major source of local income. Yet the District does not administer these taxes fairly, nor does it tax all the property it should. For example, under statehood the city might end the property-tax exemption for the profit-making holdings of otherwise nonprofit organizations and of those of non-profit but exceedingly wealthy organizations such as the National Rifle Association and the Daughters of the American Revolution. Further, the introduction of a progressive property tax, with those owning more property taxed at a higher rate, could add to receipts, as could a tax on other forms of wealth such as now is levied in several states through a surtax on interest.

• Lotteries and Race Tracks: A DC official has estimated that a locally owned lottery and race track could produce as much as $50 million a year in new revenue.

• An Improved Tax Base: The District government has done little or nothing to attract the type of employment that would enable the poorer residents of the city to pay more taxes. Unlike almost every other city in the country, our government has failed in recent years to seek light industry and service firms that require blue collar employment. Instead it has subsidized the construction of office buildings for nontaxpaying suburbanites. While businesses produce pollution, so do the tens of thousands of Maryland and Virginia cars that pour into the city daily. The encouragement of low-polluting commercial enterprises would be a net gain for the city.

• More Tourism: Perhaps the greatest potential lies in further development of the city's tourist trade. Today, the Washington tourist is shoddily treated: forced to stand in long lines to visit the major sights; hustled kitsch souvenirs and over-priced food; and carted long distances to suburban motels. Life could be made more pleasant for both the tourist and Washington if the city would provide more services, facilities, recreation, and entertainment for tourists. While the District government subsidizes the Board of Trade's tourist promotion efforts, tourist facilities have increasingly been allowed to drift into the suburbs.

Besides, the city has totally failed to take advantage of one of its unique assets: its blackness. Properly promoted, Washington could become the Quebec of America, attracting people not just because it is a center of monuments and political power, but because it is culturally unique. This would mean jobs and money for black residents.

• Land Use: In its housing programs, such as they

are, the District has failed to provide lower-income residents with a chance to become bigger taxpayers. It has failed to provide the basic equity that supports the American middle class: home ownership. Instead, the government has either done nothing or else dabbled in showcase programs for the middle class such as Southwest or Fort Lincoln.

The city's use of available land and housing has been unimaginative. Thousands of abandoned homes put a drag on the tax rolls. Public land is rented for parking lots at ridiculously low prices instead of being put to productive and higher taxed use. Housing is destroyed to make way for offices that will attract more traffic and nontaxpaying suburbanites. Meanwhile, the city fritters away time and funds on childish and costly schemes like the ill-fated sports arena which would have drained rather than filled the city's treasury.

To top it off, programs such as urban renewal and freeway construction have driven people off taxable land permanently or for years at a time. One of the prime victims of this myopic policy has been the small businessman, an important taxpayer, who must regard the District Building these days as his enemy rather than his friend.

Under statehood, it would be easier for the District to reverse the destructive policies of local planners and the federal government over the past two decades and not only make a better, more attractive city but improve the tax base dramatically as well.

To some, statehood appears as an attractive idea but politically impractical. Actually, the long-term outlook for statehood is reasonably favorable. Just one of the hopeful signs is that it has attracted interest on the left and the right. Representative McMillan's comments about statehood were not merely cant aimed at upsetting Delegate Fauntroy. To the conservative mind, statehood fits neatly into the traditional federal system. The

Taking Care of Business

Constitution made it easier to create new states than it did to allow blacks, women or those under twenty-one to vote. Each of these required a constitutional amendment; statehood can be achieved by a simple majority vote of Congress. The steady enlargement of the Union throughout its history has not been the result of radicalism; the last two states admitted, for example, joined the Union during the Eisenhower Administration. On the other hand, statehood appeals to liberals and radicals because it offers an end to the colonial administration of three-quarters of a million Americans.

If the District were admitted, it would not, in all probability, be the last state. Statehood, for example, has been seriously proposed for Puerto Rico and New York City.

Economist Richard P. Burton has gone further. In testimony before the Joint Economic Committee in October 1970, Burton proposed that "any consolidated metropolitan region whose population reaches a lower threshold of, say, 1 million, would qualify for metropolitan statehood." This would lead to the creation of seventeen new states. Burton's arguments included these:

- Metropolitan states would preserve intact the current polycentric system of local government within their jurisdictional space.
- Metropolitan states would provide metropolitan areas with a fiscally and constitutionally viable form of government.
- Metropolitan states would redress the city/suburban imbalance of political power that presently exists in state legislatures.
- Metropolitan states would provide functionally meaningful state boundaries within which comprehensive planning would be in a position to realize its potential.
- Metropolitan states would preserve the local politi-

cal gains of blacks and other minority groups. It would preserve polycentrism, unlike metropolitan reorganization with its loss of local political control. "A reorganization plan along the line of metropolitan states would not constitute a threat to the political life of any locality in the metropolitan community, and the political gains of central city blacks would be effectively safeguarded."

• Metropolitan states would force state responsiveness to the problems of the urban crisis and would obviate the need for "direct federalism."

As Alan Campbell said in *The States and the Urban Crisis,* "State governments have been described as 'the keystone of the American governmental arch.' They sit midway between the local government on the one hand, which are their creatures, and the federal government on the other, which constitutionally possesses only delegated powers. By virtue of their position, state governments possess the power, and theoretically the responsibility, for attacking practically all those problems which in sum equal the urban crisis."

In short, statehood is the great unused tool with which to make the American federal system work again. And what better place to start than in the nation's capital?

Building a political base for DC statehood has obviously just begun. The first step is to break the century-old allegiance to the belief that home rule is the best Washington can hope for. This is happening. The politicians, the local civic elite, and the media are slowly becoming aware of statehood and are being forced to deal with it. Although much of the early pressure came from the DC Statehood Party, other organizations may soon feel secure enough to add statehood to their goals, especially now that even the Board of Trade supports home rule.

Once a local consensus for statehood has been

Taking Care of Business

achieved, Congress would begin to feel the pressure. As a national issue, statehood would be an easier issue to explain and attract support for than has been home rule. Labor unions, big city mayors, black organizations and other blocs would welcome a new urban state; its votes in Congress would give them an interest in its creation. The support from these sources for traditional home rule was apathetic, largely because hardly anyone outside the District had a vested interest in home rule.

If Congress failed to act, the District could follow the pattern set by Tennessee in 1796. Tennessee held unofficial elections and sent unauthorized "members" to Congress. The elected "members" pressed for statehood and Congress granted it. The same procedure was used by Alaska. In 1956, an officially approved nonvoting delegate, Bob Bartlett, was sent to Washington, but so were "Senators" Ernest Gruening and William Egan and "Representative" Ralph Rivers. This so-called Tennessee Plan has been used on six other occasions to help obtain statehood for territories.

Those in the statehood movement would be the first to admit that statehood would be no panacea for DC's problems, any more than independence solved America's problems. In fact, their inquiry into statehood has led to a reexamination of big city government in general. One of the advantages of statehood is that it would permit a quite different structure of local government than is the case in other cities.

A major problem with our cities, for example, is the decline of local democracy. In 1790, when the United States was first trying out its new constitution, a U.S. Representative represented an average of 37,000 people. In the Jackson–Adams contest of 1824, only 356,000 votes were cast. That's less than half the present population of the District. When Abraham Lincoln was in the House of Representatives, he had a constituency equal to about a tenth the present population of the District.

As late as 1900, the average congressman represented fewer than 200,000 people. These voters, of course, also voted for state and town legislators representing even fewer persons.

Today, the average congressman represents twelve times as many people as was the case in 1790. But far more important, a city councilman in a city like New York or Philadelphia may represent 200,000 people or more.

As the nation has grown, so has the gap between the citizens and their legislators. Where once the citizen was one of less than 40,000 persons with a demand on the attention of a member of the national legislature, today the lowliest local public official for whom a citizen can vote in a major city may represent two to five times that many people. In 1816 there was one city councilman for every hundred residents of Columbus, Ohio. By 1840 there was one for every thousand residents. By 1872 that had dwindled to one for every five thousand. Today, there is one councilman for every 55,000 people.

Among the effects of this phenomenon are:

• Citizens lack access to political leaders.

• Politicians, responsible for oversized political units, rely heavily on bureaucrats who are unresponsive to the citizen.

• The expense and difficulty of making changes in the political structure is magnified.

• Unable to make an impact on the local political structure, people turn to nonpolitical techniques for changes or withdraw from any effort to participate. From civic committees to militant demonstrations, from community organizing to riots, citizens in recent years have experimented with a variety of methods to achieve the political change they could not achieve within the political system. They have had minimal success.

• Both the politician and the bureaucrat become scornful of the democratic process as they become less dependent upon it. Public involvement in government is carefully structured to ensure that the public does not get in the way. A classic example is the citizen advisory board, designed to give the public the image of power without the substance.

• The citizen's contact with politicians increasingly comes through the images of the media rather than through direct or even second-hand contact. The very size of political units accentuates media manipulation. Smaller units would make the media less important, and force media attention to focus on party platforms and programs rather than on personalities.

Even if the local politician makes a serious effort to overcome the handicap of an overgrown constituency, the job is too big. Inevitably, decisions, including a myriad of fundamentally political decisions, are farmed out to administrators without political responsibility.

That these administrators should be reluctant to give up the power they have acquired is not surprising. One should not expect that civil servants with control over schools, recreation, police, or roads should relinquish their control easily. In one of the more frank statements on the subject, Assistant Secretary of Housing and Urban Development Don Hummell told an urban renewal workshop in September 1968 that he wondered if it was inconsistent for local officials, who had been complaining about not having enough say in the formulation of HUD regulations, to be opposing a voice for their own clients —the citizens who would be most directly affected by local urban renewal programs. The *Journal of Housing* reported: "He chided his audience for not being as willing to share their authority with residents of the affected neighborhoods as they are to have him and other HUD officials relinquish their authority over federally financed programs. 'Nobody gives up control willingly,' he said, 'and I, for one, do not intend to give up all control over money I am responsible for without a struggle.'"

It is increasingly clear, however, that control must be

transferred if the American city is to become a sane and happy place in which to live and if democracy is to be reinstituted in urban America.

The primary weapon used against the people by city officials is something called "expertise." The administrator is supposed to know more about traffic flow, police policy, or educational theory than the public, and is therefore better qualified to determine city policy on freeways, police, or schools.

Armed with objective data, systems analyses, consulting reports, and all the other paraphernalia of the bureaucratic arsenal, the administrators overwhelm the public into submission. And too often, the politicians wilt before the onslaught.

When they don't they are met with contempt. Shortly after DC school superintendent Hugh Scott decided to give up his fight to have his contract extended, he told a television audience, "The election of a member of the board of education does not necessarily mean the individual understands that function. It means that individual got a certain number of votes. It's somewhat different with an educator. He comes with some degree of preparation and discipline. . . ."

He was speaking of a school board that had several times managed to bail him out of embarrassing situations, that had covered up for his underachievement as superintendent, and that had managed the complexities of a school system budget better than he had. But it lacked credentials.

The public, and the politicians who react to it, are often wrong. Sometimes they are vicious and cannibalistic toward the weak of society. But the political process offers something that is lacking in administrative decisions: the imprimateur of the governed. This stamp is not necessarily a function of efficiency or objective good; it is the sum of the objective and subjective decisions of the electorate. The fact that a community may for subjective reasons prefer small neighborhood schools to a more "efficient" educational park is one which can not be overlooked without adding to the frustration and alienation of that community. The community can't produce a consultant's report to prove the smaller schools make it happier; it shouldn't have to. And if it is objectively wrong, so what? On the average, the public hasn't done that much worse than the experts.

When the District submitted its environmental impact statement on a proposed freeway that would tunnel under the Lincoln Memorial and the Tidal Basin and carve a huge ditch through the Mall, it said that one problem was "an unspecified and subjective sense of aesthetic loss on the part of many, due to the presence of a high speed highway being superimposed on a shrine area." It added: "This, however, is a nebulous, undefined, and possibly unqualified sentiment that would be hard to measure."

In fact, it was hard to measure only because the Commissioner, the Highway Director, and the City Council didn't have to run for public office. If they had, they would quantify the sentiment pretty damn fast.

Many of the things that matter most to ordinary urban citizens, unlike planners and administrators, are nebulous and undefined. They are a feeling about the street on which you live, whether shopping is a pleasure or a chore, whether you can get where you want to go easily and inexpensively, whether your child is having trouble in school because he or she is dumb or because the teacher is no good, whether the actions of the police tend to encourage observance of the law or repel it, whether the government seems to be working for you or vice versa, whether a new road is a help or a travesty. It has been foolhardy to ignore these sentiments or to assess them without the aid of a constant, intimate political process.

One of the lessons of Washington, as the most overadministered and under-political city in the country, is that it is far less dangerous to put one's trust in politicians and their constituency than in administrators without a constituency.

After all, it was not the ignorant public that permitted the District's transportation chaos. It was not the stupid public that led to the dismal state of education. It was not the naive public that prevented the police department from controlling crime. It was not the uneducated poor who have mangled the urban renewal programs.

On the contrary, in Washington as elsewhere, the community, through organizations concerned with such issues as planning, housing, transportation, and the environment, has provided many of the solutions the government has been forced to come to.

The problem is that there is no structure through which the public can exercise political power in an intimate, direct fashion. While "community control" is the defacto form of government in most American communities outside of our large cities, it is spurned as a radical plot when applied to urban centers. Community control involves nothing more than the restoration of democracy. If one were to go to Rockville, Maryland, and suggest abolishing its local government so that all local decisions would be made by Montgomery County, the people of Rockville would justifiably rebel. Yet when a Rockville-style government is suggested for a large city like Washington it becomes the work of revolutionary devils.

Part of this reaction is racial in origin. Community control in our cities means more black power. There is also a fear of the apparently new, and acceptance of the myth perpetuated by America's corporate and planning suzerains that bigness means efficiency. Further, those who now have the power just don't want to give it up.

For Washington, the advent of statehood would

provide an opportunity to reorganize the city in a manner unique for American cities. One possible structure would be to break the city up into semi-autonomous villages or towns. The state would be relegated to strictly state functions and the local government would center on the smaller communities.

This would fly in the face of the conventional liberal wisdom that has increasingly sought release from the urban crisis by limiting local functions through such mechanisms as metropolitan governments and regional authorities. While, as Burton points out, a metropolitan government structured as a state would preserve polycentrism, the supergovernments presently favored by many would work in the opposite direction.

They already are. Washington's Metropolitan Council of Governments, although not a government and without any members directly elected to it, is rapidly gaining governmental powers. Federal housing and transportation funds hinge on COG-approved regional plans. COG even attempted to establish a police intelligence unit under its aegis.

There are several problems with such metropolitan agencies. They dilute black urban power. Just as blacks are gaining political clout in our cities, it is being dispersed through metropolitan government. Also, organizations such as COG not only further restrict community democracy, they are in themselves undemocratic. If one must have regional government, it should be, at the very least, elected regional government.

The most important supergovernment in the Washington area is Metro. Like COG, its board consists of elected officials, but not officials elected to Metro. This board has enormous discretionary powers which it can use virtually at whim, as the excessive land-takings by Metro have illustrated. At least when the bus system was under private control, fare raises had to be approved by a regulatory commission based on a close examination of the company's finances. Now, Metro can raise fares, change routes, and drop service almost without regulation. If the Metro board were elected, it would probably be more responsible than a regulatory commission. As it is, however, Metro has already shown evidence of being as contemptuous of the public as were the former private owners of the bus companies. Only now there is less we can do about it.

The problem of COG and Metro points to a peculiar obstacle in the path of Washington's drive for full self-determination. As pressure increases for self-government, more and more powers of the local government are being dispersed. Even under statehood, to regain these powers would require a struggle.

Local planning and housing authority has been diluted by COG. Authority over transportation has been diluted by both COG and Metro. Beyond this is the Pennsylvania Avenue Commission, a presidentially-appointed, congressionally-sanctioned body with extraordinary arbitrary powers over a large section of downtown Washington. And huge tracts of land, such as the three hundred acres at Ft. Lincoln or the smaller sites at L'Enfant Plaza and McLean Gardens have been turned over to developers to construct what amounts to company communities. In such places, local political authority has been delegated to corporate vice presidents.

The question arises: when DC gets full self-government, what will be left to govern? The problem is not unique to Washington, only more poignant. For as Washington inches towards self-determination, the scope of urban power generally is being contracted. The nation's cities, partly by default and partly by design, are being turned over to an oligarchy of administrators, planners, regional supernumeraries, and representatives of development conglomerates. In the name of an improved tax base, efficiency, and regional coordination, the power of urban citizens over their own destiny—urban democracy—is slipping away.

Washington, as a weak colony, is particularly defenseless. But Washingtonians may also be, because of their colonial heritage, somewhat more aware of the dangers of delegating arbitrary power than are those living in places where democracy is taken for granted even after it has begun to disappear. It is probably more than coincidence that Washington has been a leader in the fight against the freeway juggernaut and that Washingtonians are more hospitable to the idea of community control than are the residents of many large cities. A free Washington might become a leader in the fight to recover urban democracy.

But whether Washington, if granted statehood, would turn out to be an example for the rest of the country or just another journeyman city, trudging along as best it can through urban problems, is in the end irrelevant.

The demand for full self-determination rests not on the promise of excellence; Washington has as many fools, hustlers, bunglers, jivers, and merchants of myopia per capita as any city in the country. Rather, the demand rests on the simple need for equity.

We need statehood to end seventeen decades denial of rights that were set out in the Declaration of Independence and assured by the Constitution. We seek nothing less than that granted 200 million of our countrymen: full participation in the Union.

We need statehood to cure our present impotence. We need statehood because it is the one form of self-government that we can exercise in the manner of our choosing, without the threat of congressional or presidential veto and without fear of having our franchise revoked. We need statehood because anything short of it will leave us lesser citizens than other Americans.

Changes in our local government that do not result in

statehood are only colonial reform. Half freedom is half slavery, and we should not accept it. Partial self-government is no answer. Equality is not divisible.

Statehood for Washington, DC, would not guarantee a successful future; it would only make it possible.

FURTHER READING

1. History

Green, Constance McLaughlin. *Washington: Village and Capital, 1800–1878.* Princeton, New Jersey: Princeton University Press, 1962.

——. *Washington: Capital City, 1879–1950.* Princeton, New Jersey: Princeton University Press, 1963.

——. *The Secret City: A History of Race Relations in the Nation's Capital.* Princeton, New Jersey: Princeton University Press, 1967.

2. Anthropology

Liebow, Elliot. *Talley's Corner: A Study of Negro Streetcorner Men.* Boston: Little, Brown, 1967.

Hannerz, Ulf. *Soulside: Inquiries into Ghetto Culture and Community.* New York City: Columbia University Press, 1967.

3. Politics

Derthick, Martha. *City Politics in Washington, D.C.* Cambridge, Massachusetts: Harvard University Press, 1962.

4. Architecture

Jacobsen, Hugh Newell, ed. *A Guide to the Architecture of Washington, D.C.* New York City: Praeger, 1965.

5. General

Adler, Bill, ed. *Washington: A Reader.* New York City: Meridith Press, 1967.

Sennet, Richard. *The Uses of Disorder: Personal Identity and City Life.* New York City: Knopf, 1970. (In paperback as a Random House Vintage Book.)

Index